ROMANTIC BRITAIN

+

THE NATIONAL HERITAGE OF BEAUTY
HISTORY AND LEGEND

+

EDITED BY
TOM STEPHENSON

ODHAMS PRESS LIMITED
LONG ACRE, LONDON, W.C.2

THE SUPERB SPLENDOUR OF DURHAM

High above the River Wear stands the imposing edifice of Durham Cathedral, the most splendidly situated of all English Cathedrals. Adjoining is the castle of the Bishops hence the poet's line " Half church of God, half castle 'gainst the Scot." In bygone days the Prince-Bishops wielded temporal as well as spiritual power over the country between Tyne and Tees which formed the Palatinate of Durham.

CONTENTS

PUBLISHER'S NOTE

The object of this book is to give the reader a permanent record of Romantic Britain before the outbreak of war during 1939. Consequently, all the photographs used for the illustrations were taken before that date, and it should be borne in mind that many of the buildings have since been either completely destroyed or severely damaged by enemy action.

W. F. TAYLOR

TUDOR GLORY

Few places can offer such a beautiful example of Elizabethan England as is to be found at the little village of Chiddingstone, near Tonbridge, in Kent. Here, facing the church, is an ancient inn and a row of delightful old houses timbered and gabled and still retaining the leaded casement windows. Here indeed there lingers the serenity of bygone days, and the mellowed, graceful beauty of forgotten craftsmen.

INTRODUCTION

by TOM STEPHENSON

ONE of the most remarkable developments of modern times has been the great awakening to the pleasures of the countryside, and the growing recognition of the treasures with which we have been so lavishly endowed. Poets and writers in the past have paid their tribute, and in every generation there have been a fortunate few conscious of the fair face of Britain. Never before, however, has there been such widespread interest. Never has there been so much general admiration of our peaceful rural scenes, our mountain grandeur, our rivers, lakes and forests, and our numerous time-mellowed villages and pleasing towns, which, beneath their superficial modernity, still retain an air of less hurried times and many an intriguing memento of days that have been.

There was a time when Britain, with all its storied relics of the past, was appreciated more by visitors from abroad than by our own countrymen. Those who had the means would hasten to the Continent or to the far corners of the earth, woefully ignorant of the beauty and grandeur on which they turned their backs. Long ago Bacon remarked that " Travel in the younger sort is part of education ; in the elder a part of experience." This we need not dispute, but if travel is educational it does not follow that learning, like travel, may be measured by the mileage. Yet at one time there appears to have been a general acceptance of this fallacy.

The author of *Tom Brown's Schooldays* made comment on this :

" You have," he said, " seen men and cities, no doubt, and have your opinions, such as they are, about schools of painting, high art and all that ; have seen the pictures of Dresden and the Louvre, and know the taste of sauerkraut. All I say is, you don't know your own lanes and woods and fields . . . not one in twenty of you knows where to find the wood-sorrel, or bee-orchis, which grow in the next wood, or on the down three miles off. . . . And, as for the country legends, the stories of old gable ended farmhouses, the place where the last skirmish was fought in the civil wars, where the parish butts stood, where the last highwayman turned to bay, where the last ghost was laid by the parson, they've gone out of date altogether."

If Judge Hughes was living today, however, he would see how the wheel has turned. In cars, on cycles and on foot, the present generation escapes to the countryside of Britain on every possible occasion. Men and women, young and old, are to be seen following the highways to the far corners of the isle, penetrating lanes, grass-grown and at one time in danger of being forgotten, roaming the field ways and moorland trails, ever questing for the beauty of the land.

With this new awakening there has arisen an insistent and insatiable demand for information ; a thirst for knowledge of the story behind the scene and all that has gone to the making of the picture. For the artist the beauty may not be enhanced by a knowledge of how it came into being, but the average man likes to humanize his pictures and to enliven them with visions of the romance, or it may be the tragedy, the toil and strife, and the comings and goings of folk who are now little more than memories, but who in their passing added some detail to the scene. There is a desire for knowledge of the making of mountains and valleys, of the clearing of the forests and the building of homesteads, hamlets and towns. Some seek information of the men who first made the trackways and the roads, of those who discovered the fords and built the bridges, of the

STEPHENSON

A FOAMING RIVER

Amid the lonely Pennine Moors on the borders of Yorkshire, Durham and Westmorland, the River Tees at Cauldron Snout plunges down these black crags.

men who raised the earliest churches and conceived the magnificent splendour of the monasteries and cathedrals.

Within the crumbling shell of some feudal stronghold there may come a desire to picture lords and ladies, and knights in resplendent armour, jousting to gain an admiring glance from " beauty's matchless eye." We may seek to visualize the archer on the walls, the warder at the gate, and the feasting in the hall, and, not forgetting the tragic note, perhaps to sigh for the hapless captive in the noisome dungeon.

In the following pages we have sought to relate some of this long and fascinating story, to tell of

STEPHENSON

THE VILLAGE SHOP

Close to the yew-shaded churchyard in the Sussex hamlet of Bignor stands this quaint old building with its thatched roof, its diamond-leaded windows, its ancient timbers and walls of flint cobbles and herring-bone brickwork.

mountains, rivers and forests, and, as far as possible, the history and legends associated with them.

Other chapters tell of the wanderings and workings of the first men, of the Romans conquering, building and civilizing; of the ravages and subsequent settlements of Saxon and Dane, and of the Conquest by the Normans. The making of the roads, the building of the castles, monasteries and cathedrals come under review. The development of the villages and towns and the story of the bridges and inns has also been told. Scenes of history and romance, the country of poet and novelist are included, and altogether, it is hoped, the work presents a readable survey of what has gone to the making of this the " most fairy-like and romantic of all countries."

The beginnings of the story take us far back in the annals of time to a period long before man

had evolved from his lowly ancestors. With the aid of the geologist we might trace from those distant beginnings the changes and chances whereby the land was raised mountain high and carved into giant peaks which through the long æons slowly crumbled and were carried to " sow the dust of continents yet to be." We should see the land sinking beneath the sea, being elevated only to disappear again beneath the waves. By these recurring processes of denudation and periods of deposition were formed the various strata which today are the very bones of our landscape.

Intermittent with the piling up of the great thicknesses of sedimentary rocks, were the periods of volcanic activity. The rare colourful beauty of Borrowdale, the domed brow of Great Gable, and the grand crags of Scafell; the shapely peak of Tryfaen and the cwms and precipices of Snowdon, all had their origin in the ejections of primeval volcanoes. So also at a later period of the earth's history issued forth those great outpourings of lava which subsequently were carved into the jagged fantastic peaks of the Cuillin.

Coral Seas

The Black Mountains of Brecon and the ruddy loam of Hereford and Devon had their beginnings in lakes and landlocked seas inhabited by weird armour-plated fishes.

In later seas where corals flourished was formed the limestone which now provides the soaring cliffs of Cheddar, the delightful dales of Derbyshire, the great rift of Gordale and the stark terraces and numerous waterfalls of the Yorkshire Dales.

In less deep water some uncharted Amazon poured the debris of a vanished continent, the sands which were to become the millstone grits, crowning the weather-worn arch of the Pennines, and forming that long series of edges, cloughs and spacious moorlands where the cotton grass blows, where the curlew cries down the wind, and peaty burns rush over rocky ledges.

The plains of Cheshire, and the gentle undulations spreading with a rosy blush across the Midlands, tell of the making of the new red sandstone in the deserts, the torrential streams and salt lakes of Triassic times. The limestones which sweep across the country from the Dorset coast to the cliffs of Whitby affording the beauty

STEPHENSON

A CHURCH BENEATH THE DOWNS

Finely placed among venerable trees on a slight eminence at the foot of the North Downs stands the grey old church of Wotton, in Surrey. The name takes us back to pagan times for it is probably derived from Woden. John Evelyn, the seventeenth-century diarist, who attended school in the church porch, is buried here.

of the Cotswolds and a chain of lovely villages, and providing the stone out of which Wren and others have fashioned many a noble edifice—these materials also were slowly built up out of the remains of corals and molluscs which lived when the unwieldy pterodactyl was pioneering the conquest of the air. In yet later seas there was deposited through countless æons the great thicknesses of chalk which today gives us the wide reaches of Salisbury Plain, the sleek curving downs of Surrey and Sussex, the beech-clad Chilterns and the wolds of Lincolnshire and Yorkshire, Dover's famous cliffs, Beachy Head and the Seven Sisters, the jagged Needles of the Isle of Wight and the lofty white wall of Flamborough Head.

Other strata have a story to tell of subtropical times when palm trees flourished where London now stands. From those sunny days may be traced the decline into conditions of Arctic rigour, when glaciers formed on the mountains and the roar of the avalanche echoed through the hills, and great sheets of ice ploughed across the land.

Today the cwms of Snowdon, the valleys of Lakeland and the glens and corries of the Highlands, are yet eloquent of those frigid times. In Cwm Glas, for instance, above the Pass of Llanberis, the grey hummocks of rock remain smooth and polished from the passage of the ice sweeping down to the valley. At the head of Ennerdale, Greenup and other valleys in the Lake District are numerous mounds of debris left by

the glaciers in retreat, and near the head of Glen Torridon, in Wester Ross, they are so numerous as to have inspired the name of " The Corrie of a Thousand Hills."

One glacier sweeping down from Scotland filled the North Sea and overrode Snae Fell in the Isle of Man, carrying rocks from the Galloway Hills and the Lake District down into Lancashire, and even into the Midlands. Another glacier swept over the Pennines leaving boulders of granite from Shap Fell, in Westmorland, strewn along the Yorkshire coast where they may be seen today, in the neighbourhood of Robin Hood's Bay.

Glacier Lakes

The famous Parallel Roads of Glen Roy, in Inverness-shire, also tell of this period. There, like ruled lines along the sides of the glen, are the beaches of a lake formed by the water impounded by a barrier of ice. In similar fashion the valleys of the Cleveland Hills were dammed, and the wide Vale of Pickering, between the wolds and the moors, was once filled with a great lake.

Slowly the land recovered from this visitation and vegetation gradually spread over the barren earth, clothing the bare lowlands and mantling the stark hillsides. The rivers began to flow again in some places filling a glacier-gouged hollow to make a gleaming lake, and elsewhere cutting new channels where their old courses were filled with mud and clay and boulders left

STEPHENSON

A MOATED MANOR

There can be few more lovely houses than Ightham Mote, in Kent, which lies surrounded by its moat, and it is almost as secluded as in the days when its masonry was new, six centuries ago. It has been suggested that the word mote refers to its having been the Moot Hall or meeting place for the courts of the manor.

MELLOW BEAUTY

In the Wiltshire village of Potterne, south of Devizes, is preserved this lovely Tudor dwelling, now known as the Porch House. In bygone days it has served as the church house and as an inn. It has been carefully restored, and as will be seen in the above view from the garden, it retains an air of dignified old age.

STONE WALLS OF A YORKSHIRE DALE

In the hilly districts stone walls often take the place of hedgerows, and they may be seen criss-crossing in the valleys, winding along the slopes and sometimes running over the highest hill-tops. Skilfully built without any cement, many of these walls have stood for generations. Above is a scene near Grassington, in Wharfedale.

by the ice. Since then our streams have continued to flow unceasingly from the hills to the sea, deepening and widening their valleys, looping and meandering in the lowlands, and adding the finishing graces to the landscape. So have matured the delightful rivers of today, Thames, Severn and Wye ; the sweet placid flowing streams of the south country ; the brawling streams of the Pennines, that " tumble as they run " ; Tees and Tyne, Tweed and Tay and many another river which we now regard as beautifying features of the land.

With the passing of the Ice Age primeval man

Stonehenge, Rollright and Arbor Low, the stones of Callernish and Stennes and numerous other stone temples built to unknown gods.

Round those mysterious monuments there has gathered through subsequent ages a wealth of fascinating legend and mythical explanations of their origin. Curious mixtures of imaginative guesswork, and strange notions of wizardry, devils and druids.

To the land held by those Iron-Age tribes, Julius Cæsar made his flying visit and a century later Britain became part of the great Roman Empire. Time and succeeding invaders have

DIXON-SCOTT

TUDOR BEAUTY IN SUFFOLK

The lovely Suffolk village of Lavenham is well endowed with timbered buildings. The village was a centre of the cloth trade in the fifteenth and sixteenth centuries, and to that period it owes its distinctive buildings including a fine Guildhall. The handsome perpendicular church also is indebted to that old industry.

becomes more in evidence, leading his gregarious life, shaping his flints and eking out a meagre existence. Centuries after him came the better equipped men of the New Stone Age, followed in turn by the people of the Bronze and Iron Ages. Their marks still endure, for it was probably they who first blazed the old tracks along the upland ridges. They made the gentle-domed tumuli, swelling on the skyline of the downs and moorlands, the ramparts and dykes of mighty Maiden Castle and the camps of Dolebury and Hambledon and Uffington. They also left us Avebury and

largely but not entirely effaced the imprint of the legions. Watling Street and the Fosse Way, Ermine Street, Dere Street and Stane Street are memories of the roads they engineered.

Some of their towns are now green fields. Others are revealed as excavated ground plans where the curious may trace the lines of the ancient streets and the foundations of forum and basilica, baths and temples, inns and shops, and the orderly layout of an early town planning.

In many a well-chosen site may be seen the remnants of a Roman villa, with tesselated floors,

STEPHENSON

SALISBURY'S SOARING SPIRE

A landmark for miles around is the graceful tapering spire of Salisbury Cathedral which is 404 feet high, and which is the highest in England. Building of the cathedral was begun when Old Sarum was abandoned in 1220, and completed in less than forty years, but it was not until 1320 that this culminating glory was added.

the ever-present bathrooms and the hypocausts of their central heating arrangements. Hadrian's Wall crowning the crags of Northumberland and reaching from the Tyne to the Solway has been preserved sufficiently to indicate the magnitude of their defensive works.

At Porchester and Pevensey and elsewhere may be seen their ancient forts of the Saxon shore, those defences which failed to keep out the marauders from across the sea, the invaders who, "plundered all the neighbouring cities and country and spread the conflagration from the eastern to the western sea."

of the fascinating origins of the place-names of Britain, often in themselves crystallized history.

Next came the Conqueror, seizing and suppressing and parcelling out the land among his henchmen. Scattered about the land are ruins of the great feudal strongholds which arose out of those times. From those medieval fortresses as comfortless as they were impregnable, grew the more homely mansions, many-gabled manor houses dormered and mullioned, and homes of more florid but not necessarily of more graceful design.

Side by side with the building of the great castles and baronial halls and the walled towns of

STEPHENSON

SUSSEX GABLES

At the foot of the South Downs lies the little town of Steyning, a place of ancient houses with grey gables such as those seen above. Edward the Confessor gave land here to the Abbey of Fécamp. Harold the Saxon king seized the property, one of the acts said to have brought the Norman Conqueror to England.

Here and there a fragment of rudely fashioned architecture may bring to mind the days of the Saxons, of Aethelbert, diffidently receiving St. Augustine, of his daughter wedding the Northumbrian king and taking Paulinus with her to baptize the barbarians of the north. Elsewhere we may recall the saintly Abbess Hilda and the inspired Caedmon at Whitby or the Venerable Bede chronicling the story of the past and working until his last breath in the monastery at Jarrow.

Norsemen and Danes follow in turn, plundering and pillaging like the Saxons before them and eventually settling in peace to earn a hardy living from the soil.

So arose the homesteads, the hams and thwaites and thorpes of persisting villages, reminding us

the Middle Ages, we should see the developing architecture of church and cathedral and monastic splendour; the now mellowed grandeur of Ely and Wells, Canterbury and York, and Durham's stately pile above the Wear "Half church of God, half castle 'gainst the Scot."

So also must be included the stately ruins of Tintern, the splendour of Fountains Abbey, the romantic beauty of Bolton and Rievaulx and ancient Glastonbury steeped in legend, and the picturesque remains of Melrose, Jedburgh and Dryburgh, for these also are treasured features of the scene.

Another long story lies behind the making of the roads from the beginning of the prehistoric downland trails and on through Roman times.

EDGAR WARD

CLIFFS OF DEVON

At Seaton, where the River Axe enters the sea an outlier of chalk gives this bold headland rising above the curving shores of shingle in which beryls, jaspers and garnets occur. A theory with little foundation claims Seaton as the Roman Moridunum and the southern termination of the Roman road known as the Fosse Way, which ran diagonally across England by Ilchester, Cirencester, Leicester and Newark to Lincoln.

The tale would take us through the dark ages of neglect, when road making was a forgotten art and the highways of the legions lay in ruin, and on through the centuries when travel between the towns was an ordeal not lightly to be undertaken.

From the groanings and curses of sorely tried wayfarers we may learn something of the discomfort and misery entailed. The glamour of

THE VILLAGE INN

In many an old-world village the church and the inn are the two chief features and often they are close neighbours. Here is seen the "Barley Mow," at Long Wittenham, a Berkshire village.

W. F. TAYLOR

the coaching days fades before the facts of slow and cumbrous motion, and the delays due to the condition of the roads. So also the curious shifts and dodges resorted to for the upkeep of the roads make strange reading in these days.

. Along the roads we can also be reminded of many other features recalling the past, including the hundreds of famous and historic inns with memories of by-gone days. Their very names make an interesting commentary from the " Bear " and the " Ragged Staff," symbol of the ancient Earls of Warwick, down to the less imaginative " Railway Tavern " or " Bricklayer's

Arms." Many a picturesque bridge has a tale to tell, and perhaps a fanciful legend of its origin, and here and there may be seen the old toll-houses of the turnpike days.

Throughout all these centuries of development, through all the clash and strife, while others were blustering and plundering, crusading in the Holy Land or ranging the Spanish Main, generation after generation of forgotten serfs, peasant and yeomen, followed more peaceful pursuits.

Their work also must be portrayed for they cleared and tilled the land, and by their sweat and toil made meadow and cornland and sweet pasture out of the tangled forest and swamp and fen.

Village Hampdens

They dug and ploughed and drained and drove the green of cultivation up the barren hillsides. They planted the hedgerows, the beech clumps and the avenues and glades, and built the stone walls over moor and fell and across the floors of moorland dales.

They built the villages and hamlets of every size and shape, spreading round the green, drawn out in a straggling street or huddled like sheep in a gale, hiding in the vale, or standing boldly on a hill-top.

Built of whatever materials might be at hand, of brick and tile and thatch, or from the doorstep to the chimney top entirely of local stone, their homely architecture is also an integral part of the landscape.

To them also we are indebted for the preservation of many a village green and piece of common land, for many a tale could be told of stout-hearted village Hampdens who fought to save from enclosure the lands which were rightly a common heritage.

The shepherd returning from the hill, the ploughman crossing the fields to the village church or inn, the chapman journeying from one farm to the next or from village to village, the drover and the pack-horse man, and all whose business took them about the countryside—they made the footpaths and the winding by-ways, the ox roads and the White Ways and Welsh Ways, the Smuggler's Lanes and the Lovers' Lanes, which are also part of the pattern.

So through the long slow march of time, all these and other innumerable factors have contributed to the making of Britain and all its varied, appealing beauty.

A. A. MACGREGOR

A ROAD TO THE ISLES

Along the west coast of Scotland the sea runs far inland among the mountains. All traffic has to be ferried across these inlets. Above is Dornie Ferry on the coast of Wester Ross. Here Loch Alsh divides at its head into two arms, Loch Duich and Loch Long. The latter branch is seen above with Dornie on the far shore.

STEPHENSON

LAKELAND BEAUTY

From the high crags of Ashness, rising sheer above the Borrowdale Road, Derwentwater makes a delightful picture. This lake, almost completely surrounded by hills, is one of the most beautifully placed of the English lakes. In the background is the swelling mass of Skiddaw (3,054 feet) which overlooks the town of Keswick.

STEPHENSON

MIGHTY MONUMENT OF THE PAST

Many theories have been propounded in explanation of Stonehenge and, like other stone circles, it has been ascribed to the Druids. The monument, however, belongs to a much earlier period than that of those Celtic priests or " wise-men." It is thought to have been built in the early days of the Bronze Age, perhaps about 1700 B.C. Most of the stones are of local origin, but some of the smaller ones were brought from Pembrokeshire.

BEFORE THE ROMANS CAME

by TOM STEPHENSON

IT is only within recent years that it has been possible for the layman to gain an idea of the life and habits of prehistoric man. Nowadays, however, we may learn something of the long ages that elapsed before Rome was built. Painstaking workers have been patiently digging and sifting the land, collecting innumerable trifles and laboriously piecing together the details of a most intricate mosaic.

One of the first difficulties is to gain an impression of the time scale. About 2000 B.C. the Late Stone Age was merging into the Bronze Age. Beyond that date there is a backward extension into unmeasured time, and it may well be that a million years have passed since the idea of fashioning a piece of flint into a useful tool first dawned in the mind of some sub-human creature.

Of the earliest men in Britain the land today offers little evidence except to the expert who is willing to make a minute scrutiny. We will, therefore, only outline the story in brief, and mention some of the places which have provided interesting clues.

In the little Kentish village of Ightham lived Benjamin Harrison, a village grocer who was also a keen archæologist, and whose discoveries set the experts debating at great length. On the North Downs Harrison found some flints which he believed had been roughly shaped by man. Today, while the authorities are not unanimous, many accept these stones as primitive tools.

These flints, possibly the earliest indication of man as a tool-making animal, are termed *eoliths* from two Greek words meaning " dawn of stone."

In the neighbourhood of Ipswich, beneath a deposit known as the Suffolk Crag, Mr. J. Read Moir discovered flint implements which he considered the connecting link between eoliths and tools undoubtedly shaped by man.

Of these discoveries Mr. T. D. Kendrick has written :

> " Pre-Crag man stands forth suddenly, unheralded and astonishing, revealed, as it were, by the swift drawing aside of a curtain ; his background is the darkness of the immeasurable past and he inhabits a land which was believed to be untenanted by the human race."

From this faintly visualized dawn of tool-making man, we pass to the *Paleolithic* (Greek *palaios* = old, and *lithos* = stone) or Old Stone Age.

Anyone familiar with the Norfolk coast at Cromer will remember the accumulation of flint fragments along the foreshore. Among this shingle have been found orange-coloured flints evidently shaped by primitive man. It has been

W. F. TAYLOR

A STONE CIRCLE IN LAKELAND

Scattered about the country there are many stone circles where our prehistoric forefathers carried out unknown rites. None of these ancient temples, not even Stonehenge, is situated in more impressive solitude than the so-called Druid's Circle at Keswick. Here one appears to be completely ringed with high and mighty hills.

suggested that here was a workshop where those early artificers fashioned their implements. Many of the tools, including huge rough hand axes and scrapers and choppers, are so large that it is considered that the people who made and used them were men of exceptional strength with big and powerful hands.

Subsequent to the coming of the first tool-makers, Britain, in common with Northern Europe, suffered conditions similar to those of the Arctic regions of today, and glaciers ploughed across the land.

In those times Britain was still part of the Continent, unsevered by the English Channel. Therefore the animals, driven southwards by the advancing ice-sheet, or returning northwards in the warmer intervals, had no sea barrier to interrupt their passage. This land bridge would also facilitate the migrations of Paleolithic Man, for he also at times was, no doubt, compelled to retreat to a more endurable climate.

He was, it must be remembered, a hunter depending on the chase for his food, augmenting his larder probably with fish, berries, nuts and roots. He had not discovered the arts of cultivation or domestication of animals, and, at best, his existence could only have been a very lean one. A wanderer, with nothing more permanent as a home than a rude shelter of twigs covered with grass or skins, he had no anchorage, but roamed as he was led by his quest for food. Generally he appears to have lived in the vicinity of rivers, and the most abundant finds of flint implements have been located in such places.

So far, prehistoric man appears to have lived in the open, but towards the middle of Paleolithic times the Ice Age reached its greatest intensity, and the hardy individuals who remained to face its rigours were driven to seek shelter, and this brings us to the period of the Cave Men, perhaps 20,000 years ago.

Probably they inhabited mouths of caves and hollows under overhanging rocks. At Oldbury Hill, near the village of Ightham, previously mentioned, we may see one of these rock shelters. Since it was inhabited some of the overhanging

STEPHENSON

A STONE-AGE DWELLING

These overhanging rocks on Oldbury Hill, at Ightham, Kent, provided a home for prehistoric men whose implements have been found nearby. At the time it was inhabited it was no doubt considered a desirable residence, well placed on a hill-side, affording shelter from the weather, with an adjacent water supply.

W. F. TAYLOR

A COMMUNAL GRAVE

Communal burial was a practice of the people of the Late Stone Age, and over their dead they raised large mounds of earth, now known as Long Barrows. Some are 300 feet or more in length. Many of them contain stone passages and burial chambers. Above is the Long Barrow of Belas Knapp, in Gloucestershire.

rock has fallen down the hillside. Sufficient remains, however, for the imaginative mind to picture a family living here ; man, the hunter, ranging the adjacent country for his prey, and the woman busy with household life, dressing the food, scraping skins and fashioning them into clumsy garments. Some of their weapons lost and perhaps trampled in the mud, remained buried on the slopes beneath until Benjamin Harrison found them ages later and recognized the story behind them.

Kent's Cavern, near Torquay, was another habitation, and remains have been found there belonging to several distinct periods, and the implements range from the early drift period to the New Stone Age. This does not mean that the cavern was continuously occupied by man through such a lapse of time. In fact, from the bones which were found, it was evident that it had also served as a retreat for animals such as the cave-hyena, rhinoceros, bison, bear, cave lion, wolf, fox and reindeer. Another cave at Brixham provides a similar story, and the limestone caves in the Mendips have also yielded many clues of early habitation.

This Neanderthal Man, as he has been named, appears to have been a most unprepossessing creature. He had a flat receding forehead, with a heavy continuous brow ridge protruding over large eye sockets, a chinless jaw and thick neck,

and a head thrust forward. His arms were long and his thighbones curved, and he probably shuffled along with a stooping gait.

Neanderthal Man completely vanished with the arrival of a superior type known as the Cro-Magnon Man. This newcomer was tall and had a well-developed forehead and a strong chin. The first discovery of Cro-Magnon man in Britain was made at Paviland Cave, near Rhossilly, in South Wales. The skeleton was found associated with a skull and tusk of a hairy mammoth, and his bones had been stained red with oxide of iron which suggests the existence of some ritual connected with burial. Near the thighs were a number of small shells which may have formed a waist girdle, and there were also some small rods of ivory, perhaps the remains of a necklace.

An Artistic People

Thus we come to the latter stages of Paleolithic times which were eras of remarkable development. A higher standard of tool making is evident and implements fashioned of bone, such as harpoons, are found, and eventually bone needles appear and there is, moreover, an indication of artistic tendencies.

Among these artistic folk there came from the east a horde of invaders, who have been likened to Philistines or prehistoric Huns. For a time

ANCIENT DWELLINGS

A Skara Brae, Orkney, there is a remarkable group of prehistoric dwellings.   The photograph shows Hut 7, the best preserved of them.   In the centre is the rectangular fireplace, and on each side of it is a bed which would be filled with heather.   At the back is a stone cupboard or dresser, possibly used for the storing of food.

these barbarians dominated Western Europe and evidence of their influence has been discovered at Kent's Cavern and in the caves of Creswell Crags, in Derbyshire. With the passing of these people their predecessors rose again and developed a most amazing culture. In France and Spain, caves have been discovered in which are engraved and painted on the rock face pictures of remarkable artistic merit and small statues of ivory and stone have been found.

In Britain, so far, there have been no discoveries of caves decorated by these artists, but the Creswell Caves have yielded carved bone implements of the period.

A process of degeneration appears to mark the close of the Old Stone Age. Man the hunter and the artist passes from the scene and his place is taken by people in some respects his inferiors yet in others marking very definite advances. Thus we pass into the *Neolithic* Period (Greek *neos* = new, and *lithos* = stone) or New Stone Age, a time when Britain was emerging from the final rigours of the Ice Age.

It may have been about 5000 B.C. when these long-headed Neolithic men reached Britain, but some authorities put it as late as 3000 B.C., and suggest that the period may only have lasted about 1,000 years until the beginning of the Bronze Age.

These newcomers may rightly be said to have introduced the first civilization in these islands for they brought with them a communal life not likely to have been known in the Old Stone Age. They had learned something of agriculture, and certainly before the end of the period they were cultivating cereals. Unlike their nomadic predecessors, they were farmers and herdsmen. Pottery they knew how to manufacture, and their stone implements were polished instead of being merely shaped by chipping. Whilst their clothing in the main probably consisted of skins, they had discovered the uses of flax and acquired a knowledge of weaving.

Early Villages

Their primitive dwellings were often sunk in the ground, and the depression was surrounded by piled stones upholding the walls and roof which consisted of a timber framework, perhaps filled with wattle and daub, or thatched with turf. The huts were generally grouped in villages, sometimes on sites which lent themselves to defence, and where some attempt at fortification was made.

Windmill Hill, near Avebury, in Wiltshire, appears to have been such a site and the camp was surrounded by three oval concentric ditches, the outermost of which had a diameter of about 1,200 feet.

The Trundle, near Goodwood racecourse, in

Sussex, was another site with an inner ditch and two incomplete outer ditches, interrupted by causeways, and it has been suggested that these barriers formed part of a defence with wooden towers. Another theory is that there were probably dwelling places situated between the causeways.

Another aspect of the settled life of those days is the evidence of the organized industry of the flint mines from which the raw materials for implements were obtained. One of these was at the famous Grimes Graves, near Brandon, in Suffolk, where the workings cover about twenty acres. As many as three hundred and sixty-six circular depressions have been counted, marking the spots where shafts were dug down to the level of the flint and then opened out into galleries.

A number of these flint mines have been excavated in Sussex, and one of the most interesting is that of Cissbury Ring on the South Downs, near Worthing. Picks made from the antlers of red deer, shovels fashioned from the shoulder blades of oxen, and fitted with handles made

from deer antlers, have been found on this site as well as an interesting specimen of a prehistoric miner's lamp. In one of the galleries, the roof was found still blackened with soot from such a lamp used by a miner who possibly worked there 4,000 years ago.

" Giants' Graves"

One of the outstanding features of Neolithic times was the practice of communal burial, and the erection of large mounds over the dead. Many of these Long Barrows, as they are termed, still remain and whilst they are of most frequent occurrence in Wessex and the Cotswolds, they may be traced from Lincolnshire to Wales and from Cornwall to the far north of Scotland.

For an illustration we might take the Long Barrow at West Kennet, close to the Bath Road, in Wiltshire. This was excavated in 1860, and then had a length of 336 feet tapering from a width of 75 feet at the east end, where it was 8 feet high, to a width of 40 feet at the western extremity. Near the eastern end some stones

DIXON-SCOTT

THE DEVIL'S DEN

Dolmens, or stone tables, such as this one on the downs near Marlborough, in Wiltshire, are probably the remains of Neolithic Long Barrows. The covering mantle of earth has been ploughed away or removed by the action of the weather, leaving exposed some of the stones which formed the burial chamber.

ORDNANCE SURVEY   BY PERMISSION H.M. STATIONERY OFFICE

THE OLDEST MONUMENT IN BRITAIN

Avebury, in Wiltshire, was an important place in Neolithic times.   Towards the close of this period and at the time when bronze implements were coming into fashion, this great temple was built.   This view from the air shows the ditch and rampart which surrounded the stone circle from which an avenue of stones led to Overton Hill.

were found protruding from the soil, and others were lying about on the mound, and from these it was possible to reconstruct the original work.

From the east end a double row of upright stones extended 60 feet into the mound and there terminated in a burial chamber. Both the chamber and the corridor were roofed with large flat stones, some of them a ton in weight. Over this the earth had been heaped in a mound, round the outer edge of which was a ring of standing stones and between these were courses of dry walling.

Another interesting specimen is at Capel Garmon, in Denbighshire. This had a side entrance and a passage leading into a chamber with three divisions. A series of Long Barrows have also been recognized on the Lincolnshire Wolds, some of them having significant names such as " Deadman's Graves," " Hills of the Slain " and " Giants' Graves."

Many other Long Barrows have lost their coverings, and sometimes the stones as well have been removed, and it is probable that the many dolmens (stone tables) as they are termed, are relics of Long Barrows. Such a one is Kit's Coty, between Chatham and Maidstone, in Kent, which

Pepys believed to be the monument of a Saxon king. In plan this is like a broad H with a large cap-stone set across the three upright stones.

Cornwall has several examples, one of the best known being the Lanyon Quoit. Wales is well sprinkled with them, many having interesting legends. Among them may be mentioned the Tinkinswood Dolmen at St. Nicholas, Glamorgan, the Maen Cetti, or Arthur's Stone, in Gower, and the one at Clynnog Fawr, in Caernarvonshire. In Ireland, about nine hundred dolmens have been catalogued and one at Mount Brown, near Carlow, has a cap-stone weighing one hundred tons.

Temple Builders

The period during which prehistoric man, aided with only the simplest of engineering devices, expended such an enormous amount of labour in erecting these great tombs, has been termed the *Megalithic* Age (*megas* = great, *lithos* = stone). Before considering other relics of this period, it should be mentioned that the Megalithic culture did not terminate with the end of Neolithic times, but was carried forward into the subsequent Bronze Age.

The best known, and most popular, remains of this kind are the numerous stone circles, the Druid's Circles as they are often termed, examples of which are found in many parts of the country from the south of England up to the Orkneys.

It is now generally believed that these served as temples or places of assembly, and were the outcome of some deep-seated feeling which was sufficiently strong to impel men to co-operate in the gigantic labour involved in the erection of structures which still endure as tribute to their endeavours.

The first and foremost of these temples in magnitude and in antiquity are the Avebury ruins, in Wiltshire. Of the five hundred great monoliths which comprised the temple, only about two dozen remain, but by excavations and examination of earlier records, it has been possible to create pictures of its former splendour.

for about one mile to another stone circle on Overton Hill, known as the Sanctuary. Recent excavations have been made along this line, and some of the stones have been restored to their original position. These can now be seen alongside the lane connecting Avebury with the Bath Road.

Stonehenge, the most famous of all the circles, is probably the latest in date, and is certainly the most elaborate. Avebury and Stonehenge may be regarded as the two extremes of circle architecture, the one the prototype and the other the culminating masterpiece. The former consisted

TEMPLE OF MYSTERY

This sketch gives an impression of Stonehenge in its complete state. The outer ring consisted of thirty upright stones carrying horizontal stones. Inside them was a ring of smaller stones. Next were five Trilithons in a horseshoe, then a horseshoe of smaller stones and finally a flat slab now termed the Altar Stone.

Round the modern village may be seen the great ditch and rampart which surrounded the temple, enclosing some twenty-eight acres, and having an average diameter of 1,200 feet. Within the ditch was a large circle of massive unhewn stones, enclosing two smaller double circles. From the temple an avenue of stones extended

of rough hewn blocks and the latter of squared and dressed stones arranged in a more complicated plan. At Avebury and in most other circles, the stones are of local origin, but at Stonehenge some of the blocks were brought from the Prescelly Hills, in Pembrokeshire, nearly one hundred and fifty miles away. These stones, it is believed, were brought to Salisbury Plain in the time of the Long Barrow men, and as the monument was not completed in its final form until the Bronze Age, it is possible they were part of an earlier circle which was incorporated in the later work.

Much has been written of Stonehenge, and many speculations have been made regarding its purpose. But the precise object for which it was built is still a subject of conjecture. The fact that at the summer solstice the sun rises over the Hele Stone in a line with the axis of the monument has been used to formulate a theory of sun worship. At the heart of the monument is a flat stone known as the Altar, and outside the ring is another recumbent slab termed the Slaughter Stone, and these have been incorporated in fanciful notions of Druids and sacrificial rites.

Whatever the nature of the ceremonies, there can certainly be no doubt that it was a place of supreme importance in its day; an object of veneration, possibly a place of pilgrimage and, as the number of burial mounds in its vicinity suggest, a desirable and hallowed resting place.

The Beaker Folk

The Bronze Age, to which we have referred, is believed to have opened in this country about 2000 B.C. or possibly a little later. The first implements of bronze from which the period takes its name were introduced by round-headed stocky people who have been labelled the "Beaker" folk from the beaker-shaped pottery which they brought with them. The main stream of immigrants is believed to have reached our eastern shores from the Rhinelands and to have established themselves among the Long Barrow folk on the Yorkshire Wolds. From there they afterwards spread northwards, westwards into Wales, and southwards to Wiltshire.

For the wayfarer the most obvious relics of the Bronze Age are the innumerable Round Barrows scattered about the countryside. These circular, domed mounds are particularly conspicuous on the smooth turfed downland where they may often be seen as gentle swellings above the general level of the land, and sometimes standing out clearly as rounded elevations on the skyline. In Wiltshire alone there are said to be 2,000 Round Barrows and about three hundred have been enumerated in the vicinity of Stonehenge.

Like the Long Barrows they served the purpose of burial mounds, and have afforded interesting information of their times. The beakers were buried with the dead, and may have held refreshment intended for the departed spirit.

Many of these Bronze-Age folk appear to have been sufficiently wealthy to adorn themselves with numerous ornaments. Fragments of leather garments, and of linen and woollen clothes have been found. Some of the chiefs fastened their tunics with buttons of gold, ivory and amber. Necklaces of jet have been discovered as well as beads of amber, glass, and various gold ornaments.

W. F. TAYLOR

BRONZE-AGE BURIAL MOUNDS

In many parts of the country and especially on the chalk uplands, may be seen domed mounds known as Round Barrows. The majority of these are burial mounds of the Bronze Age, and the relics found in them have provided information of that period. Above are some typical examples at East Kennet, in Wiltshire.

HOME OF BRONZE-AGE MAN

At one period prehistoric men built themselves dwellings similar to the one above which are known as Beehive Huts. These consist of slabs of stone set in a ring with a horizontal stone over the low doorway, the roof being covered with turf and supported by a centre post. This example is to be seen on Bodmin Moor, Cornwall.

For a glimpse of a Bronze-Age habitation we may journey to Dartmoor where there are a number of hut circles believed to date from this period. Grimspound, four and a half mile south-west of Moretonhampstead, appears to have been a village of twenty-four huts surrounded by a dry stone wall. These huts consisted of a circle of upright slabs of stone about 3 feet high, backed with turf, a space about 30 inches high being left for a doorway. Near the centre of the circle was a stone on which may have stood a centre-post supporting a roof of boughs covered with turf or bracken.

Travelling Tinkers

On Bodmin Moor, in Cornwall, are other examples where stone foundations may be seen in walled enclosures and, as on Dartmoor, the fields of the villagers may be traced.

Considerable light has been thrown on the period by the discovery of numerous collections of implements which had been buried by their owners, perhaps during times of crisis and not afterwards recovered. Some of these consist of broken or disused implements collected by travelling tinkers for remelting.

The travelling tinker and the tribal smith, it has been said, stand for hitherto unknown conditions, both social and economic, and there is abundant evidence of the commerce which

developed in these times. At Bologna, in Italy, there were large depots to which were brought for re-smelting old bronze collected from all over Europe including Britain.

Cornish tin was doubtless exported to Ireland, possibly in exchange for Irish gold, but it may be that the gold ornaments found in Cornwall were specimens lost by the Irish traders on their way to the Continent, for these people are assumed to have crossed the peninsula instead of rounding Land's End by sea.

There has been much speculation regarding the antiquity of the Cornish tin trade, and there have been fascinating theories about dark Phœnicians venturing so far for the metal as early as 1200 or 1500 B.C. Imaginative writers have given us pictures of these folk bartering for tin, and carrying it overland by ancient tracks to the Isle of Wight, or even to the Straits of Dover before they took to the sea for their home voyage.

Pytheas, the Greek explorer, appears to have reached these shores about 325 B.C. From Land's End, he says, the natives carried ingots of tin to an island called Ictis, which at low tide was left dry, and there they sold the metal to the merchants. Ictis is considered to be the little island of St. Michael's Mount, in Mount's Bay, although the Isle of Wight has been claimed as the site, largely on the basis of the similarity of its own name Vectis, to Ictis. This commerce had no doubt been in existence for some time before the voyage of Pytheas, but for how long we must leave in conjecture.

For fifteen centuries the Bronze Age developed and matured in Britain before the coming of iron. This metal which had been in use for some time on the Continent is believed to have reached England about 500 B.C., and with its coming a new era opened.

Skilled Craftsmen

Bronze still remained in use during the Iron Age, and was fashioned into various articles including helmets, shields, mirrors and other objects. Iron, however, was used where its greater hardness and durability was advantageous. Beautiful specimens of the artistic work of this period, including some excellent enamel work, have been found. These testify to the skill of the early British craftsmen who were unsurpassed by any of their continental contemporaries.

Iron-Age villages and towns have been located in various parts of the country. At Chysauster, in Cornwall, may be seen the remains of a typical village. This consisted of eight large houses, four on each side of a street. One of the houses is an oval enclosure 90 feet long with masonry still standing in places to a height of 6 feet. A passage led into a central chamber which apparently was not roofed. On each side of this were rooms built into the thickness of the walls. Excavation revealed paving, hearths, ashes, a granite basin and a drain along the west side of the house. Behind the houses were artificially terraced garden plots surrounded by stone walls.

At Carn Euny, four and a half miles southwest of Penzance, are traces of a village similar to that at Chysauster, and in one of the houses a doorway in the wall afforded entry into a fogou or underground dwelling. This was a stone-lined tunnel about 60 feet long and 6 feet high. Near the eastern end a side passage leads into a circular chamber 16 feet in diameter. This room was partly paved and under the flagstones was a drain extended along the passage. Another fogou at Halligye, near Trelowarren, is well preserved and may be explored with the aid of a torch or candle. In the tunnel of this one there is a ridge of rock across the passage, evidently intended as a booby trap or stumbling block to give warning of the approach of a stranger.

For the layman the most impressive remains of the Iron Age are the great earthworks which crown many a hill-top and which, with their mighty swelling ramparts and deep ditches contouring the flanks of the hills, present an air of permanence and of enduring harmony with the landscape.

There are more of these structures than we could include even in a bare catalogue, and mention of a few must suffice. Along the Berkshire and Wiltshire Ridgeway there are several outstanding examples, one of the finest being Uffington Castle. This stands on the edge of

W. F. TAYLOR

PRE-ROMAN EARTHWORKS

On many a hill-top may be seen the earthworks of prehistoric men. Most of these were probably built in the five hundred years before the Roman Conquest, but some are considered to have had their beginnings in the Late Stone Age. The photograph shows the ramparts of the British Camp on the Herefordshire Beacon.

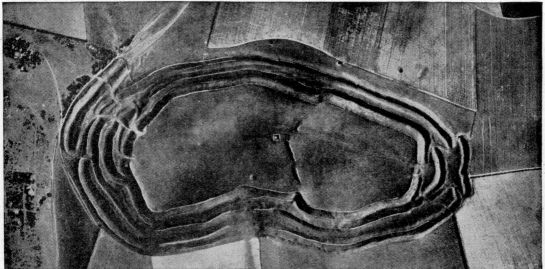

ORDNANCE SURVEY BY PERMISSION H.M. STATIONERY OFFICE

THE GREAT RAMPARTS OF MAIDEN CASTLE

This aerial view of Maiden Castle, near Dorchester, affords some idea of this great earthwork which is by far the largest in Britain. In late Stone-Age times there was a town here. For 1,500 years it appears to have been deserted, and then from about the fifth century B.C. *it was again occupied until Roman times.*

the downs overlooking the spreading Vale of the White Horse. That famous animal, in fact, is carved in the chalk slopes beneath the ramparts. He would be dull indeed who could pace that great circling bank and look down on the outer ditch and the gateway leading to the camp without wondering by whom, and for what purpose, such a place was constructed by the forgotten inhabitants of the downs.

From that vantage point, nearly 900 feet above sea-level, we may gaze to westward along the line of the Ridgeway and pick out the ramparts of Liddington Castle, a similar structure where Richard Jefferies loved to bask and daydream on the smooth grassy walls of the camp. A few miles westwards again and we reach Barbury Castle, with double ditch and rampart encircling about twelve acres.

Salisbury Plain has several of these great earthworks, including Bratton Castle overlooking the vale of Pewsey, and the great upstanding camps of Battlesbury and Scratchbury, near Warminster, and the lonely camp of Yarnbury with triple ditches and double ramparts and complicated entrances as if designed to baffle unwanted visitors.

On the western edge of the Mendips stands Dolebury, with stone-faced ramparts, and west of this, overlooking Weston-super-Mare, is the similarly engineered Worlebury. In Dorset, at the eastern end of the vale of Blackmore, the twin heights of Hod Hill and Hambledon Hill are each crowned with a conspicuous camp.

Some of these may have had an earlier origin, and in some instances there is evidence of Bronze

Age and even Neolithic occupation, prior to the building of the ramparts, but generally these works are believed to date from the Iron Age. Although in the past they have been referred to as camps, this term is now considered misleading and it is suggested that " hill-forts " or " hill-towns " would be a more accurate appellation, for the earthworks were the walls of villages or towns.

A Prehistoric Town

By far the greatest and most imposing of all these earthworks are those of Maiden Castle, near Dorchester. Recent excavations have established that here, 4,000 years ago, was a town covering about fifteen acres and enclosed within triple entrenchments. This Neolithic settlement was apparently raided about 1,900 B.C. Then for fifteen centuries the site was abandoned. Towards the end of the fifth century B.C. it was again occupied and developed into a town with upwards of 4,000 inhabitants. The innermost rampart was given a stone parapet and entrance was gained through a passage between massive stone walls. Inside the great gateway there was a sentry-box on each side. Nearby was a pit containing thousands of sling stones stored ready for defence. Only in Roman times was the place finally abandoned for a site now occupied by modern Dorchester.

Here, perhaps more than anywhere else in Britain, is evidence of the long drawn out centuries and of the labour and life of our prehistoric forefathers.

Based on Ordnance Survey Map by permission H.M. Stationery Office

BRITAIN OF THE ROMANS

by TOM STEPHENSON

THROUGHOUT Britain there yet remains many an interesting memento of those three and a half centuries during which this country was a part of the great Roman Empire, enjoying the advantages of that amazing civilization, and developing under its rule to an extent not generally realized.

In many places we see relics of the days when soldiers and merchants from the far corners of a wide-spread empire wandered through the land, of the days when the toga was worn, when Latin was the recognized tongue and Roman culture prevailed, and men congregated at the baths, or worshipped strange gods in Roman temples.

Confronted with a straight stretch of road, we immediately hazard a guess as to its Roman origin, and frequently we are not mistaken. Camps and forts where the Legions stayed are not difficult to recognize. Here and there we may discern the bare outlines of a town, perhaps only faint markings in the soil or a few fragments of masonry tell the tale of vanished glory.

Along the moors and basalt crags of Northumberland we may walk the ramparts of Hadrian's Wall, the greatest of all our Roman relics. There we may linger within the confines of a fort or town whose lowly foundations tell of the mighty past. There we may trace the plans of barracks and granary, the commandant's quarters and the regimental chapel ; the forum and the temple, the shops and houses and baths, and, beyond the fort, the village where dwelt the soldiers' native wives and the various camp followers.

Elsewhere we may stand amid the ruins of Roman villas where mosaic floors, the elaborate

ROMAN BATH
W. F. TAYLOR
According to legend the warm mineral springs at Bath were discovered by Bladud, father of King Lear. The waters were appreciated by the Romans, who erected bath houses and made the place a spa.

arrangements for the all-important baths, the central heating systems and other details may tell of the domestic arrangements of a wealthy citizen of the Empire.

On the Ordnance Survey maps are indicated Romano-British villages where the native population lived and worked, and where excavations have revealed the shards and weapons and tools of the common people.

Before Cæsar made his hurried invasions in 55 and 54 B.C., arts, industry and commerce had been developed in Britain. Kings or tribal chieftains governed from their respective capitals, and they had close connections with kindred tribes across the Channel.

Cunobelinus (Shakespeare's Cymbeline) who reigned until A.D. 43, gained some ascendancy over his rivals and was regarded by Rome prior to the conquest, as king of England and Camulodunum, the Colchester of today, where he had a mint, was considered the virtual capital of England.

In A.D. 43, during the reign of Claudius, it was decided the time was opportune for bringing Britain within the Roman Empire. Four Legions with auxiliary troops landed on the Kentish coast, possibly at Dover, Richborough and Lympne. After defeating the native forces commanded by two sons of Cunobelinus, they advanced to the Thames. There Claudius joined the Legions with additional troops, including the impressive elephant corps. Although Claudius was only in the country sixteen days, within that time the Thames had been crossed, Camulodunum seized and south-eastern England was under Roman rule.

Colchester has many reminders of its early days. Even the modern by-pass named in one

PHOTOCHROM

NEWPORT ARCH, LINCOLN

*Once used by the legionaries and citizens of the Roman city of Lindum Colonia, this gateway which has stood for
nearly nineteen centuries was the northern gate of the city and is still an exit from modern Lincoln. This was
probably the inner gateway, the outer having disappeared. From here Ermine Street continued northwards.*

portion Cymbeline's Way, recalls Cunobelinus,
whose capital was most likely at Lexden, two
miles west of Colchester. A mound there,
traditionally known as Cunobelinus's circus is
thought to have been his tomb.

The existing city has grown on the site of the
town founded by Claudius as the first Colonia or
Roman colony in Britain. There the retired
legionaries were comfortably settled with grants
of land, and in the centre of the town was erected
a temple dedicated to the deified Claudius.
Beneath the Norman castle may be seen the
vaulted crypt of this temple which, according
to Tacitus, was regarded with hatred by the
Britons as " a stronghold of eternal tyranny."

At first the town was unfortified, but after the
disastrous events in A.D. 61, it was surrounded
by a massive wall 10 feet thick and 30 feet high,
and making a circuit of nearly two miles. One
well-preserved length of the wall may be followed
from the cattle market to the Balkerne Gate,
the main gateway of the Roman town. The
gate towers, the guard room, the arches over
the stone-paved carriage ways and the smaller
arches for pedestrians, stand as an imposing
memento of the days when within the wall,
warriors from distant lands bowed to strange

deities including the invincible Sun-God Mithras.

Other remains in the Castle Park include ruins
of houses with mosaic floors. These dwellings
were part of a street 300 feet of which was
uncovered in 1920, when it was found that the
houses had been built about A.D. 75 over the
ruins of an earlier street which had probably
been burnt down when Boudicca sacked the
town.

Advance of the Legions

With a base securely established at Colchester,
the Romans set out to overcome the rest of the
country, and dividing their forces they pushed
outwards on radiating lines, one section advancing to the south-west, another to the west, and
the third northwards. After four years' cam-
paigning they had advanced as far as the line
now represented by the Fosse Way, the Roman
road running from Lincoln by way of Leicester,
Cirencester and Bath to Axminster, in Devon.

Leicester, the Ratae of Roman times, has a
number of mosaic pavements which suggests that
the town had some affluent citizens. The Church
of St. Nicholas is partly built of Roman materials,
and recent excavations have established that the
Jewry Wall, a large mass of masonry, was part

of the entrance from the Roman basilica, or town hall, to the forum.

Lincoln, whence the Ninth Legion advanced from Leicester, was first established as a military centre, but later developed into Lindum Colonia, a privileged colony of retired Legionaries similar to that at Colchester. Except for a few fragments the defensive walls have disappeared, but in the street now known as Bail Gate, circles in the roadway mark the sites of the pillars of a colonnade which fronted a building nearly 300 feet long, and which is believed to have been the basilica, a usual feature in the forum of a Roman town.

Slaughter of the Druids

Before continuing the westward advance the Romans deemed it advisable to turn about and subdue the Iceni or East Anglia rather than proceed with such a warlike tribe in their rear. This accomplished, a campaign was opened which was to last for thirty years before the intractable tribes of Wales led by Caractacus were finally conquered.

By A.D. 61 the legions had advanced through North Wales to the shores of the Menai Straits. Tacitus tells of the Druids and their followers gathered on the Anglesey shore, the women with dishevelled hair carrying flaming torches and dashing through the ranks like furies, while the priests poured forth curses on the invaders.

While the luckless Celts of Anglesey were being exterminated there came news that sent the Roman general hastening back to England. In the interval since the coming of Claudius wealthy towns had sprung up at Verulamium (St. Albans), Colchester and London, and these were now threatened by the rebelling Iceni, led by the redoubtable Queen Boudicca, the Boadicea commemorated by the chariot memorial near Westminster Bridge.

"Mighty in stature, terrible in aspect; her voice was harsh and her countenance savage," says the historian, Dion Cassius, of this fierce amazon who wreaked terrible vengeance for her wrongs before she poisoned herself in despair.

At Colchester strange omens and portents foretold her coming and a statue of Victory fell to the ground with its back to the enemy. With fire and sword Colonia was reduced to ruins, its inhabitants slaughtered, and the altar and temple to the deified Claudius were razed to the ground. London and Verulamium suffered a similar fate before this devastating revolt was quelled.

Each of these towns, however, rose again out of its ashes. London doubled its size and became the largest town in Britain, a city well planned and complete with adequate drainage and water supply.

Verulamium, near St. Albans, still offers

STEPHENSON

ROMAN THEATRE AT ST. ALBANS

On the edge of St. Albans are many evidences of the Roman town of Verulamium. Most interesting of them all is this second-century theatre which stood by Watling Street. Excavation of the site revealed striking evidence of the decline of Roman civilization. In the fourth century the theatre became a municipal refuse dump.

VALENTINE

MULTANGULAR TOWER, YORK

The lower portion of this tower consists of Roman masonry and is part of the legionary fortress of York which was surrounded by a wall with towers and gates.

evidence of its historic and prehistoric past. The original town of the British Catuvellauni occupied the brow of the hill at Prae Wood, south of the present town. The town which Boudicca sacked stood a little lower down the hill near the River Ver. In the second century Verulamium became a walled city standing on the ancient Watling Street, and rose to considerable importance. It was, in fact, the only Roman town in Britain to be constituted a self-governing *municipium*.

Portions of the Roman Wall may be seen, and excavations are each year revealing more of the ruins including the lines of the streets, and the buildings with beautiful tesselated floors.

By far the most interesting feature is the Roman theatre built about A.D. 141, and so far the only building of its kind discovered in Britain.

There one may walk round the smooth grassy banks of the auditorium and look down on the circular orchestra, the gangways and the foundations and piers of the stage, the green room and dressing rooms, and the slot into which the curtain was lowered. Confronted with these ruins no great amount of imagination is required to picture the Roman citizens of Verulamium, perhaps joined by a merchant or soldier on his way north, sitting here and witnessing Greek dramas or pantomimes and burlesques.

The famous Agricola, who took a prominent part in the conquest of Britain, arrived in A.D. 77 or 78, and after completing the conquest of

Wales, he set out to subdue the north of England and eventually to advance into Scotland.

Chester, Agricola's starting-point for the north, had already been established as a fortress on a bluff of red sandstone by the Dee, then a broad arm of the sea, up which the Roman galleys came to moor beneath the fortress on a site now silted up by the sands of Dee to form the level ground known as the Roodee.

Deva, as this fortress was termed, from the River Dee, was one of the three legionary fortresses in Britain, a distinction it shared with York and Caerleon on Usk.

The existing medieval walls of Chester follow the lines of the earlier walls of the east and north sides. Roman masonry has been exposed in several places and the foundations of a Roman tower may be seen at the New Gate. The main streets in the centre of the city evidently coincide with the Roman streets and the picturesque Rows, of which Chester is proud, are built over the ruins of second- and third-century buildings.

In some of the shops in these thoroughfares may be seen odd remnants of this erstwhile city of the legions.

Agricola, in A.D. 79, overcame the Brigantes, and in the following year made his headquarters at York as being better suited for his further campaigns.

Ultimately he overran the north of England, and consolidated his position with roads and chains of forts. One of these may have been at

STEPHENSON

ROMAN MASONRY IN VILLAGE SCHOOL

Schoolchildren at High Rochester have a reminder of Rome's departed glory. The school porch is built of stones from the adjacent fort of Bremenium.

Ribchester on the banks of the Ribble, in Lancashire, where the ancient time-worn parish church stands on the site of a temple dedicated to Minerva.

From here one road was driven up the west side of the Ribble Valley across the vale of the Hodder and through the moorland country of Bowland on its way to Overborough. Another road ran on the other side of Ribblesdale to Elslack, in Yorkshire, and through the Aire gap at Skipton. Beyond there the road divided, one branch continuing across the Wharfe and over Blubberhouses Moor where a straight length of seven miles is still termed Watling Street, and on to Aldborough. The other branch proceeded to Ilkley and on to York. Agricola is believed to have established forts at Ilkley which would guard the route through the low Pennine Pass of the Aire gap.

Farther north another road was driven over the Stainmore Pass with forts at Greta Bridge and Bowes, and at Rey Cross on a commanding site overlooking the wide vale of the Eden, whilst another was located on the western side of the Pennines at Brough under Stainmore. These roads and forts are considered part of a strategic plan to encompass the great block of hilly country between the Aire Valley and Stainmore, the two natural routes through the Pennines.

When Agricola went to York, or Eboracum, as it was known, a military base was already established there with the Ninth Legion in occupation. In later years York developed into the chief military centre of Roman Britain, the " Altera Roma," or other Rome. Four emperors are known to have visited it. Hadrian was there in A.D. 121 or 122, and he it was who made it the naval headquarters. Severus stayed there, and there he died. Outside the walls, according to legend, his body was burnt and his ashes were carried to Rome in an urn, to which before his death he had addressed the words, " You are about to contain a man for whom the world was too small."

York's most prominent relic of Roman days is the Multangular Tower which formed the south-west bastion of the city wall. In the museum, as might be expected, are numerous objects, including altars to Mars, Hercules, Jove and Britannia, and a touching inscription " To the gods, the Shades ; for Simplicia Florentine,

VICTOR AND VANQUISHED

In Hexham Abbey may be seen this tombstone of Flavinus, a standard-bearer of the Ala Petriana, a cavalry regiment stationed on the wall. It depicts a mounted Roman kicking a naked Briton, who is crouching on the ground and looking rather woe-begone.

a most innocent being who lived ten months. Her father Felicius Simplex, of the VI Legion, dedicated this."

About sixteen miles north-west of York, the village of Aldborough occupies the site of Isurium Brigantium, the Romanized capital of the Brigantes where many mosaic pavements have been discovered. Aldborough stands on the road which remains to mark the line followed by Agricola in his advance into Scotland.

On the north banks of the Tyne, near the present-day village of Corbridge, Agricola founded the fort of Corstopitium, which later grew into an important military town and a base for the soldiers who were later stationed on the wall.

Excavations have unearthed the foundations of a forum and huge granaries as well as temples, shops and houses. One building, evidently a pottery shop, had its wares arranged in rows, and in the floor were found coins, perhaps dropped by the shopkeeper or intending purchasers in the second century.

Corstopitium knew some troublous days and was sacked on at least three occasions, and each time was rebuilt before being finally left to decay about A.D. 395.

From there Agricola drove his line into the wild and hilly country of the North Tyne and the barren solitudes of the Cheviots. At West Woodburn the fort of Habitancium is to be seen, and at High Rochester are the more imposing remains of Bremenium. This site has yielded a number of inscribed stones and altars which tell something of its story. Here were installed great catapults or stone-throwing machines and a number of stone balls used as projectiles, some of them weighing more than a hundredweight, have been unearthed.

On the roadside near the fort stands the base of a circular tomb believed to be that of Severus Alexander, a third-century governor of the fort.

High amid the Cheviots on the lonely heights at the head of the Coquet Valley, stands Chew Green Camp or Camps, which have been described as " the most perfect group of Roman earthworks that exist, not merely in this kingdom, but perhaps anywhere in the Roman Empire." From this desolate spot Dere Street crossed the Scottish Border and ran down to the Tweed and on towards the upstanding Eildon Hills. Those triple peaks suggested the name of Trimontium for the great fort which Agricola established at Newstead, near Melrose. Unfortunately no signs of this are visible today, but excavations in the past have yielded innumerable relics of the days when centurions of the Twentieth Legion dedicated altars to Silvanus and other gods.

A Scottish Frontier

Still northwards Agricola thrust his way to Stirling, on to Perth and as far north as Inchtuthill, where another of his forts was established. Somewhere in the Highlands in A.D. 84, and after he had constructed a chain of forts from the Forth to the Clyde he fought the famous unlocated battle of Mons Graupius.

After Agricola's recall to Rome, there were frequent revolts which eventually compelled the Romans to consider the establishment of a definite frontier. In A.D. 121 or 122 the Emperor Hadrian visited Britain, and to him is ascribed

W. F. TAYLOR

RUINS OF CILURNIUM ON HADRIAN'S WALL

At Chesters on the North Tyne near Chollerford are the remains of one of the most interesting forts on the Roman Wall. The photograph shows a street of the fort with bases of pillars and remains of buildings. From burnt debris found during excavations, it is surmised the fort was burnt on three occasions by the Picts.

D. MCLEISH

ROMAN WALL AT HOUSESTEADS

Along the heights of Northumberland runs Hadrian's Wall, the greatest and most spectacular of Roman frontier works, extending from the mouth of the Tyne to the Solway Firth. The builders took advantage of the natural features by taking the wall along the highest ground which presents a steep escarpment towards the north.

the famous wall which was built across England from the mouth of the Tyne to the Solway, and which is now known as Hadrian's Wall.

This mighty piece of engineering, the grandest of all our Roman remains, and the one most likely to rouse the imagination and bring to mind visions of the Legions, the Tungrians, the Asturians, the Thracians, Dalmatians and Batavians, is even yet a splendid witness of the power and infinite resources of Imperial Rome.

Hadrian's Wall

Recent work has established that the wall, with its chain of forts, mile castles and turrets, extending for seventy-three miles from sea to sea, was completed within a period of five years. The borough of Wallsend, as its name implies, was the eastward termination of the wall. Newcastle took its Roman name of Pons Aelius from the bridge built across the Tyne in Hadrian's reign, Aelius being the family name of the Emperor.

Westwards from Newcastle for about twenty-seven miles, the line of the wall is now covered by an eighteenth-century road, and we may start our brief survey at the point where the

wall crossed the North Tyne at Chollerford.

There was situated the fort of Cilurnium, occupied by Asturian cavalry. This site on the private estate at Chesters, has been carefully excavated and in the adjacent museum is a splendid collection of inscribed stones, votive offerings and jewellery, and a reproduction of a bronze tablet, the "discharge certificate" of a time-expired legionary. Within the grounds may be seen the foundations and lower walls of the buildings, including barracks and remains of a colonnade, and the regimental chapel from which a stairway led down to the strong room which housed the pay chest. The commandant's house with hypocaust for central heating may be recognized, and near the river stands the regimental bath-house with seven small recesses which may have been lockers for the bathers' clothes. On the opposite bank of the Tyne is the abutment of the bridge which crossed the river, and three stone piers are sometimes visible in the water.

About six miles west of Chesters there begins the best preserved length of the wall, and from Sewingshields as we walk the wall along those heights, and gaze northwards across the brown waste of moors towards the distant Cheviots, we may well wonder what were the effects of such a bleak and cheerless prospect on the minds of legionaries from Spain and other southern climes. Did they with native oaths curse the bogs and sombre moorlands, and grey weeping skies of this northern frontier?

On this length there is sufficient to indicate the nature of the wall, and it has been discovered that the Second, the Sixth and the Twentieth Legions were engaged in its construction, aided no doubt by auxiliaries and native slaves.

Building of the Wall

Stone was quarried in the locality, dressed and shaped and carried to the required site. At first the wall was intended to be 10 feet thick, but later this was altered to 8 feet. North of the wall a V-shaped ditch about 30 feet wide and 10 feet deep was excavated.

South of the wall runs the Vallum, a ditch which was crossed at intervals by roadways spanned by ornamental arches. This work is considered earlier than the wall, and may have marked the frontier in the reign of Trajan (A.D. 98-117). Throughout its length the wall was guarded by a chain of forts, and at each Roman mile stood a milecastle, providing quarters for the men on sentry duty. Between each mile-castle two turrets divided the wall into three equal lengths, and it is supposed these turrets were used for signalling by fire or smoke.

From Sewingshields we follow the wall to Housesteads, the ruins of Borcovicium. This famous fort, now owned by the National Trust, is one of the most fascinating ruins on the wall. Careful exploration has brought to light the structure of the fort, and there we may wander in and out of the various buildings all neatly labelled. Here was stationed the First Cohort of the Tungrians (from Tungres, Belgium), one thousand strong and housed in ten long, narrow barracks. Three other similarly-placed buildings were probably workshops and stables. In the centre of the fort stood the commandant's quarters with courtyard and colonnade. North of this were two granaries, their floors raised to keep the grain dry. Some of the masonry of the four gateways remains, and in the south entrance the pivot holes of the gates may be seen and the central stone against which the doors closed. On each side of this stone are grooves worn by Roman wheels, seventeen or eighteen centuries ago.

Outside the fort were other buildings, and on the south slopes was a considerable settlement of civilians. Some of the houses there have been uncovered, and one is known as " the Murder House," from the fact that the skeletons of a man and woman were found beneath the floor. The broken end of a sword was found between the man's ribs, and, as by Roman law, burial was forbidden within the town, these two victims had evidently been concealed by the unknown assassin.

Westwards along the wall from Borcovicium is one of the best illustrations of a milecastle

STEPHENSON

A MILECASTLE ON THE WALL

At intervals of a Roman mile these buildings are found along the wall. About 20 yards square, these structures served as quarters for those on sentry duty. The gate of this milecastle near the fort of Borcovicus has evidently been narrowed at some period. On each side may be seen the beginnings of the arch of the gateway.

A ROMAN AMPHITHEATRE

At Caerleon-on-Usk, once an important fortress of the legions, this amphitheatre has been excavated. It was probably constructed before the end of the first century. The arena, 184 feet long and 136 feet wide, was hollowed out of the hillside and was lined with smooth masonry 12 feet high to prevent the hunted animals from escaping.

with walls and gateways still standing. Onwards we might still follow the wall on over Winshields, its highest point (1,230 feet), and on by the Nine Nicks of Thirlwall, by Great Chesters, and on to Birdoswald and close by the ruined Priory of Lanercost, built in the main of stones from the wall, and finally by Carlisle and out to the Solway at Bowness.

Antonine's Wall

Less than twenty years after the completion of this enormous work, it was decided to establish a frontier farther north along the line of Agricola's forts from the Forth to the Clyde. This was built of turf instead of stone, and the forts were much closer together. Today Antonine's Wall, as it is known, is not so conspicuous a feature as Hadrian's frontier. A few meagre evidences may be seen at Mumrills, near Falkirk, at Bar Hill, near Kirkintilloch, at Castle Carey and on Ferguston Moor.

By the time the Antonine's Wall was completed Britain had known a century of Roman rule, and great strides had been made in the Romanization of the country, and a number of towns had developed into important centres. York and Chester have been referred to as legionary fortresses, and the third place of this type was Caerleon-on-Usk, known to the Romans as Isca

Silurium. Very little of the walls of the fortress which once held 5,000 soldiers is now visible. Although barracks and baths, temples and shrines have tumbled down, there remains an interesting feature in the Roman amphitheatre, long associated with later fables and legends.

Where once the officers and men of the second August Legion gathered to witness gladiators in combat, the baiting of animals and possibly the torture of prisoners, we may walk the grass-grown banks and gaze upon the arena and the masonry of the entrances, and see the inscriptions still in position recording by whom the walls were built.

Another town of considerable importance though never of military or commercial eminence was Bath, the Aqua Sulis, so named from the British goddess of the waters, Sol or Sulis. Even in those days this was a place of widespread fame, where strangers came from overseas to take the waters. The "great bath," partly restored, indicated the grandeur of the original structure, which covered more than one and a half acres, and included in addition to the swimming baths, vapour baths, hot chambers and other rooms.

A number of small towns served as tribal capitals in the same way as Aldborough, to which reference has already been made. Silchester, on the northern edge of Hampshire, was, as its name, Calleva Atrebatum, implies, the Calleva of the Atrebates. This, the most completely excavated Roman town, has unfortunately been covered over again, and instead of beholding the ground-work of its methodical town planning, its streets of shops and houses, its inns and forum, and baths and temples, only a crumbling section of the town wall is now on view.

Chichester, which was linked with London by the Stane Street, was called Regnum, and served as a tribal town of the Regni. There, in the middle of the first century, the British chief, Cogidubunus, ruled by Roman authority. An inscribed slab preserved in the walls of the council house at Chichester, records that on a piece of ground given by one Pudens, King Tiberius Claudius Cogidubunus, dedicated a temple to Neptune and Minerva.

Cirencester, that picturesque old town on the southern edge of the Cotswolds, was " Corinium of the Dobuni," the second largest town in Roman Britain, rich and prosperous and standing at the junction of several important thoroughfares. One more town which must be mentioned is Uriconium, which stood on Watling Street, near its crossing of the Severn, and not far from the Wrekin, in Shropshire. Much of this site is now exposed, to reveal the bases of the pillars of the colonnade which formed one side of the great forum. One of the finest Roman inscriptions yet discovered came from here. This was a slab of stone, 12 feet wide and 4 feet high, which was placed over the main entrance of the forum, recording its erection by the " Cornovii," the local tribe, in honour of the Emperor Hadrian in A.D. 130.

Besides the evidences of town life there are many indications of life in the country under Roman rule, the most interesting features being the Roman villas, of which about five hundred have been discovered.

Luxurious Villas

These villas, it is now considered, were not the homes of Roman officers or settlers, but domiciles of native landowners who had adopted Roman fashions and ways of living. Many of these gentry would have learned the Latin tongue, and some maybe read Latin authors.

One of the best preserved of these houses is at Chedworth, in the Cotswolds. There may be seen the general plan of the house and its associated buildings ; its courtyard with a corridor on three sides, the dining-room with mosaic floor, and the bath-house with hot room and warm

STEPHENSON

CRUMBLING WALLS OF A ROMAN TOWN

On Watling Street, near Wroxeter, stood the Roman Uriconium which may have had its beginnings in A.D. 47 as a base from which to quell the native tribes of Wales. Eventually the town covered 170 acres and was surrounded by a wall three miles long. The photograph shows the remains of the basilica, or public hall.

STEPHENSON

HOME OF WEALTHY CITIZEN

Numerous villas of wealthy Roman-Britons have been discovered, and one of the finest examples is that of Chedworth in the Cotswolds. The photograph shows the bases of two pillars of a colonnade, and remains of the buildings of the north wing. The dining-room has a mosaic floor with representations of the four seasons.

room, and a plunge bath with outlet and drain pipe complete.

On the north side of the courtyard was the blacksmith's forge, and blooms of iron are preserved in the museum on the site. Along this side also was a fulling establishment for the cleaning of cloth, the manufacture of which may have been the source of the owner's wealth. Adjoining this building was the bakehouse, and next came the servants' quarters. At Bignor, in Sussex, the largest villa in the country has been unearthed, exposing some excellent mosaic work. Folkestone possesses a fine example, and others may be visited at Brading in the Isle of Wight, at Darenth in Kent, at Spoonleywood in the Cotswolds, North Leigh in Oxfordshire, and many other places.

The Roman Occupation, however, was by no means a period of unbroken peace and prosperity, and there are many evidences of uprisings of the local tribes, of invasions of the barbarian Picts and Scots who stormed Hadrian's Wall, and who burned and plundered as far as they could reach.

More serious dangers arose when Saxon raiders from overseas began to harass our eastern shores, and to meet this danger a series of forts was erected from the Wash to the Solent, and placed under the control of an officer known as Count of the Saxon Shore.

Forts of Saxon Shore

In several places there are relics of this phase of Roman Britain. Burgh Castle, near Great Yarmouth, still displays portions of the walls and bastions of one of these forts.

Richborough, already mentioned as a landing-place of the Romans in A.D. 47, subsequently developed into Rutupiae, the chief port of the period, although the receding sea has since left it amid the marshes. Here also a Saxon shore fort was built, and its ruins are sufficiently substantial to indicate the magnitude of the work. Long lengths of the wall are standing, in places to a height of 25 feet, and defended by external ditches. The entrances and lower portions of the towers or turrets on the wall are also exposed, and various buildings, including the inevitable baths, have been unearthed.

A Roman Lighthouse

Dover was another fort, and tiles which have been found inscribed CL.BR. indicate it was a station of the Classis Britannica, the Roman "Channel Fleet." Like Richborough it was fortified against the Saxons, though its fort has vanished. On Castle Hill, however, there is a relic, the only one of its kind in Britain. This is the pharos or Roman lighthouse, which must have been 80 feet high when, with its companion on the opposite headland, it served to guide the Roman vessels to the harbour of Portis Dubrae. The existing structure is 62 feet high, but only the lower 40 feet consist of Roman masonry, and this portion has been faced with later work.

At Pevensey, the walls of Anderida, another fort of the Saxon shore, are still standing. Portchester, near Portsmouth, was yet another of these forts, and there, as at Pevensey, a Norman castle was later built within the fortifications.

Despite these elaborate precautions, Britain proved insecure, and in A.D. 367 it suffered severely from a disastrous raid by the Picts and the Scots, who swept across Hadrian's Wall while simultaneously Saxon raiders landed on the east coast. Together they ravaged and thieved and destroyed what they could not pillage. The forces of the Duke of Britain and the Count of the Saxon Shore were put to flight, and their leaders fell in battle, and when Count Theodosius arrived to put matters right he found the invaders hammering at the gates of London.

It was after these foes had been driven out and order restored that a series of signal stations were erected along the Yorkshire coast, where their remains may be seen at Castle Hill, Scarborough, and at Hunt Cliffe, near Saltburn. The purpose of these structures was to give warning of the approach of hostile fleets, but Rome's power was waning, and her rule in Britain was drawing to its close. Today these ruined stations afford tragic evidence of the final days of Roman Britain for they disclose that they were overrun, their watch towers burnt, and the inhabitants slaughtered, the corpses of men, women, children and dogs being flung unceremoniously into the wells of the forts.

So Rome's glory departed. Her troops were gradually recalled, and in the fifth century Britain was left to her fate, to lapse from a high standard of civilization to a state little less than barbarian.

By permission of H.M. Stationery Office　　　　　　　H.M. OFFICE OF WORKS

RICHBOROUGH CASTLE

Richborough, the Roman port of Rutupiae, bears witness to the decline of Rome. In the above photograph are seen the ditches and the massive walls of a fort of the Saxon shore, one of the strongholds raised to withstand the raids of pirates from across the North Sea. The walls have an average width of eleven feet.

LANDMARKS OF SAXON AND DANE

by TOM STEPHENSON

SAXON England arose from the ashes and ruins of Roman Britain. During the period of the Roman occupation our eastern shores had suffered raids by fierce pirates from across the North Sea. But after the withdrawal of the Legions " a flock of cubs burst forth from the lair of the barbaric lioness " and the land was at the mercy of the relentless Saxons, Angles and Jutes.

It would be easy to present a picture of the period as one of continuous destruction, of sacking, burning and slaughtering and for this the early Chronicles would provide many lurid details. The Romano-British civilization, we know, was swept aside. Towns, temples and villas were overthrown, priests, we are told, were slain before the altars and the people cruelly slaughtered.

Even a race of warriors, barbarians as they may be, cannot, however, live entirely by the sword. If they were pirates and vandals, these invaders were also farmers and husbandmen. They soon began to cultivate the land, to build homes for themselves, not of stones such as those they found in existence, but of wood from the forests. Split logs of oak, like those to be seen in Greensted Church in Essex, served for the walls of the humble dwellings of the people, and also for the hall of the lord. Clearings were made and townships established and in later days a little church, at first also of wood, but afterwards of stone, became the centre of the village. Gradually the land was divided into parishes, each with its church and priest, and many of our existing churches stand on the sites of Saxon structures, though nothing may remain of the original foundation. Some retain odd fragments of the early masonry, and in a few places an ancient edifice has weathered the storm and neglect of centuries.

These primitive little buildings and odd remnants, a window or door or crypt incorporated in a medieval church or cathedral; hog-backed tombstones and weather-worn crosses, with ancient carvings and strange runes— these are some of the clues to the days when the land hitherto known as Britain was beginning to be known as England.

Such relics enlivened with stories from the Chroniclers may recall for us the times of the possibly mythical Hengist and Horsa, the days of ealdormen, thegns and ceorls, who worshipped Woden and Thor ; of St. Augustine converting an English king or Paulinus baptizing the pagans in the cold rivers of Northumbria ; of Penda and Offa, the fighting kings of Mercia or Alfred confronting the ruthless Norsemen.

Of the two centuries between the abandoning of England by Rome and the coming of St. Augustine in A.D. 597, we have but vague notions, and it is not always possible to discriminate between the facts of history and the fancies of legend and tradition.

Kent was the gateway for the Saxons, just as it had been for the Romans and for prehistoric

D. MCLEISH

ALFRED THE GREAT

Winchester was Alfred's capital and at the foot of the High Street stands this imposing statue inscribed, " To the founder of the Kingdom and the Nation."

STEPHENSON

GREENSTED CHURCH

The nave of this little church near Chipping Ongar, Essex, is probably 1,200 years old.   The walls consist of split logs of oak placed close together in upright position.   In 1013 the remains of King Edmund were deposited in the chapel for the night whilst on the difficult journey from London to Bury St. Edmunds.

adventurers long before Cæsar came. Between Sandwich and Ramsgate, within sight of the Roman fort at Richborough, lies Ebbsfleet. Today this place is a mile from the sea, but in A.D. 449 according to the Anglo-Saxon Chronicles, it afforded landing for three shiploads of Jutes under the brothers Hengist and Horsa. Vortigern, the British king, accepted these people as allies, and, for their services, allowed them to settle in the Isle of Thanet. Soon, however, the newcomers turned on their host and fought against Vortigern at a ford over the Medway, at the place now known as Aylesford. There, it is said, Horsa was slain and Hengist with his son Esc or Oisc, afterwards ruled the kingdom.

Founding of Sussex

Sussex, or the kingdom of the South Saxons, had its reputed beginnings in A.D. 477, when Ella came to Britain with his three sons, Cymen, Wlenking and Cissa. Cymens-shore, the place of their landing, is supposed to have been near Selsey Bill, and from there they first advanced eastwards and captured the fortified town of Regnum, which may have taken its new name of Chichester from Cissa, just as Lancing may commemorate his brother Wlenking.

Cerdic and his son Cynric are two other chiefs who, according to the Chronicles, came with five ships and landed at Cerdic's-Ore. This may have been in the vicinity of Totton at the head of Southampton Water, whence, it has been suggested, they advanced northwards along the ancient track known as the Cloven Way.

A little north of Salisbury, and overlooking the valley of the Avon, there stands a prominent landmark long famous as Old Sarum. This was the Searoburh where Cynric defeated the Britons in A.D. 552. From prehistoric time onwards Sarum was an important site. In Saxon days Alfred is said to have repaired the fortifications. The Danes, under Sweyn Forkbeard, found it worth sacking, and later both Canute and Edward the Confessor had royal mints there. In Norman times it became a fortified city complete with castle and cathedral, and today the most obvious features are the ruins of those buildings standing grey and forlorn within the great earthworks.

At Barbury, a few miles south of Swindon, and at Durdham, near Bristol, the British were also defeated and so the kingdom of Wessex was established from the English Channel to the Severn, and the upper valley of the Thames.

This is the version of the Chronicles, but in recent years suggestions have been put forward that Wessex was overcome by an advance from the east coast which followed the line of the Icknield Way, along the foot of the Chilterns and on to the upper reaches of the Thames.

Meanwhile, similar developments had taken place elsewhere. The immigration had continued and thousands of Anglo-Saxons had landed along the east side of Britain, slaughtered or driven westwards the native tribes, and established new kingdoms in the land they found full of promise. East Anglia was the home of the East Angles, and Norfolk and Suffolk the divisions of the north and south men of the kingdom. Essex and Middlesex were occupied by the East and Mid-Saxons respectively, and in the valley of the Trent was founded the kingdom of Mercia which later spread over the whole of the midlands, westwards to the borders of Wales, and then northwards to the Humber.

Beyond that river other tribes had founded the kingdom of Deira reaching up to the Tees, and Bernicia extending northwards again beyond the Tees.

About this time Rome once again exerted its influence, sending on this occasion instead of the conquering legions, a small band of missionaries to convert the pagan Saxons. When Augustine and his monks arrived in Thanet in A.D. 597, Aethelbert was King of Kent and also recognized as overlord of Britain. He had married a Christian wife, Bertha, daughter of the king of the Franks, and she practised her religion at Canterbury under the guidance of a French bishop Luidhard.

A few days after the arrival of Augustine, Aethelbert went to hear his message. This the king apparently did with some diffidence. Sitting in the open air, he ordered Augustine and his companions to be brought into his presence, " for he had taken precaution that they should not come to him in any house lest, according to an ancient superstition, if they practised any magical arts, they might impose upon him and so get the better of him."

Historic Canterbury

Although Aethelbert did not at once accept the new religion, he gave the monks lodging in the city of Canterbury and licensed them to preach, and win as many as they could unto their profession.

Equally cautious was the king's reply to the address of Augustine : " You give us very fair words and promises ; but yet for that they are strange and unknown to me, I cannot rightly assent unto them, forsaking that ancient religion which this long time both I and all English men have observed."

Canterbury, among all its memories of later days, has many indications of its religious beginnings. Most famous is the Church of St. Martin where the Christian legionaries once worshipped, for, as Bede says, it had been built whilst the Romans were still in the island. There eventually Aethelbert was baptized perhaps with water from the font still preserved.

In the same historic city are the ruins of the

FELTON

OLD SARUM

Surrounded by ditches and ramparts this famous landmark above the Wiltshire Avon, was probably occupied in pre-Roman days. Throughout Saxon and Norman times it was a place of note and grew into a city with castle and cathedral before it was abandoned in the thirteenth century for the present site of Salisbury.

VALENTINE

A CHURCH ON A PAGAN SITE

The Yorkshire village of Goodmanham was the Godmundingham where the pagan priest of Edwin, after hearing Paulinus preach, profaned and destroyed the altars and temples of his old gods.

Church of St. Pancras which is believed to have served Aethelbert as a pagan temple before being dedicated by St. Augustine. The remains of a Norman Abbey occupy the site of the monastery founded by Augustine. There Aethelbert and his queen were buried and four empty tombs, which are preserved in the grounds, are believed to be those of Augustus and his successors.

Among Augustine's monks was one described by Bede as " tall of stature, a little stooping, his hair black, his visage meagre, his nose slender and aquiline, his aspect both venerable and majestic." This was Paulinus destined to take a prominent part in the conversion of the north.

Pagan Northumbria

When Edwin, King of Northumbria, married Aethelberga, the daughter of Aethelbert, it was stipulated that she should retain her Christian faith, and that she should be allowed to take her priests with her, and for this purpose Paulinus was made bishop in A.D. 625 and accompanied the bride into pagan Northumbria.

Edwin, like his father-in-law, was no impulsive proselyte, and for two years he clung to his old gods, but in A.D. 627 he called a Witan or Council of his wise men and asked them what they thought of the new doctrine. At that meeting was made the famous speech, " The present life of man, O King, seems to be in comparison of that time which is unknown to us, like to the swift flight of a sparrow through the room

wherein you sit at supper in winter, with your commanders and ministers, and a good fire in the midst, whilst the storms of rain and snow prevail abroad ; the sparrow, I say, flying in at one door, and immediately out at another, whilst he is within, is safe from the wintry storm ; but after a short space of fair weather, he immediately vanishes out of your sight, into the dark winter from which he had emerged. So this life of man appears for a short space, but of what went before, or what is to follow, we are utterly ignorant. If, therefore, this new doctrine contains something more certain, it seems justly to deserve to be followed."

Paulinus then addressed the assembly and after his exhortation Coifi, chief priest of the king, was first to cry for the destruction of the old temples and altars.

Edwin and his court were baptized at York and the king, under the direction of Paulinus, began the building of a larger and nobler church of stone in place of the previous wooden structure. So were laid the foundations of the forerunner of York's present-day glorious Minster.

W. F. TAYLOR

ST. PETER ON THE WALLS

Since Saxon days this church near Bradwell, Essex, has served various uses, but was restored in 1920. Built of stone, it remains as a landmark overlooking the low-lying fields and mud flats of Essex.

W. F. TAYLOR

A THOUSAND-YEARS-OLD CHURCH

The Saxon church of St. Lawrence at Bradford-on-Avon, described as " the most ancient unaltered church in England," probably dates from the tenth century and may have replaced an earlier wooden structure. For years the nave and porch served as a charity school and the chancel was used as a dwelling place.

To continue the story of Northumbria, we might journey to Bamburgh, where a modernized castle crowns a rocky eminence overlooking the North Sea. On that craggy height Ida, the Flamebearer, first Anglian king of Bernicia, founded a stronghold in A.D. 547. A later castle there was occupied by Queen Bebba, wife of Ida's grandson. So the place became known as Bebbanburh, or Bebba's Burh, and later as Bamburgh.

Holy Isle of Lindisfarne

From Bamburgh we may gaze across to the Holy Isle of Lindisfarne, which for centuries was a great religious centre of the north. There, Aidan, who became Bishop of Northumbria, founded a monastery in the seventh century. Many stories are told of Aidan's piety and abstinence and his supposed divine powers. From one of the Farne Isles during the reign of Oswy, he beheld Bamburgh being attacked by Penda and his Mercian army. When Aidan saw the flames of fire and smoke carried by the boisterous wind above the city walls, he lifted his hands to heaven and cried, " Behold, Lord, how great mischief Penda does," which words were hardly uttered, says Bede, " when the wind immediately turning from the city, drove back the flames upon those who had kindled them," and they forebore any further attempts against the city.

With a successor of St. Aidan, the Bishop Colman, we might travel to Whitby where, on a headland overlooking the sea, and high above the red roofs of the town, stand bare and forlorn the ruins of a medieval monastery.

Beneath those ruins have been found stone foundations of the Anglo-Saxon monastery established by the Abbess Hilda in A.D. 657. There, as a modern cross reminds us, Cædmon, a tongue-tied lay brother, received heavenly inspiration, and he who had hitherto been dumb at the feast, found himself gifted with the eloquence of the poet.

It was in A.D. 664 that Colman came to Whitby for a great religious gathering, the Synod of Streonshalh, for so Whitby was then known. Among the noted churchmen there assembled was Wilfrid, Abbot of Ripon, a stormy restless soul, frequently in trouble. Twice he was deposed from the Bishopric of York and eventually he was excommunicated. But despite his varied life Wilfrid was a great builder, and is said to have travelled his diocese always accompanied by a number of skilled masons. Some remains of his work may be seen in the crypt beneath Ripon Minster, but the best example of his skill is to be found in the church and monastery he established at Hexham, in Northumberland, in the year A.D. 673.

The dominant feature of this picturesque old town by the Tyne is the Abbey Church standing on the site of the structure built by Wilfrid. Of the original building it was said that "of all others throughout England, this church was deemed the first for workmanship, design and unequalled beauty; and lastly, that in those days nothing equal to it existed on this side of the Alps."

Underneath the church is preserved the crypt of Wilfrid's edifice into which we may descend by the same stone steps used by the pilgrims who centuries ago came to visit the holy relics of St. Andrew.

Seat of Sanctuary

Above ground is Wilfrid's font, made from the inverted base of a Roman column. Another interesting relic is his episcopal chair carved out of a block of stone and still adorned with scrolls. This is known as the Frith Stool or Seat of Sanctuary, a reminder of the Saxon custom of sanctuary which gave protection to the fugitive from his pursuers.

Cedd, Bishop of East Anglia, who was also at the Synod of Whitby, had his centres in Essex at Tilaburg, the modern Tilbury, and at Ythanceaster, this being the Saxon name for the Roman fortress of Othona at the mouth of the River Blackwell. Tilbury offers no clues of Cedd, but near the village of Bradwell there stands the rude Saxon church known as St. Peter on the Walls.

Cedd also had a monastery among "craggy and distant mountains, which look more like lurking places for robbers, and retreats for wild beasts, than habitations for men." Thus does Bede describe Lastingham, now a pleasant moorland village, seven miles north-west of Pickering in Yorkshire. There Cedd died and a few remnants of his monastery may be seen in the crypt beneath the village church. Two wells in the village commemorate St. Cedd and his brother, St. Chad, who became Bishop of Lichfield.

The Saxon villages have endured in name only and it would be fruitless to search for the homes of our early forefathers, the wooden dwellings, or the painted halls where the mead cup went round, and the gleeman's song echoed among the smoked rafters. These have gone, but here and there may be seen crudely-built churches where the priest preached of Christ

W. F. TAYLOR

A SAXON TOWER AT SOMPTING

The little village of Sompting, at the foot of the downs near Worthing, has an ancient church with a curiously gabled tower which is generally believed to have been built prior to A.D. 1000.

EARLS BARTON

On a grassy height above the Northamptonshire village of Earls Barton, stands this medieval church with its impressive Saxon tower rising some seventy feet above the ground, and which is said to be " the most noteworthy architectural monument of the Saxon period."   The mound was probably a prehistoric stronghold.

to people who would not have completely forgotten the pagan gods of their ancestors.

One of the most notable of these buildings is the small church at Bradford-on-Avon, which is said to have been founded by St. Aldhelm, a Bishop of Sherborne, who died in A.D. 709. The village of Wing, near Leighton Buzzard, has a church dating from the eighth century with a crypt beneath the chancel.

Saxon Churches

Northamptonshire offers some interesting illustrations as at Earls Barton where the church tower still stands as a splendid monument of Saxon craftsmanship. Barnack also has a Saxon tower and Brixworth, between Northampton and Market Harborough, has a church which was built of Roman masonry about the end of the seventh century.

Roman ruins often served as a quarry for these buildings, and the mining village of Escombe, in Durham, has an eighth-century church built of stones from the Roman fortress of Vinovia, and

the chancel arch appears to have been rebuilt from one of the gateways of the fort.

The churches of Jarrow and Monkwearmouth in the same county also contain Saxon work and are of especial interest for their associations with Bede.

The Venerable Bede, the learned monk, whose *Ecclesiastical History of the English Nation* is our chief source of knowledge of Anglo-Saxon times down to A.D. 731, died at Jarrow where he had laboured so long, and there he was buried in A.D. 735. The monastery of Jarrow has gone, but the church of St. Paul possesses a chancel founded in A.D. 685. Within those ancient walls which the boy Bede saw being built nearly thirteen centuries ago, there is preserved a straight-backed chair which is said to have belonged to him.

Another phase of Saxon sculpture is expressed in the stone crosses many of which are still in existence, some of them elaborately decorated with interlacing scrolls or adorned with carvings of birds, beasts and human figures. One excellent specimen is preserved at Bewcastle, a little

Cumberland village north of the Roman wall. An inscription on this cross records that it was erected by Hwætred and Wothgær in honour of King Alcfrith, son of Oswy.

At Gosforth and at Irton, also in Cumberland, are other fine crosses, and at Ruthwell, in Dumfriesshire, a remarkable specimen is now preserved in the church. In the market place at Sandbach, in Cheshire, two restored crosses standing in the market place are said to have been raised by the seventh-century Peada, King of Mercia.

In the latter half of the eighth century the central kingdom of Mercia was ruled by the warlike Offa who established himself as overlord of England. The closing years of Offa's reign saw the coming of the first Danish marauders. Three ships came to the Dorset coast in A.D. 789 and the reeve, or sheriff, as he would be termed in later days, " rode thereto and wished to drive them to the king's town, because he knew not what they were ; and they slew him ; and those were the first ships of Danish men that sought the land of England."·

A SEVENTH-CENTURY CRYPT
The Church of St. Wystan at Repton, Derbyshire, has a Saxon chancel beneath which is this interesting crypt. Here the Bishopric of Mercia was established.

Dread prodigies, we read, appeared over Northumbria in A.D. 793. There were whirlwinds beyond measure and lightnings ; and fiery dragons were seen flying in the sky, and in the same year, " the heathen men miserably destroyed God's church at Lindisfarne through robbery and slaughter."

Those first despoilers of the monasteries returned to their fjords and creeks across the sea, carrying with them, in addition to their loot, stories of the wealth they had found ready for the taking. So began the long series of raids and bloody conflicts equalling if not surpassing the ferocity with which three centuries previously the Anglo-Saxons had ravaged the land.

Bury St. Edmunds, in name at least, commemorates an incident of those troubled times, for it takes its name from the last Saxon king of East Anglia. The Danes, after sacking the monasteries at Peterborough and Ely in A.D. 870, took up winter quarters at Thetford, in Norfolk, and there in the same year came in conflict with Edmund's army. At Snareshill, some mounds on the heath are said to mark the graves of those who fell in this battle.

ANGLIAN CROSSES AT ILKLEY
The Saxons after their conversion to Christianity erected many elaborate crosses. On the tallest of those at Ilkley the four evangelists are represented.

There Edmund was slain, having been, according to tradition, tied to a tree to serve as a target for the Danish archers who afterwards cut off his head. At Hoxne, a stone cross is reputed to mark the site of the tree to which he was bound. Thirty years later the dead king was revered as a saint and a martyr and his remains acquired miraculous propensities. A church was built to house his shrine at Beodricsworth, which later became known as St. Edmunds Burh, and eventually as Bury St. Edmunds; now the seat of the Diocese of St. Edmundsbury.

Alfred the Great

It was the famous King of Wessex, Alfred the Great, who ultimately checked the inroads of the Danes and laid the foundations of a united England. Wantage, a little town in the vale of the White Horse, prides itself on being the birthplace of Alfred, and a statue of him overlooks the market place. Somewhere on the Berkshire Downs, south of the town, was fought the battle of Ashdown in A.D. 871, when the Danes were invading Wessex.

The Chronicles tell how four nights after a battle at Reading, King Aethelred and Alfred his brother fought with the whole body of Danes at Ashdown. Aethelred fought against the host in which were the heathen kings Bagsecg and Healfden, and Alfred fought against the host of the earls, and both of the hosts were routed; and there were many thousands slain and they were fighting till night.

The curious White Horse carved in the chalk near Uffington, though now considered a prehistoric work, was formerly held to commemorate this defeat of the Danes, and about three miles to the south-west, the name Ashdown still persists and a nearby mound is known as King Alfred's Castle.

Healfden and his army spent the following winter in London and some of the coins he struck there may be seen in the British Museum.

Four years later the same king fixed his winter quarters by the Tyne, and in A.D. 876 he dealt out the lands of the Northumbrians. So the Danes were established in Yorkshire, and subsequently the ancient kingdom of Deira was divided into thridings or ridings.

York, which Healfden made his capital, was for nearly a century ruled by Scandinavian kings. Today the venerable city offers no tangible evidence of its Viking times when fleets from Norway and Denmark anchored in the Ouse, but the names of some of its quaint streets commemorate the times of Ragnvald and Sigtryg and Eric Bloodaxe. Goodramgate takes its name from one Gothomr, Fishergate was the street of the

W. F. TAYLOR

SCENE OF MARTYRDOM

Near the attractive Suffolk village of Hoxne, Edmund, the Anglian king, was martyred by the Danes in A.D. 870, *because, it is said, he steadfastly refused to renounce his faith or hold his kingdom as a vassal from the heathen overlords. A stone cross marks the site of the tree to which he was bound by his captors.*

PHOTOCHROM

SAXON EARTHWORKS AT WAREHAM

The " Green Walls " of Wareham, in Dorset, served as the earthworks of the Wessex fortress of King Alfred, but their origin may be Roman or prehistoric. In the parish church lies the marble coffin of Edward the Martyr, who, at the age of thirteen, was murdered at Corfe Castle in A.D. 978 by his stepmother's retainers.

W. F. TAYLOR

SITE OF DANISH DEFEAT

The picturesque little village of Edington by the northern edge of Salisbury Plain is believed to be the Ethandun, where Alfred overcame the Danes in A.D. 878. After the conflict the Danes swore that they would withdraw from Alfred's kingdom in the south and west and the Danish king, Guthrum became a Christian.

Fiskare, or fisherman, and Skeldergate, the street of the Skjaldari, or shieldmaker.

In the same year that Healfden shared out the land of Yorkshire, the Danes entered Wareham, in Dorset. There Alfred made peace with them, but the truce did not last long, and in A.D. 878 the Danes seized Chippenham, in Wiltshire, and Alfred and his chiefs fled to Athelney, in Somerset. There for some months they stayed in the marshes by the River Parret. It was there that the legendary incident of the burnt cakes is supposed to have occurred, and from there that Alfred is said to have visited the camp of the Danes disguised as a harpist. A farmhouse now

was baptized and afterwards signed the famous Treaty of Wedmore which defined the boundaries of the Danelaw or Danish territory and provided that Guthrum should withdraw from Wessex.

Alfred's further campaigns, his taking of London from the Danes in A.D. 885, his raising of the siege of Exeter and his diversion of the River Lea to leave the Viking ships high and dry and easy to capture, we cannot attempt to describe. Mention must, however, be made of Winchester, the historic city which for long served as the capital of Wessex kings.

There Alfred founded the Abbey of St. Mary, and built the new Minster, both of which were

W. F. TAYLOR

WHERE ALFRED MADE PEACE WITH THE DANES

In the Somerset village of Wedmore, Alfred and Guthrum the Danish king came to terms after the battle of Ethandun. There they agreed to the famous Treaty of Wedmore, whereby the boundaries of the Danelaw were defined, and after which Guthrum retired from Wessex and settled in East Anglia in comparative peace.

stands on the site where Alfred founded Athelney Abbey and a monument is all that marks his refuge.

From this retreat Alfred rallied his men, and the banner of the golden dragon, the emblem of Wessex, was unfurled for a decisive onslaught on the Danes at Ethandun. The attractive village of Edington, which lies beneath the Wiltshire Downs, near Westbury, is believed to have been the site of this conflict, where Alfred fought with the whole force of the Danes and put them to flight.

Three weeks after this battle the Danish king, Guthrum, was lavishly entertained by Alfred at Aller, a Somerset village near Athelney. Guthrum

destroyed at the Reformation. There also he initiated the recording of the Anglo-Saxon Chronicle and the compilation of books for the education of his people.

Edward the Elder and his sister Ethelflaed continued the work initiated by their father Alfred by fortifying the English burghs, restoring the crumbling fortifications of the Romans or erecting new earthworks where necessary.

Tamworth, the old capital of Mercia, was so fortified by Ethelflaed and in A.D. 907 she restored the Roman city of Chester. Runcorn and Eddisbury, in Cheshire, and Shrewsbury and Bridgnorth, in Shropshire, were other places strengthened by this lady. Under Edward the Danelaw was brought under English rule and the Danish burghs became the centres of the shires named after them as in Lincoln, Derby, Leicester and Nottingham, and for each shire of the Danelaw a Danish earl was responsible to the English king.

Aethelstan succeeded his father, Edward, and according to the Anglo-Saxon Chronicle he was crowned at Kingston-on-Thames. An interesting relic of those days is a stone preserved in the market place, where seven Saxon kings are reputed to have been crowned.

Battle of Brunanburgh

Somewhere in the north, Athelstan fought the unlocated Battle of Brunanburgh, where five kings lay on the field of battle in the bloom of youth, as well as seven of the earls of Anlaf. Before this conflict Athelstan is said to have visited Beverley Minster and to have placed on the altar the sword given to him by his grandfather, Alfred, and there the weapon lies in the tomb of St. John of Beverley.

The interesting old town of Malmesbury, in Wiltshire, also claims association with this monarch, for there he restored an ancient monastery and in the parish church, itself part of a medieval abbey, Athelstan's tomb may be seen.

Towards the end of the tenth century the Danes were again on the warpath, reckless and ruthless as ever. The pleasant little Berkshire town of Wallingford, which, like Wareham, still preserves its old earthworks, was one of the many places to suffer in these later campaigns. On the downs south of Wallingford stands the burial mound of Cuichelme, a Wessex king. This was supposed to be an ominous spot for the Danes, for it was foretold that if they ever came there they would never get back to the sea. But the plunderers scorned the old wives' tale, and in defiance went to Cuichelme's Low, or Cuckamsley Hill, and after a battle at Kennet, returned to the coast by Winchester where the people might see the rank and iniquitous foe as they passed by their gates carrying their meat and plunder to the sea.

Ten years after this episode England was ruled by the Danish king, Canute. In 1013, his doughty father, Sweyn Forkbeard, had been accepted king, but his reign was brief and after his death an attempt was made to reinstate an English monarch.

At Ashingdon, in Essex, Canute battled with Edmund Ironside, and Canute, we are told, had the victory, though all England fought against him. Edmund thereupon fled to the village of Deerhurst, south of Tewkesbury.

Two centuries previously a monastery had been founded in Deerhurst, and the Abbey

HUMPHREY AND VERA JOEL

A STREET IN SHAFTESBURY

" One of the queerest and quaintest spots in England " was Thomas Hardy's description of this ancient Dorset town which overlooks the picturesque vale of Blackmore. Here Alfred founded an abbey on the site of a pagan temple and this was probably the nucleus of the town. Canute is said to have died here in 1035.

Church, restored, of course, in subsequent ages, now serves as the Parish Church and is a beautiful and interesting structure. Not far from the church is another Saxon building, known as Odda's Chapel, which according to an inscription found in an adjacent orchard, was built by Earl Odda in the reign of Edward the Confessor.

South of the village, in a meadow now known as the "Naight," but then termed "Olney," an island in the Severn marshes, Edmund Ironside and Canute met in 1016. There they became allies and sworn brothers, and it was agreed Edmund should rule Wessex, and Canute Mercia and the north. Only a few months after this Edmund died and was buried with his grandfather, Edgar, at Glastonbury. Canute thereupon became King of England, and for a time he also ruled Norway and Denmark.

Palace of Canute

The charming village of Bosham, near Chichester, also has memories of Canute. Whether he ever rebuked the waves may be questionable, but Bosham, like Southampton, claims to have been the scene of that incident. There he had a palace, and through the centuries there was handed down a tradition that his infant daughter had been buried in the church. During restorations in 1865 a stone coffin and some bones of a child were found on the legendary site, and this spot is now marked by a tile bearing the Danish raven.

Bosham also serves as a reminder of the closing days of Saxon England, for its little church is figured in the famous Bayeux tapestry. In Bosham, it is said, there was of old a palace belonging to Harold Godwinson, the ill-fated monarch who in his brief reign made that famous march from Sussex to Yorkshire, there to overcome at Stamford Bridge the Norsemen under Tostig, his brother, and Harold Hardrada of Norway.

HUMPHREY AND VERA JOEL

BOSHAM HARBOUR
The church of this Sussex hamlet dates from early Saxon times. In the seventh century Bishop Wilfrid found a colony of Irish monks there. Tradition makes it a home of Canute, and Harold had a palace there.

The Saxon Chronicle in its usual terse style tells of one brave Norwegian who held the bridge over the Derwent. "An Englishman aimed at him with a javelin, but it availed nothing. Then came another under the bridge and pierced him terribly inwards under the coat of mail. And Harold, king of the English, then came over the bridge followed by his army." Both the king's brother and Harold Hardrada of Norway were killed in the battle.

These foes conquered we may picture Harold hastening southwards again to that battle on the outskirts of Hastings where he was to meet his death and the era of Saxon England was to come to its close.

W. F. TAYLOR

TINTAGEL

" Wild Tintagel by the Cornish seas " figures in legends of Uther Pendragon and Ygerne, the parents of Arthur, of the wizard Merlin and the romance of Tristram and Iseult.   It was the supposed birthplace of Arthur, and, according to the old tales, he still haunts the scene in the shape of a bird—the Cornish chough. The castle was most likely a Norman building and was once a stronghold of the Earls of Cornwall.

KING ARTHUR AND HIS KNIGHTS

by TOM STEPHENSON

ARTHUR of Britain, however insubstantial a figure he may be in history, is commemorated in folk lore and legend throughout the land. This mysterious, perhaps mythical hero of romance and fable, this champion of many wondrous exploits, the favoured of the fairies and most glamorous of kings, yet lives in the tales that are told of Tintagel and Glastonbury and " many towered Camelot." In placenames and stories his name occurs from Cornwall to Caerleon and Carlisle, and even beyond the Border, for has not Edinburgh its Arthur's Seat and Argyll its Ben Arthur?

Whether Arthur ever lived has long been debated. Caxton stated " that diverse men hold opinion that there was no such Arthur, and that all such books as be made of him be but feigned and fables."

The ninth century Welsh Nennius makes Arthur a " Dux bellorum " or war leader who led the Britons against the Saxons in twelve battles, the last of which was fought at Mount Badon, possibly near Bath. Gildas, another historian, says this battle was fought at the time of his nativity, about A.D. 516. Gildas, however, makes no mention of Arthur.

Allusions to Arthur occur in the songs of the earliest Welsh bards, some of whom lived in the sixth and seventh centuries, but it is in the twelfth century that he attains his full heroic prominence with the appearance of Geoffrey Monmouth's *History of the Kings of Britain*. In 1485 Caxton printed Mallory's *La Morte d' Arthur*, and by that time innumerable legends had gathered round the supposed erstwhile British king. Arthur had become a phantom monarch and leader of a goodly array of noble knights, and fairy tales and notions of intervening ages had been taken to embellish the tale.

One of the best known of Arthur's haunts is the Castle of Tintagel on the Cornish coast. It matters not that the masonry is of Norman or perhaps later date. The legends assert that Arthur, with Lancelot and Gawaine, came to a little chasm in the combe and saw that the enclosure of the castle was fallen down into an

PHOTOCHROM

SLAUGHTER BRIDGE

This bridge near Camelford, in Cornwall, is claimed to be the scene of Arthur's last battle when he was mortally wounded by his rebel nephew, Mordred. According to one version, the stricken king was borne to Tintagel and all the time he lay dying the sea and winds moaned unceasingly until the hero was buried at Glastonbury.

abysm. A priest told them it was the great Tintagel, and when they asked how it was the ground was caved in, he gave the following explanation.

"King Uther Pendragon, that was father to King Arthur, held a great court and summoned all his barons. The king of this castle that then was here was called Gorlois. He went to the court and took his wife with him that was named Ygerne, and she was the fairest dame in any kingdom.

"Gorlois liking not Uther's overtures to

it was not for himself but for his uncle. On the voyage home, however, Tristram and Iseult drank a love potion which had been prepared by Iseult's mother, and which was to have been given to King Mark and his bride on the nuptial night. By the virtues of that drink, 'happed the love first betwixt Sir Tristram and La Beale Isoud, the which love never departed the days of their life.'

"Iseult, nevertheless, married the Cornish king, and there is a long story of the lovers' intrigues and escapes until they are caught in guilt. Tristram

EDGAR WARD

GLASTONBURY AND ITS FAMOUS TOR
This ancient town is the supposed Avalon, the fairyland or paradise to which the dying Arthur was borne by fair maidens. There Arthur and his Queen Guenevere were said to have been buried. On the Tor, seen in the background, was buried, according to tradition, the Holy Grail brought by Joseph of Arimathea.

Ygerne, left unceremoniously and brought her back to Tintagel. Uther demanded that she should be returned to the court, and, on being defied, came and besieged the castle. Now Uther had with him the crafty Merlin who changed the king into the semblance of Gorlois and so he gained access to Ygerne and 'begat King Arthur in the Great Hall that was next to the enclosure where this abysm is. And for this sin hath the ground sunk in this wise.'

Tristram and Iseult

"'Tyntagel, on its surge-beat hill,' also figures in the romance of Tristram and Iseult. Tristram was the son of a British prince and nephew of King Mark of Cornwall, who had a stronghold at Tintagel. In early life Tristram proved his prowess by overcoming an Irish giant and shortly afterwards he journeyed to Ireland and met Iseult, La Beale Isoud as Mallory names her.

"Of all earthly men Iseult loved Tristram most, but when the knight asked for her hand

subsequently withdrew to Brittany, where, believing himself forgotten by his uncle's wife, he wed the Iseult of the White Hands, who, however, was but wife in name. In the end, dying of a poisoned wound, Tristram sent for Iseult. If she came the ship was to bear a white sail, but if she refused then a black sail was to be shown.

"Tristram is falsely told by his wife that the ship is returning with a black sail, and his hope departs. Iseult arrives too late to save him and dies by his side, and so in a ship they bore those lovers cold and

"'In Cornwall Tristram and Queen Iseult lay;
In King Marc's chapel in Tyntagel old.'"

Camelford, a few miles inland from Tintagel, has been claimed as the original Camelot, where "the joyous court of knights and beauteous ladies of Arthur's day, held high revelry." But there is little ground for the assumption, and Cadbury, in Somerset, is a more likely locality.

Near Camelford, however, is Slaughter Bridge, with its tradition of being so named from the site of Arthur's last conflict. Four miles from Camelford, amid the shaggy brown moors, is Dozmary Pool. There exists the general belief that this was the mere in which the dying Arthur bid Sir Bedivere fling the brand Excalibur, the famous weapon bestowed on Arthur by the Lady of the Lake.

This story, however, is also localized in the ancient city of Glastonbury. There the River Brue is spanned by a bridge known as " Pomparles." The meaning of the name is said to be the " Bridge Perilous." Leland, the king's antiquary, about 1542, refers to the bridge of his day as " Pont Perlus, wher men fable that Arture cast in his Swerd."

For seven centuries at least Glastonbury has been supposedly the island valley of Avilion, or Avalon, the vague and shadowy Celtic paradise, " Where falls not hail, or rain, or any snow,
  Nor ever wind blows loudly ; but it lies
Deep meadowed, happy, fair with orchardlawns
And bowery hollows crown'd with summer sea."
And that last battle where " there were slain all the brave ones, Arthur's warriors, high and low, and all the Britons of Arthur's board," Arthur declared he would " fare to Avalon, to the fairest of all maidens, to Argante, the Queen, an elf most fair, and she shall make my wounds all sound ; make me all whole with healing draughts, and afterwards I will come again to my kingdom and dwell with the Britons with mickle joy."

The Passing of Arthur

Even as he spoke, " there came from the sea a short boat, borne on the waves, and two women therein, wondrously arrayed and they took Arthur anon, and bare him quickly and softly laid him down and fared forth away. Then was brought to pass that which Merlin whilom said, that there should be sorrow untold at Arthur's forthfaring." This is Layamon's version and Mallory tells much the same story with a few additional details.

Amid Glastonbury's monastic ruins may be seen the reputed grave of Arthur, for, although his burial place had for centuries been considered beyond human ken, the monks who claimed Joseph of Arimathea as their founder, did not find it beyond their ability to locate the grave

STEPHENSON

WHERE ARTHUR SLEEPS
Snowdon figures in Arthurian legend, and in a cave on the peaks of Lliwedd, seen in the above photograph, Arthur and his knights lie in magic sleep awaiting recall. On the right of Lliwedd, between that peak and the highest point of Snowdon, is Bwlch y Saethau, the Pass of the Arrows, where Arthur is said to have fallen in battle.

of the legendary monarch within their walls. At the command of Henry II they sought the burial place as indicated by Welsh tradition.

First they found a leaden cross, recording the interment of Arthur and his queen. Next they unearthed a stone coffin containing the bones of a woman with beautiful golden locks which crumbled to dust at the touch of a monk. Beneath this was found a coffin of hollowed oak containing the remains of a huge man with an enormous head bearing twelve wounds, all of which had healed save one. But there are other places where Arthur is supposed to rest, not dead but lying in enchanted sleep.

Glastonbury links Arthur with a yet earlier figure, and on Weary-All Hill, a stone marks the spot where Joseph of Arimathea is said to have planted his staff which thereupon took root and flourished. In the Abbey grounds, and in St. John's churchyard, are preserved offshoots of this Holy Thorn which blossoms at Christmastime.

Joseph brought with him the chalice or Holy Grail used at the Last Supper and in which he collected the blood of Christ from the Cross.

It was at the Vigil of Pentecost, when all the fellowship of the Round Table were come unto Camelot, that the Quest of the Holy Grail was inaugurated. To the court was brought " a young knight, the which is of Kings lineage and of the kindred of Joseph of Arimathea,

whereby the marvels of this court and of strange realms shall be fully accomplished." This was Sir Galahad, son of the fair Elaine and Sir Lancelot.

After the tournaments in which Sir Galahad proved himself, and surmounted all other knights save Sir Lancelot and Sir Percevale, the Holy Grail passed through the hall but none might see it and " then was all the hall fulfilled with good odours and every knight had such meats and drinks as he best loved in the world."

Then the knights pledged themselves to labour in quest of the grail, and one hundred and fifty of them, to Arthur's sorrow, mounted upon their horses and rode through the streets of Camelot.

Many Towered Camelot

The site of Camelot has long been considered to be the ancient camp of Cadbury about four and a half miles south of Castle Cary, in Somerset.

An old track from Camelot is still known as King Arthur's Lane, and the village of South Cadbury has a King Arthur's Well.

Camelot today presents no evidence of the " dim rich city " with " tower after tower, spire beyond spire " climbing to the mighty hall that Merlin built. Nor shall we find St. Stephen's Church where Arthur wedded Guenevere, despite

W. F. TAYLOR

BAMBURGH CASTLE

This restored castle on the Northumbrian coast stands on the site said to have been first fortified by the Anglian king, Ida the Flamebearer, in A.D. 547. Possibly this was the " Joyous Garde," the castle from which Sir Lancelot of the Lake, "flower of all knighthood," rode to Carlisle to return Queen Guenevere.

DIXON-SCOTT

RICHMOND CASTLE
The romantic Yorkshire Richmond, with its mighty castle standing high above the River Swale, is another reputed burial place of Arthur with its story of a luckless wight who discovered the sleeping warriors but failed to break the magic spell. Had he done so, he would have been " the greatest man that ever was born."

the warnings of Merlin that she would prove unfaithful and would love Sir Lancelot. But beneath the grassy slopes Arthur and his mailclad knights are sleeping still, and, according to tradition, when the moon is full, the ghostly company still ride the ramparts on horses shod with silver.

Fair City of Caerleon

Arthur's Court was not permanently fixed at Camelot, and frequent mention is made of Caerleon-on-Usk, near Newport, in Monmouthshire. "In those days," says Layamon, "no burgh so fair was in any land, nor so widely known, as Caerleon by Usk, unless it were the rich burgh that is named Rome." Thither came many kings and earls of noble cities to see Arthur crowned, and as he was led to the church four kings " went before him, bearing before him, as was their right, four golden swords."

The hollow in a field at Caerleon, which in recent years has been excavated to reveal the remains of a Roman amphitheatre, has long been known as the Round Table. Many other sites are similarly named, but in the Great Hall at Winchester, there hangs on the wall a table top long claimed as " Arthur's Board." This table, eighteen feet in diameter, is divided into sectors for the king and twenty-four knights, but the Round Table of the legends was a far larger piece of furniture.

At one of Arthur's feasts there had been a great slaughter of knights arising from disputes as to precedence. Afterwards there came to the king a Cornish craftsman who said he would make a table at which sixteen hundred or more might sit, "and then thou needest never fear, to the world's end, that ever any moody knight may make fight, for there shall the high be even with the low."

Throughout Wales, Arthur's memory is maintained by place-names and features with associated legends. Gower was the Gore of which the sorceress, Morgan le Fay, was queen in her own right. On Cefn Bryn, near Swansea, is a dolmen known as Arthur's Stone and Guenevere has her monument at Llantilern, near Cardiff. Between the peaks of the Brecon Beacons is

R. M. ADAM

THE EILDON HILLS, MELROSE

A cavern in these hills is another supposed resting place of Arthur, where the monarch and his retinue await one who will sound the horn " that bids the charmed sleep of ages fly " and " rolls the long sound through Eildon's caverns vast."   According to another legend, these hills were cleft in three by the wizard Michael Scott.

Arthur's Chair and on Cefn Carn Cavall, near Builth, is the footprint of Cavall, " Arthur's hound of deepest mouth."

Snowdon, formerly known as Caer Eryri, has numerous legends. One of them localizes Arthur's death on Snowdon. Up the valley of Cwm Llan, Arthur and his knights drove the enemy, up to the dip between Y Wyddfa and Lliwedd, two of the peaks of Snowdon. There, Arthur fell before a shower of arrows and so the place is named Bwlch y Saethau, or the Pass of the Arrows. Then Arthur's knights carried his body over Lliwedd and interred it in a vast cavern, " The Cave of the Young Men of Snowdon." In this undiscovered recess the warriors still sleep in their armour awaiting Arthur's re-awakening.

In the far north of England we are still in Arthur's country, and there are many references to Carlisle and its neighbourhood. The ballad of " The Marriage of Sir Gawaine " tells that,

" King Arthur lives in merry Carleile,
     And seemly is to see ;
And there with him Queene Guenever
     That bride so bright of blee."

In the Castle of Carlisle Sir Mordred and Sir Agravaine and twelve other knights surprised

Sir Lancelot in the chamber of Guenevere. Sir Agravaine and the twelve knights were slain, but Sir Mordred, sore wounded and smitten, fled to Arthur and told him the news. So the king ordained that Guenevere should be burnt to death for her sins.

Rescue of Guenevere

" Then the queen was led forth without Carlisle and there she was despoiled into her smock," and there was " weeping and wailing and wringing of hands." But Lancelot came to the rescue, slew another batch of knights, had a kirtle and gown cast about the queen, and so rode away with her to his castle of Joyous Gard " and there he kept her as a noble knight should do."

Of Joyous Gard, according to Mallory, " Some men say it was Alnwick and some men say it was Bamburgh," both in Northumberland. Whichever it was, Arthur ventured there ; but was unhorsed by Lancelot, and only by the compassionate nature of the knight was Arthur's party permitted to withdraw. After that the Pope intervened, and Lancelot and Guenevere returned and Lancelot " rode throughout Carlisle, and so in the castle that all men might behold; and wit you well there was many a weeping eye." So was Guenevere returned to Arthur.

Between Carlisle and Penrith, in Cumberland, is the region of Inglewood Forest, where in the vicinity of the village of Upper Hesket has been located the Tarn Wadling, or, as it is sometimes called, Tarn Wathelayne, which is mentioned in the Ballad of Sir Gawaine, son of Loth and nephew of Arthur.

Castle of the Grim Baron

On an island in this tarn stood the castle of "The Grim Baron, a churlish knight, whom Arthur was only able to overcome by the aid of a 'foul ladye.'" For her services Arthur was to find her a fair and courtly knight for husband. Gawaine alone of all the knights would undertake to wed the repulsive hag to absolve Arthur of his pledge. But Gawaine had the reward of discovering on the wedding night that instead of the loathly dame, he had for wife "a young ladye faire,"

"Her eyen was black as sloe ;
The ripening cherry swellde her lippe,
And all her neck was snow."

From Carlisle we may journey into Northumberland, and there, near Housesteads on the Roman Wall, is the lonely farm of Sewingshields.

"Immemorial tradition has asserted that King Arthur, his Queen Guenevere, his court of lords and ladies and his hounds were enchanted in some cave of the crags or in a hall below the castle of Sewingshields." There they will continue entranced until someone first blows a bugle and then with the sword of stone cuts a garter to be found in the hall.

A shepherd, so the story goes, found his way into the place and withdrew the sword from the scabbard. Thereupon the sleepers awoke and sat upright. He then cut the garter, but as he sheathed the sword the enchanted ones fell back in slumber, but not before Arthur had cried,

"O, woe betide that evil day
On which this witless wight was born,
Who drew the sword, the garter cut,
But never blew the bugle horn."

Across the Scottish border we find the same story, for in the Eildon Hills, the triple peaks that rise above Melrose, the sleepers await one who shall peal

"proud Arthur's march from fairyland."

There, with much left unsaid, with no mention of the luckless maid of Astolat or Sir Gawaine's encounters with the Greene Knight, with many a strange adventure and many a pleasing story not even hinted at, we must say farewell to Arthur and his fellowship of famous knights.

VIOLET BANKS

ARTHUR'S SEAT, EDINBURGH

Overlooking the Scottish capital, this famous landmark which has been likened to a couchant lion, is a remnant of an extinct volcano. It is said to take its name from the legendary monarch. According to the story, Arthur stood on the summit of the hill, watching the tide of battle as his followers overcame the opposing Picts.

EDGAR WARD

IMPRESSIVE RUINS OF CASTLE HEDINGHAM

This great Norman keep, with walls twelve feet thick and archway thirty-two feet across, was built by Alberic de Vere in the twelfth century. Queen Maud, wife of King Stephen, died there and the castle also figures in the wars of King John. Henry VII was sumptuously entertained there, and for centuries it was a seat of the Earls of Oxford. With the exception of the keep the castle was reduced to ruins in 1666.

SCENES OF NORMAN TIMES

by HAROLD SHELTON

THE walls of Anderida, looking out over the waters of Pevensey Bay, recall the first event in the occupation of Britain by the Normans, for it was here in September of 1066 that William landed on the shore of Sussex and inaugurated an era of change which was to prove the most complete upheaval of custom and tradition that the island had witnessed since the coming of the Romans under the Emperor Claudius, almost exactly a thousand years before.

If we make Pevensey Bay our starting-point we can follow the course taken by William on his first victorious progress to London. We follow him first to the hill of Senlac overlooking the Hastings plain. On this exposed plateau we see him in conflict with Harold, last of the Wessex kings, who had raised an army in London and marched southward to meet the invader. Harold's infantry armed with scythes, sticks and battle-axes proved but a poor match for the cavalry and bow-men of the Normans. Harold fell, pierced by an arrow in the eye, and his troops retreated in disorder. The splendid pile of Battle Abbey which today dominates the village, marks for us the place where tradition relates the battle was fought. It is said that, faithful to a vow which he made before the battle, William founded an abbey to commemorate his victory.

Next we follow William as he marches directly to London, first over the tumbled hills of the Forest Ridge, then across the Weald of Surrey, finally breasting the steep slopes of the North Downs. With Sussex, Kent and Surrey owing allegiance to him, he found no opposition until he attempted to cross the river at London Bridge.

DIXON-SCOTT

A BEAUTIFUL NORMAN DOOR
The late Norman church of Kilpeck, near Hereford, possesses this richly sculptured doorway, one of the finest specimens of Norman moulding in the country.

Here the citizens of Saxon London, built north of the river on the twin summits of Cornhill and Ludgate Hill, met him in battle and drove him back.

So with William we must retrace our steps and leave the smouldering ruins of Southwark (which was then a flourishing town independent of London). We follow the south bank of the river to Wallingford, which is the first place where it could be forded, and then re-approach London from the north. We must imagine the Normans once more meeting the Saxons in battle, this time a few miles to the west of London in the open fields where Hammersmith and Wandsworth now stand. Resistance soon ceased and Edgar, who had acceded to the crown of Wessex on the death of Harold, abdicated. Our journey ends at Westminster Abbey, where on Christmas Day of 1066 William was crowned.

The first stage of the Norman Conquest was over. Yet it was not a conquest of alien wresting the throne from its rightful holder, for William had been nominated to the crown of England by Edward the Confessor, and Harold had promised William his support.

It is a sardonic fact that the Normans who brought unity to an England which had not been united since the departure of the Romans should come of the same stock as the Norsemen or Danes who had spread desolation throughout the land at the time when the Saxons had been building a new civilization in the seventh century; for the word Norman is a corruption of Northman—the Viking stock of Scandinavia and Denmark.

The White Tower of the Tower of London,

W. F. TAYLOR

ANCIENT WALLS OF PEVENSEY

Pevensey has a long and stirring history. There the Romans built their great fortress of Anderida which was later overrun by the Saxons who " slew all that dwelt therein." William the Conqueror landed in Pevensey Bay and within the Roman walls his half-brother built the Norman castle which was frequently besieged.

DIXON-SCOTT

CASTLE RUINS AT HASTINGS

This shattered stronghold, possibly founded by the Conqueror not long after the Battle of Hastings, is said to have been built for the purpose of obtaining unrestricted passage across the Channel for the royal messengers. The first tourney ever held in Britain is supposed to have taken place there in the presence of King John.

rising majestically above the broad waterway of the Thames, the great bulk of Castle Hedingham, most impressive landmark in Northern Essex, the still more solid though more battered ruins of Colchester Castle—all recall the efforts which William made to hold the country in check. All three are early Norman fortresses where garrisons were established to hold the conquered Saxons in subjection.

William utilized and enlarged the Saxon earthworks where these existed, as at Corfe Castle. The grand position of the mound commanding the whole of the Isle of Purbeck shows how well the Saxons chose their sites. Sometimes, as at Pevensey, William built within the confines of a Roman fort. Where new sites were chosen he constructed the rectangular Norman keeps of which the Tower of London was one of the first and one of the largest, as befitted a place which was the only considerable town of the Saxons and the only one which resisted his progress.

If we journey northward from Castle Hedingham along the boundary of East Anglia we shall come ultimately to the fen country, which covers more than half of Cambridgeshire and Huntingdonshire. Today it is level pasture, well drained and fertile. But in Norman times before the dykes were cut and the rivers persuaded into their present channels the whole district was an impenetrable swamp, above which only the Isle of Ely emerged as dry land. It was here that Hereward the Wake, immortalized in the work of Charles Kingsley, led a rebellion which has assumed a significance as great as the rising of Boudicca against the Romans. In 1071 Hereward, at the head of several hundreds of the oppressed, established himself in the island and defied the Normans for nearly a year. When at last he was forced to submit, his courage won him a place in the army of William the Conqueror, who declared Hereward was " a man of noble soul and a most distinguished warrior."

The New Forest, most gracious of England's

woodland country, owes its origin to an act of the first Norman king. Hunting was the chief sport of the Norman nobles as it had been of the Saxons. A great part of England was set apart as royal preserves where the red deer and wild boar continued undisturbed and woe betide the impetuous serf who dared to loose an arrow at the king's deer.

PHOTOCHROM

CRUMBLING RUINS OF CORFE CASTLE

In a commanding position overlooking a gap in the Purbeck Hills this ruin founded by William the Conqueror was for centuries an impregnable stronghold. King Edward was murdered by his stepmother at Corfe.

Within a hundred years of the Conquest about seventy royal forests had been established, and special courts were instituted where the harsh forest laws of Normandy were rigorously applied. Of the Conqueror the Anglo-Saxon Chronicle says, " He made many deer-parks ; and he established laws therewith ; so that whosoever slew a hart or hind, should be deprived of his eyesight. As he forbade men to kill the harts, so also the boars ; and he loved the tall deer as if he were their father. Likewise he decreed by the hares, that they should go free. His rich men bemoaned it, and the poor men shuddered at it. But he was so stern that he recked not the hatred of them all; for they must follow withal the king's will, if they would live, or have land or possessions, or even his peace."

Barons in Revolt

The square bulk of Rochester Castle, overlooking a broad reach of the Medway recalls the troubled reign of William II, surnamed Rufus from his red complexion, which suspicious historians have hinted might spring from too great an attachment to the red wine of Normandy. It was at Rochester that Baron Odo flew his flag for six months in open rebellion against the king, who from the beginning of his reign met with more resistance from his own nobles than from his subjects at large—a state of affairs which was characteristic of the later Norman days. Bamburgh too is the scene of another siege in which the Earl of Northumberland held out manfully against the king's men until Rufus built another castle mound, overlooking Bamburgh, and there laid wait until Northumberland sallied forth for provisions. The traces of this second mound, a kind of counter castle, are a unique monument of Norman warfare.

In the Welsh Marches we shall find a more lasting reminder of Rufus in the temper of the countrymen and the tales that are still told of the stern Norman rule. As he was unable to subdue the indomitable spirit which has always marked the hill men of Britain, he laid a charge on his barons to conquer what land they could on the borderland of Wales and hold it for their own. Thus arose the rule of the Marcher Lords who, removed as they were from the centre of government, gained for themselves a great measure of independence, so that each became virtual king in his own right. They built castles at Gloucester, Pembroke and Chester, and, descending from them upon the villages and settlements, slew the men and violated their women folk, returning always to their strongholds as soon as the news came of an organized resistance. Hamelin de Baladun held sway over Breconshire and Monmouthshire from the castle of Abergavenny. Fitzhamon, Earl of Gloucester, Fitz Osborne of Chepstow, Roger de Montgomery of Shrewsbury—all did irretrievable damage which has lived on in tradition and which has tended to make the peasants of the Welsh Marches more insular and more race conscious than the subjects of "wildest" Wales.

Abergavenny, a little town on the Usk, and overlooked by the Sugar Loaf, was later held by William de Braose of whom a tale is told which well illustrates the spirit of the times. This de Braose, during one of his expeditions, was captured by the Welsh and later ransomed by his own people. With an admirable gesture

D. MCLEISH

COLCHESTER'S MIGHTY KEEP

The massive keep of Colchester Castle, by far the largest in Britain and about twice the size of the White Tower of London, is built partly of Roman materials. Perhaps because of its tremendous strength it never experienced a serious siege, although it was defended by the Royalists for three months during the Civil War.

W. F. TAYLOR

DEATH SCENE OF A MONARCH

The arrow shot by Sir William Tyrell is said to have glanced from a tree and mortally wounded the king, William Rufus. Near Stoney Cross the Rufus Stone marks the traditional site of the tree. According to another version, Rufus was killed by a discontented Saxon for, it is said, Rufus was loathed by the people.

he invited the Chief who had held him to ransom, and the leading men of his clan, to a feast. In the midst of the banquet soldiers entered the hall and slew every guest except one who escaped to perpetuate the story.

The effigies of the crusaders, of which there are several in the cathedrals and in some of the parish churches too, show better than anything else how Norman knights went into battle swathed in armour from head to foot and armed with the destructive battle-axe. They recall the time when the Norman nobles answered the call of the first religious war. Though many of the unorganized armies, which at the invitation of the Pope and the Emperor of the Eastern Roman Empire set out to rescue Jerusalem from the Mohammedans, never reached the scene of their activities, it was still the first attempt on the part of Britain since Roman days to take part in continental wars.

The Rufus Stone, halfway between the bleak crossroads at Stoney Cross and Cadnam, in the midst of the most desolate part of the New Forest, where the woodlands begin to thin out and their place is taken by mile after mile of windswept heather-covered heath, marks the spot where Rufus fell. An inscription on the stone tells us that he was mortally wounded by a stray arrow from the bow of one of his companions, Sir Walter Tyrell, when hunting in the forest.

His tomb is in Winchester Cathedral where he was buried without ceremony. He was unloved at his death as he had been unpopular in his life, owing to the severity which he showed in the exaction of the utmost farthing from his subjects and in the prosecution of the Forest Laws.

The castles of Arundel and Shrewsbury, the former constantly rebuilt in later centuries and today a palatial residence rather than a fortress, are remembered for the part they played in the struggle between Henry I and Robert of Bellême, pretender to the throne. For it was at Arundel that Robert was besieged for nearly a year before making good his escape, whilst at Shrewsbury he finally took refuge and surrendered.

Siege of a Castle

We can easily imagine the stern struggle before one of these early castles was captured. No siege passed without hand to hand battles and the employment of every available means of offence and defence. When Rochester Castle was besieged in 1215 the besiegers tunnelled under the castle, filled the tunnel with brushwood and set a light to it, so that when the beams that supported the tunnel were burnt, one corner of the keep subsided into the tunnel and fell in ruins.

The battering-ram was used also. This was crashed against the sides of the castle until a

W. F. TAYLOR

GUILDFORD CASTLE KEEP

This ancient keep, now a picturesque ruin, is almost all that remains of the castle built in the reign of Henry II. It was a residence of Henry who converted the adjacent caverns into wine cellars. On one occasion the castle fell into the hands of Louis of France.   It also served as the county gaol and is now the property of the town.

breach was made in the walls. Catapults hurled rocks into the ward and moving towers were brought up to the gates so that the attackers could reach the walls. During all these operations defenders and attackers alike kept up a continuous fire of arrows and the besieged replied also by dropping heavy missiles, boiling water, or molten lead on the heads of those intrepid soldiers who came too near the walls, and by catching up as many of the attackers as they could with the assistance of grappling irons.

How well the castle could be defended against a formal siege is shown by the fact that Exeter Castle, a fortress of no great strength, was held for five months against King Stephen. Even then it was only a failure of the well with which every castle was provided that hastened the final surrender. When, as sometimes happened, the infuriated peasants made a more or less organized attack on one of the castles, it was fatally easy for the defenders, standing on the ramparts of the walls and protected by the embrasures, to pick them off with arrows as they advanced.

The Norman House of Christchurch, which was built inside the outer wall of the castle, shows how towards the middle of the twelfth century, when the danger of revolt from the peasants was growing less, the Norman nobles began to change their mode of living. They started to build manors and granges which had greater comfort than the stonework of the castles, and which were modelled rather on the lines of the Anglo-Saxon Hall which had been constructed of timber after the style of the later medieval barns. In much the same way the abbot of the monastery frequently built himself a separate residence outside the confines of the convent.

The Jew's House at Lincoln belongs to the twelfth century, and with its windows of two lights on the first floor shows the growing tendency to comfort rather than defence. The Old Hall at Ower Moigne, in Dorset, illustrates how this tendency developed still further in the course of the next century.

Great Architects

When we come to consider the life of the poorer people we are on less sure ground. Towns were still small and few in number, and the townsmen were forced to become servants to the baron in his castle. In town and country alike they lived in wooden houses with thatched roofs, consisting of a hall with alcoves which served for kitchens, and drawing-rooms, and of a loft built over the hall.

The Normans were great architects. They re-introduced into England the art of carving in stone, and we can trace their handiwork in the ruins of abbeys, in cathedrals and in parish churches, for as in every age of architecture the greatest works were the monuments which were raised for religious devotion.

No single Norman church has been preserved

D. MCLEISH

JEW'S HOUSE, LINCOLN

One of the oldest inhabited dwellings in Britain is the twelfth-century house at Lincoln. In the reign of John it was occupied by a Jewess named Belaset, who was hanged in 1290 for debasing coins.

intact. There is no church in England so characteristic of the Norman style as the Church of Greensted, in Essex, or the Church of St. Lawrence at Bradford-on-Avon is of the Saxon. But what they lack in completeness they amply compensate for in number and in the beauty of the fragments which survive. If we go to Barfreston, in Kent—a tiny village set at the foot of the rolling country, where the downs reach to the edge of the Thanet marshes—we shall find a church which shows much of their artistry and craftsmanship. Here in a small circular window we shall see the beginnings of the stone tracery which was to prove the most fascinating attraction of the later Gothic style.

Barfreston shows, too, the tendency to

subdivision which gave all Norman building its great symmetry, and, at the same time, rendered it a style which can easily be distinguished from any other. So in Chichester Cathedral the wall above the main arcade is divided into several arches, and they in turn into smaller arches, each dependent on the other, and each contributing to the beauty of the whole. We can see this subdivision carried out even in the stone vaults with which the Normans roofed the nave.

The little Church of Walsoken, in Norfolk, shows well how the chancel arch is broken up and supported on columns in the same way as the great vault of St. Albans is supported on the vast square columns which rise from the aisles of the nave. The very mass and solidity of these columns, so perfectly proportioned to the magnificence of the abbey is an integral part of the beauty of Norman building. We need only go to Waltham Abbey or the Cathedral of Durham to see how much is added by the great circular piers whose only resemblance to the classical column is that they have the same base and capital.

Imaginative Sculptors

So long as they were concerned with construction in detail, and until they had mastered the principles of vaulting, the Normans gave little attention to decoration. Even so, if we look at the Norman font in Lincoln Cathedral, we cannot fail to marvel at the technique and delicacy with which the figures moulded upon it are picked out. Still more, if we visit Ely Cathedral and find the Prior's Doorway, with its beautifully carved tympana set in the ornamented semicircle of the Norman arch, we shall realize the full imaginative capacity of the Norman sculptors.

How beautiful even the simplest arch can be is shown by the chancel arch of Rainham Church, in Essex, which throws an interesting light, also, on how the people worshipped in Norman times. For the chancel was the place of devotion for the priests, where the altar was set against the east end, whilst the lay brethren in the monasteries, and the country people in the parish church must needs be content with sitting in the nave and watching the Elevation of the Host through the chancel arch.

It would take many months to visit all the sacred buildings which show Norman workmanship, either in the general plan of the church or perhaps in a single rounded arch, or perhaps in the narrow windows of two lights set high in the church wall which were so typical of their art. Especially worthy of a visit, however, is the Church of St. Cross, Winchester, where the nave is almost entirely Norman and shows the generous proportions of which the builders were capable.

We must also see the splendid arcade and the rounded porch of the priory church at Castle Acre, the splendid arch of the porchway to Selby Abbey, and the grand Norman tower of St. Albans, built before the end of the eleventh century from Roman tiles stripped from the ruins of Verulamium. Even at Canterbury,

W. F. TAYLOR

SOUTHWELL MINSTER
The beautiful austere nave of Southwell presents an excellent example of Norman church architecture, with the massive piers of the nave arcade surmounted by the lofty triforium and clerestory.

FELTON

HISTORIC HALL OF WESTMINSTER

This famous Hall, built by William Rufus, was completed in 1099. The beautiful timber roof dates from the end of the fourteenth century when the Hall was restored by Richard II. Westminster Hall served for centuries as the chief law court of England, being abandoned for this purpose when the present Law Courts were built in the Strand.

though the splendour of the Gothic Cathedral will enthral us most, we shall remember that it was originally the church of a Norman monastery of which the round arches of the ruins to the north-east of the cathedral are our sole reminder.

It was perhaps natural that the Normans should build more and more monasteries, for they offered the only profession which gentlemen could follow, apart from that of the soldier. So one county alone can show four such monasteries which were founded before the last of the Norman kings. Yorkshire will reveal the illustrious ruins of Rievaulx, Roche, Fountains and Kirkstall, all founded by one Order—the Cistercian. We must remember when we visit them that the first buildings were of wood, and that most of the majestic ruins date from the end of the twelfth and the thirteenth centuries.

STEPHENSON

NORMAN GATEWAY, CASTLE ACRE

The Conqueror granted the Norfolk Manor of Castle Acre to William de Warenne, who built a castle on a mound flanked by earthworks. This gateway, which afforded access to the stronghold, spans the village street.

Domesday Book

Our chief link with the life of the people is the Domesday Book, the minute survey of the land and its resources which William initiated in 1086. The Anglo-Saxon Chronicle says he sent his men all over England into each shire. " So very narrowly, indeed, did he commission them to trace it out, that there was not one single hide, nor a rood of land, nay, moreover (it is shameful to tell, though he thought it no shame to do it) not even an ox, nor a cow, nor a swine was there left, that was not set down in his writ. And all the recorded particulars were afterwards brought to him."

The whole country was divided into counties, the counties into Hundreds and the Hundreds into manors. Only in a few cases have the Hundreds been preserved on the modern map— the Three Hundreds of Aylesbury, the Chiltern Hundreds and the Hundred of Hoo, in Kent, are instances where the titles have survived even though the political significance has disappeared. Everything in the manor belonged to the lord of the manor, held in trust by him for the king. Apart from the land which he ploughed himself, most of the manor was granted by him to his followers in return for their services.

The Domesday Book shows several classes among the retainers of the lord of the manor including the villeins who held about thirty acres, the cottars who held about five acres as well as a number of bondsmen who held no land and were, in fact, slaves or serfs who worked in return for board and lodging, and were never allowed to possess property of any kind, but had their freedom.

Probably the life of the villein or cottar was no harder than that of the modern labourer. As today he depended for his prosperity on the goodwill of the landowner, but, he had his house, he ploughed his own land and raised his own vegetables, and, in return for these privileges, he ploughed the land of his lord and was plighted to follow him into battle. Even though he had no money with which to buy pleasures, in a simple age there were no pleasures to be bought and he enjoyed the protection without which life would have been impossible. Nor must we take too seriously the dire tales of rape and oppression which are perpetuated in legend and story. It is certainly true that the Norman lords brooked no opposition. To have done so would probably have cost them their lives ; for the countrymen, as ever conservative, looked on them as interlopers and continued to do so even though their life under them may have been easier than under the Saxons. In any case, we must remember that the Feudal System effected a vital change towards unity and co-operation which would have been impossible in a purely individualistic manner of life.

A drive along the byways of Central Essex, or in the Vale of Blackmore, or the Valley of the Ouse, in Bedfordshire, reveals a curious link

ESSEX MEMORIES OF CANUTE

DIXON-SCOTT

Said to have developed from a church founded by a standard-bearer of Canute, Waltham became an Augustinian Abbey in Norman times. The parish church seen in the background formed the nave of the abbey church. Waltham also has Saxon associations, and King Harold, who fell at Hastings, is said to be buried there.

GREY RUINS OF OLD SARUM

W. F. TAYLOR

In Norman times this ancient site near Salisbury grew into a walled city and was an episcopal see from 1072. After disagreement between the castellans and the clergy the site was abandoned and the cathedral was pulled down in 1331, the materials being used again in the building of Salisbury Cathedral.

with Feudal England. The villeins tilled their land in long, narrow strips, and there was always a Right of Way at the sides and ends of the strips. These Rights of Way in later times were turned into roads which so took on the typical appearance of an English country lane—straight for a quarter of a mile down the side of one strip, turning through a right-angle bend along the bottom of the strip for perhaps a hundred yards or so, and straight for another quarter of a mile down the next strip.

During the closing years of the Norman era, there was a great increase in trade. In Saxon days England had been self-supporting, and even under the Normans the manor required little that was not raised within its confines. But gradually markets were established in the towns where goods were bartered, and market crosses, with roofs to protect the buyers and sellers, were raised.

DIXON-SCOTT

WHITE TOWER OF LONDON

Within the south-east angle of the Roman walls the Conqueror raised the great edifice of the Tower of London The White Tower, seen above, was designed by Gundulf, Bishop of Rochester.

Foreign trade was developed and London, we are told, was a city to which " merchants rejoice to bring their trade in ships," and " ships and merchandise of foreign merchants " were present at Boston Fair in 1196.

Annual fairs were established and granted royal charters. All ports and roads William " ordered to be open to merchants, and no injury to be done to them." In one charter the king says, " I will and ordain that all who come to the fair, remain at it, and return from it have my firm peace."

Winchester had its St. Giles Fair, licence for which was granted to Bishop Walkelin by the Conqueror. Cambridge had its widely famous fair of Stourbridge which flourished through the Middle Ages, and only dwindled in comparatively recent days. In Defoe's day it was a tremendous gathering, a " prodigious resort of the trading people of all parts of England, with streets of booths and tents."

Such was the life in Norman times. Even with men's thoughts turning naturally to warfare, life may have been on the whole more peaceful, more leisured and (who shall say otherwise?) happier than it is today.

FELTON

ROCHESTER'S MASSIVE KEEP

This impressive Norman keep, 120 feet high and overlooking the Medway, is an illustration of the military architecture of the period. Built in 1125 the walls at the base are 12 feet thick.

THE STORY OF THE CASTLES

by HAROLD SHELTON

OF the many contributing factors to the beauty and splendour of Britain, the remains of the castles and ancient strongholds are among the most popular features. Frequently, because of their well-chosen position they remain, even in ruin, a dominant note in the landscape. Their weathered and perhaps decaying masonry, their embattled towers and walls and remnants of barbican, drawbridge and portcullis may still conjure from the past visions of pomp and pageantry, and of tales of tyranny and feudal subjection.

The evolution of the castle is part of the great struggle between the means of offence and those of defence. Each stage of development represents a further effort to overcome the available means of attack, from the puny earthworks of Neolithic man to the culminating strongholds—the concentric castles of the Edwardian period. By that time defence had become stronger than offence, so that the castle could withstand a siege of many months, and was virtually immune to the engines of warfare.

The modern castle is no longer a stronghold, but a dwelling-place, whose battlements are an idle show which could not withstand a determined siege for a day. Steel has taken the place of masonry, and the mobile tank which can spread destruction as it goes and yet afford protection to the destroyers has more in common with the castle than any other means of warfare.

The castle ruins have much in common with those of the monasteries. Just as the latter epitomize the art of religious architecture, so, from Roman times onwards, castles are the sum total of military architecture. The civil life of the Early Middle Ages centred round the convent; so the military life centred round the castle. The monasteries later attracted townships because the abbot was the principal buyer of the district and labour was wanted to work the monastic land. So towns often arose near the castles because the castle was the home of the lord of the manor, and there was protection in living under the castle walls. To complete our comparison, just as the monasteries were allowed to fall into decay through the avarice of one man, Henry VIII, so the hand of man—Oliver Cromwell—was responsible for the decay of the castles when, at the close of the great Civil War, they were slighted at his command, which means that their roofs were stripped, their battlements destroyed, and the fabric made unfit for future defence.

Those which at first glance seem to have survived miraculously, such as Windsor and Arundel, to name only two of the finest, closer inspection shows to have been rebuilt again and

DIXON-SCOTT

HENRY VIII GATE AND ROUND TOWER, WINDSOR

Overlooking the Thames, Windsor Castle, which down through the centuries has served as a royal residence, was founded by William the Conqueror. Parts of the structure date from the reign of Henry III.

DIXON-SCOTT

FORMIDABLE GATEWAY OF LEWES CASTLE

One of the earliest of Norman castles, this Sussex stronghold, on a height in the middle of the town, was built by William de Warenne, the first Earl of Surrey, who died in 1088. The inner gate is part of the original work, but the outer gate is Edwardian.   De Warenne and his wife, Gundrada, daughter of the Conqueror, also founded the priory at Lewes.   Their coffins, found in the ruins, are preserved in St. John's Church, Southover.

again, so that little of the original building can be discerned. Even so, the massive ruins that remain are a testimony to the skill of the Roman and Norman builders who constructed buildings of a solidity which has withstood the ravages of weather and men for a period of six hundred to sixteen hundred years.

The hilltop fortresses of Prehistoric Britain are the earliest attempts at castle building. The second era was begun with the advent of the Romans. The Romans inherited the traditions of the great castle builders of Asia Minor, of Troy and Tiryns and of Phœnicia. They brought to Britain an art which was already fully developed. Their own great contribution lay

the Stour and the Thames, that the Romans turned of necessity to defend the coast and appointed a Count of the Saxon Shore, who was responsible for the line of citadels which extended from the Wash on the east coast to the Solent on the south.

In the north and north-west the position was very different. Here the country was never Romanized, but was held with more or less success in face of constant opposition from the Picts and Scots and from the Celtic tribes of Wales. The walls of Hadrian and Constantine were efforts to define the Roman boundary for close on two hundred years. Along the former castella were constructed at intervals which

DIXON SCOTT

SPLENDOUR OF WARWICK CASTLE

" The fairest monument of ancient and chivalrous splendour " was Scott's description of this noble structure with its embattled walls and stately towers. Probably replacing a Saxon stronghold, the foundations were laid by Earl Turchil in the days of the Conqueror, but the fortifications are chiefly fourteenth century.

in the construction of walled cities with defensive turrets at intervals rather than in the erection of single fortresses. The multi-angular tower on the Roman wall at York is more significant than even Richborough.

The history of the Roman occupation, too, is reflected in the distribution of castles. The south of England was quickly won over by a peaceful, rather than a military, occupation. Hence in the south there was no need for fortresses to quell the spirit of the insurgents. It was not until the fourth century, when marauding tribes of Saxons were beginning to sail up the eastern estuaries and penetrate into the country by the Blackwater,

constituted the largest and most important scheme of Roman castle building.

With the weakening of the Roman influence the second period of castle building came to an end. The Saxon invaders burned and pillaged the Roman castles with the same ruthlessness as they overthrew their towns and houses. Perhaps they even manned once more the deserted earthworks of the downs. The Vikings, who in turn came to harry the Saxon chieftains, were just as ignorant of the art of castle building as the Teutonic tribes.

The Norse tribes who settled in Normandy developed a new art of fortification. Their

FEUDAL FORTRESS OF THE PERCYS

The restored Alnwick Castle in Northumberland was founded by Ivo de Vescy, the Norman Baron of Alnwick, about 1096. After frequent assaults by marauding Scots, it was rebuilt by the famous Percys between 1310 and 1350. It once ranked as one of the most formidable strongholds in the North of England.

influence impelled the Saxon chieftains in the tenth century to strengthen naturally strong positions with artificial aids, nearly a hundred years before William of Normandy led his army to victory at Senlac. The method adopted in those last years of the Saxon Kingdoms was to raise a mound and surround it with a deep moat, further strengthening the top of the mound with a wooden palisade. Probably the earthen mound and timber stockade was the only type of castle known in this country before the Norman Conquest.

Norman Strongholds

The landing of William and his rapid conquest of the country heralded the third and greatest period of castle building, continuing intermittently until the reign of Henry VIII. William had two problems to solve. He needed garrisons to be the headquarters of his soldiers and he needed some visible strength to overawe the countryside. The Norman castle satisfied both these needs. Under the government of one of the Norman barons it held undisputed sway over the rural population. William de Braose ruled Sussex from Bramber—a great man who won the name of "Just" because he did not kill everyone who chanced to stand in his way, and refrained from pillaging the homes of the old and infirm. If we journey to Bramber today we shall still

find the castle ruins dominating the quiet village. Raised high on a grassy mound from which there is a long view over the Sussex Weald they command the river where in medieval days there was an important ford, and so stand guard over the gap between the two spurs of the South Downs which stretch eastward towards Lewes and westward to Chanctonbury Ring and Washington.

Two distinct types of early Norman fortress survive in most parts of Britain, one distinguished by a " shell " keep, the other by a " rectangular " keep. The shell keep was by far the more numerous. Where William or his lieutenants found Saxon mounds, they reoccupied them and strengthened the palisades which surmounted them, digging a wide bank and ditch to protect the earthwork and a considerable portion of land as well. The wooden structure on the top of the mound became known as the keep, the rest of the enclosure as the ward. Within the ward dwelling-places of wood were built for the knights, and enclosures made for cattle and stores. So within a couple of days William could devise a rough-and-ready fortification which could resist unexpected attacks.

Thirty or more years afterwards, when their position was stronger, the Normans started to replace the timber palisades and buildings with masonry, constructing a roughly circular building

DIXON-SCOTT

CARISBROOKE CASTLE.   PRISON OF A KING

"*I do not think I shall ever see a ruin to surpass Carisbrooke Castle,*" remarked the poet Keats of this Norman stronghold in the Isle of Wight.   Charles I was held a prisoner here during the Civil War and twice attempted to escape.   The photograph shows the formidable gatehouse with the battlemented towers.

on the summit of the mound, and the living accommodation in the ward. The keep on the mound was only a last line of defence in which the garrison could take refuge when the outer ward had fallen before the enemy. But so strong did the timber palisade prove that the Normans showed no haste to build the structure of masonry. Hence these shell keeps are often a little later in date than the rectangular keeps which were not preceded by timber defences. Corfe Castle, which dominates the gap in the Purbeck Hills in just the same way as does Bramber the gap in the South Downs, must have been one of the earliest. If we approach it along the main road from the direction of Wareham

by treachery from within, was it reduced to its shattered state.

Although more numerous at the date of construction, the shell keep has not survived so frequently. This is partly because the construction was less massive, but chiefly because this type, like the Saxon mound, was practically confined to towns. So when the castles were dismantled after the Civil Wars, the ruins were not allowed to occupy for long what was obviously a fine building site. First they were used as quarries—it is said that the Seaford Road is built from the stones of Lewes Castle. Then, if they escaped that fate, they were rebuilt to form prisons or courts of justice, so perpetuating

W. F. TAYLOR

HISTORIC KENILWORTH

Founded about 1120 by Geoffrey de Clinton, Kenilworth was granted to Simon de Montfort in 1234. John of Gaunt made additions, including the banqueting hall and two towers, one of which bears his name. Elizabeth granted it to her favourite, the Earl of Leicester. The oldest part is the Norman keep of 1180.

its gaunt ruined outline stands out clear against the sky. From its mound we look over the sandy wastes of Dorset's heathlands with the same sweeping views as at Bramber we look over the Sussex Weald.

Solidly built by the Conqueror and well placed on a height, Corfe proved unconquerable to Stephen. King John who used it as a residence considered it offered safe storage for his regalia during his dispute with the barons, and he also decided it was a useful prison, for there he is said to have starved to death twenty-two French prisoners. Down to the days of Cromwell it stood intact. Then, only after it had been taken

the custom by which the Lord of the Manor was both the dispenser of justice and the jailer of the local folk. Even when the castle remained a castle until modern times, it became first and foremost a prison.

The Tower of London, for instance, has in turn been fortress, royal palace and prison house. Stephen was the first king to reside in it. Henry III and the three Edwards all held court there. Richard II was in residence when he abdicated. Henry VI died there, put to death, so tradition relates, by the Duke of Gloucester. Another regal victim was the child King Edward V, slain side by side with his brother. Anne Boleyn and

PHOTOCHROM

KINGMAKER'S YORKSHIRE FORTRESS

This imposing ruin in Wensleydale, probably founded about 1170, came into the Neville family in 1270 and was a stronghold of Warwick the Kingmaker. His daughter, Anne, married Richard III and their only son was born and died at Middleham. In 1539 it was reported that there was at Middleham a castle highly decayed and in ruin and thereunto adjoining six Parks and six Chases otherwise called Forest or dales.

DIXON-SCOTT

CONWAY'S ROMANTIC RUINS

As part of his plan for the subjugation of Wales, Edward I completed this embattled pile in 1284 on the site of an early fortress built by Hugh Lupus, Earl of Chester, in the reign of the Conqueror. When the Welsh Prince Llewelyn was slain, Edward is said to have received the head of his foe in the banqueting hall of Conway.

Katherine Howard lived here in solitary confinement before being executed. In later days a long line of distinguished prisoners came to know its walls only too well—Sir Thomas More, Sir Walter Raleigh, Perkin Warbeck, Lady Jane Grey, Guy Fawkes, and many others.

Windsor and Arundel were both originally castles of the shell type. Their chequered history is typical of every type. Windsor was founded by William the Conqueror, and has been the royal palace of almost every king since that time. It was rebuilt entirely by Edward III, and again by the architect Wyatville in the early Victorian era. Even his " cruel " restoration was unable to spoil its magnificence ; seen from the river it appears the veritable prototype of all castles.

Arundel, too, has suffered many vicissitudes. There are still considerable portions of the Norman keep intact, and of the Edwardian defences, though the imposing pile of the present castle—all that can be seen from the road—was constructed in the nineteenth century. Here it was that Robert of Montgomery won such an unenviable name for cruelty and rapaciousness.

In 1102 it was besieged by Henry I. Thirty-seven years later King Stephen beleaguered it, but it bravely withstood his onslaught. It was only at the end of the great Civil War that it surrendered to the Roundheads, and was " slighted " after the manner of all the other medieval strongholds. Tradition relates that the circular hole in the keep was the entrance to a secret passage leading to the banks of the Arun. Alas for tradition ! It is more probably the entrance to the Norman dungeons which have since been filled in.

A Magnificent Palace

The magnificent palace of the Earls of Warwick, which stands upon a cliff almost overhanging the Avon, is yet another of this type of Norman fortress which has lived through the stirring history of all the castles, declined and then risen again to become one of Britain's most splendid castle mansions. The gatehouse which bears the crest of the Warwick family, a bear and a ragged staff, is a worthy entrance to the warm grey pile of the castle itself. A road hewn out of the

PHOTOCHROM

COURTYARD, SKIPTON CASTLE

This Yorkshire stronghold occupies a strategic position in the gap carved in the Pennines by the River Aire. Founded in the eleventh century by the Norman, Robert de Romille, it later became the homes of the warlike Cliffords, Earls of Cumberland. Of the original structure, only the western doorway of the inner castle remains.

living rock leads into the outer court, where the two great towers, Cæsar's and Guy's, dominate the whole building. The mansion is unique if only because it is raised on a wonderfully vaulted undercroft beneath which are the vast cellars, these too being hewn from the rock on which the castle stands. It was Thomas Beauchamp who rebuilt the Norman fortress and so laid the foundations for the present edifice, which is surely the most splendid example of Gothic domestic architecture in the country.

There are many lesser castles which fall into this group. Leeds, in Kent, is unique because instead of the artificial mound we find a natural island in a lake doing justice for it. The later medieval mansion which stands on its site, whether we view it from the main Ashford-Maidstone road or approach it by the footpath which runs through the park, has the same air of an island fortress which the Norman castle must have had. It is only when we reach the very fringe of the lake that we discern the art of the later builder, the large windows and spacious rooms which belong to an age when attack was no longer feared. Alnwick, Carisbrooke, and Berkeley Castle, in Gloucestershire, though these, too, have been reconstructed, all retain the shell keep. Perhaps it was because this type combined the functions of palace and fortress and was thus the forerunner of the castellated manor house that where it has survived it has never survived without reconstruction.

Thus Alnwick was the medieval home of the Percy family who were permitted to fortify the town in the fifteenth century, as witnessed by the Bond Gate which bears the armorial lion of the Percys. Prior to the fourteenth century the castle was held by the de Vescys, descended from the great Ivo de Vescy who was Baron of Alnwick at the beginning of the twelfth century. It passed into the Percy family by chance; for it was bequeathed by the last of the de Vescys to the Bishop of Durham to hold in trust for de Vescy's bastard son, William. Perhaps it was moral disapproval which led the bishop to sell the estate to Henry de Percy and apply the proceeds to his privy purse!

A Royal Prisoner

Carisbrooke (where the sombre ruins of the old are in marked contrast with the later mansion, yet each throws into relief the beauty of the other) became the seat of the Governors of the Isle of Wight when it had ceased to be necessary as a fortress. It was here that Charles I was imprisoned for a time in 1647, and here, too, that his daughter Elizabeth met her death three years later. Berkeley again has been the manorial seat of the Earls of Berkeley ever since it was granted to Roger de Berkeley by William of

STEPHENSON

FOURTEENTH-CENTURY CASTLE
Bodiam, near Robertsbridge in Sussex, was one of the latest of the great fortified houses. Among the defences were drawbridges, barbican and portcullis.

Normandy. Even in the Civil Wars the tenure was not broken, for the castle was given back by Cromwell to the eighth baron on condition that the battlements were destroyed. In history it is remembered as the place where Edward II was murdered in 1307. The blackest deeds always seem to win most fame.

The castles with rectangular keeps were military strongholds primarily and dwelling-places only when need arose. They were built on sites where no previous fortifications existed, often in a commanding position in a thinly populated part of the countryside. Awe-inspiring, spectacular, magnificently constructed, they stand today as a supreme memorial to the Norman masons' work. Although they, too, were surrounded by an encircling wall, they differed from the castles with " shell " keeps in that residence was taken up in the keep itself instead of in the outer ward. The entrance was guarded by a strong forebuilding, presenting an almost insuperable obstacle to any foolhardy enemy who hazarded to attack it. The White Tower of the Tower of London and the keeps of Rochester and Colchester, and lofty Castle Hedingham are

HUMPHREY AND VERA JOEL

PICTURESQUE CASTLE OF HURSTMONCEAUX

This restored fortified manor on the edge of the Pevensey Levels in Sussex, built of warm red brick, was founded by Sir Roger Fiennes in the fifteenth century and dismantled in 1777. The castle, recently restored, is two hundred feet square and has four corner towers. The photograph shows the lofty gate towers with machicolated parapet through the openings of which missiles could be dropped on the enemy at the gates.

.EDGAR WARD

ENGLAND'S OLDEST MOATED MANOR

Stokesay Castle, in Shropshire, dating from the thirteenth century and the oldest fortified manor in Britain, has a romantic, fairy-like charm. It was probably built as a moated dwelling by John de Verdon about 1270. Seventy years later it was fortified and embattled by Lawrence, a merchant of Ludlow who then owned it.

a few of the most beautiful. Each shows a thickness of wall twenty or more feet in places which seems incredible in an era of jerry-built residences. How mighty they were we can well judge from the fact that all Norfolk was held in subjection by three great fortresses—Castle Rising, Castle Acre, and Norwich.

Kenilworth, too, was originally a rectangular Norman keep, and the most vital stronghold of the later Norman period in the midlands. John of Gaunt and Simon de Montfort both held it for a time; the work of the former being perpetuated in the range of buildings known as Lancaster's Buildings. But it is due to the genius of Sir Walter Scott that Kenilworth springs to the mind among the foremost of English castles. In *Kenilworth* we read of the magnificent entertainment which was offered Queen Elizabeth by Robert Dudley, a degenerate descendant

of John of Gaunt. In Scott's pages the splendour and pomp of castle life live again.

Farther north, amid the characteristic scenery of the Yorkshire dales, Middleham in the valley of the Ure, better known as Wensleydale, was for centuries the home of the Neville family, and once one of the strongholds of the Earl of Warwick, nicknamed the Kingmaker. Here is a castle which has never been rebuilt since the thirteenth century. Raised on a plateau which overlooks the valley, it is the most conspicuous feature of the landscape. Its rough stone architecture is typical of northern strongholds. No trace of ornament relieves the grim outline. The keep, of which the outer faces of two stories are nearly intact, rises from the centre of a great ward seventy yards long and sixty yards broad, itself surrounded by a wall nearly thirty feet high. As if to emphasize its great bulk flanking towers protect the outer wall, and vast buttresses project from the corners of the keep. There is no more forbidding edifice in England, nor one which allies so much beauty with its strength.

Towards the end of the Norman period a new type of castle appeared. It was found that when once the outer wall of the shell keep castle had been overthrown, the keep itself offered but a poor further defence. By the reign of Henry II, too, there was less need of such impregnable fortresses as Rochester or Hedingham. Accordingly the shell keep was discarded and the rectangular keep was replaced by a circular one with walls much less thick, which could be roofed in by masonry instead of by the timber roofs which were the only ones possible in the rectangular shape. The cost of raising such a castle was less than half the cost of raising a rectangular keep and its defensible strength nearly as great. So we find castles like Pembroke and Conisborough and Orford which mark a distinct step in the evolution of design.

Yet no one would judge them insignificant despite their less massive construction. The castle of Pembroke stands over the town with just as much majesty as does Rochester. Conisborough seems no less impressive than Hedingham. Orford is still the most striking feature of the decaying coastal town which came into being when it was built and declined as soon as it fell into ruins.

The great era of building in central and southern England soon came to an end. The country was more settled, and the king found that it was not an unmixed blessing to have powerful nobles esconced in fortresses which could not be subdued without a six months' siege.

Conquest of Wales

Richard I and Henry III discouraged further building, and it is only in the north of England and on the borders of Wales that we find progress maintained. Throughout the thirteenth century systematic attempts were made to complete the conquest of Wales, and, to this end, lines of castles were built to keep open the means of communication as well as to serve the prime purpose of sheltering the barons and their retainers. New influences were at work in determining design. A greater standard of comfort

DIXON-SCOTT

SUPERB RUINS OF RAGLAN CASTLE

On the site of an earlier structure, William Herbert, Earl of Pembroke, erected this picturesque stronghold in Monmouthshire, completing it shortly before his execution in 1469. Converted into a mansion in Tudor times, it was still strong enough in the Civil War to withstand for ten weeks the Parliamentary forces under Fairfax.

DIXON-SCOTT

DECAYING GLORY OF NUNNEY

In the Somerset village of Nunney may be seen the picturesque ruins of this moated medieval castle which was completed about 1373. Rectangular, with a round tower at each angle, it was a compact and well fortified manor, and even in ruins is invested with dignity and grandeur. It was besieged by Cromwell's forces.

was expected than had been possible in the earlier Norman castles. Great strides were being made in manufacturing engines of attack so that fresh means of defence were required. The result was that the keep was discarded entirely and the main line of defence provided by a far stronger outer wall flanked by mural towers and embrasures which commanded the attackers who brought battering rams or scaling ladders to bear upon the walls. The moat was still a vital part of the fortifications and often natural hills were cut away so as to fall with the steepness of a precipice.

Welsh Fortresses

A number of these fortresses in the Marcher Country have survived, Skenfrith and Grosmont on the Monnow, Kidwelly, and Lougharne overlooking the Pendine Sands ; Caerphilly and Carric Cennen each adding immensely to the charm of the scenery in which it is set.

The concentric castles of Edward I are in the same tradition and represent the highest pinnacle to which medieval military architecture attained. They, too, are built without keeps and depend for their might on the strength of the encircling walls, but instead of these being protected merely by the mural towers, they are surrounded by other complete walls, these too being defended with

embrasures and turrets. How well they served their purpose we may judge from the contemporary record that Harlech Castle was held by no more than twenty-five men and held successfully. Many of the castles built in the preceding reign were rebuilt or enlarged as at Caerphilly ; others, as Beaumaris and Conway, were built on fresh sites. Perhaps the most remarkable feature to be noted in these Edwardian fortresses is the gatehouse which, as the ruins of Harlech testify, was a veritable castle in itself.

Caernarvon Castle, by far the most spectacular and most complete of the medieval ruins in Wales, was built in the reign of Edward I on a different plan and defended by a single encircling wall of immense strength. But even this single wall was proved adequate when, in 1403, the castle was besieged in the Welsh rising under Owen Glyndwr, and, though manned only by a few loyalists, held out magnificently until the siege was raised. Right through that period of revolt Caernarvon and Conway remained loyal in the face of an almost united Welsh nation. It was at Caernarvon that the first Prince of Wales was born in 1284.

All that comes after is anti-climax. A licence from the king was necessary before fortified residences could be erected, and so carefully was

DIXON-SCOTT

A GATEWAY OF ENGLAND

Dover has long been the " Key of England." The Norman castle, built by Henry II, was strengthened in later Norman days. The Constable's Gate seen above was added in the fourteenth century.

masonry. Tongue ferns grow on the ledges, a few trails of ivy serve as tapestry, and moss and lichen pattern the walls of hall and kitchen alike, and a thorn tree grows in what was the Lady's Bower.

Half the south side of the castle was taken up with the great hall. At the eastern end of this would be the dais with the lord's table and at the opposite end are the doorways through which food and drink would be brought from butlery and kitchen.

The kitchens with their huge fireplaces a dozen feet across and arched like pack-horse bridges ; the flues still black with the grime of ancient fires, the butlery and pantry and cellars may help to give some idea of the domestic side of the establishment.

In the north, Bolton Castle, in Wensleydale, where in later years Mary Queen of Scots was held captive, was built about the same time. Though its beauty cannot vie with that of Bodiam it is imposing enough and in the general style of northern castles, rougher and less ornate than those of the south. So strongly was Bolton fortified that every gate, even those in the outer courtyard, was protected by a portcullis.

By the end of the fifteenth century the visible means of defence were only to give a show of magnificence, and the timbered banqueting-hall with minstrels' gallery, like that of Penshurst Place, was far more important than the guard room or the dungeons.

Bodiam in the south and Bolton in the north were the last of the purely military strongholds. The brick-built castle, manor house of Hurstmonceaux—the first house to be built of brick since Roman days—was erected in the same century. Its genial grace in contrast with the grim splendour of the earlier fortresses is testimony enough to the changing times and man's growing taste for comfort and spaciousness.

Our story is completed by a passing reference to the line of castles which were built by Henry VIII to defend the coast against the attacks of the French. Walmer, Deal, Sandown and Camber form just such an epilogue to the third era of castle building as did Richborough and the others raised by the Count of the Saxon Shore to the second era. Once again it was to ward off attacks from the other side of the Channel that recourse was had to an art which had almost been discarded and was never revived.

the licence reserved that only those families received it whose loyalty was assured.

Sir Edward Dalyngrigge, who had fought at Crécy and Poitiers, and who was a favourite of Richard II, was in 1386 given licence to crenellate and make into a castle his manor house of Bodiam. From a lily-decked moat Dalyngrigge's masonry still rises sheer and smooth, presenting at once an aspect of stern and yet graceful beauty, and an air of unassailable strength. It stands on a slight eminence above the valley of the Rother. As we approach it from the village no other building can be seen, and thus its apparent size is magnified.

So complete are its walls that, until we are on the very edge of the moat, we might believe it still inhabited. Once we have passed the fragment of the barbican and beneath the iron teeth of the portcullis, and through the gatehouse, we find, however, that we have entered an empty shell.

In the grass-grown court are fragments of

THE BEAUTIFUL ABBEYS
OF BRITAIN

by HAROLD SHELTON

THE monastic ruins of Britain are a vital part of the heritage which the Middle Ages have handed down to the present. If only because we find in them a beauty of architecture allied with beauty of situation, they have a double claim on our appreciation. So Tintern Abbey in the Valley of the Wye, Bolton in Wharfedale, Strata Florida in Cardiganshire and Llanthony in the Black Mountains add enormously to the beauty of the scene. Rievaulx, Abbey Dore, Fountains or Mount Grace, to name only four out of very many, are as important as the annals of contemporary chroniclers in helping us to understand the life of the monks and the difficult times in which they lived.

The beginnings of monasticism are to be found in the rebellion against the false values of an age when Christianity was beginning to spread a humanizing influence over the western world, but Paganism still held undisputed sway over the people at large. The solitary hermits are the first sign of such a rebellion. They lived a solitary life, existing on the bare necessities, devoting their lives to reflection on God and seeking peace in the midst of strife. The transition from the state of these solitary hermits to organized communities of devout men is a simple one and inevitable.

Towards the end of the fifth century, when most of the civilized Romano-British inhabitants had been driven into Wales or Ireland, many communities were founded with the object of providing missionaries to reintroduce Christianity into Saxon England. Names such as St. Columb and St. Patrick associated with these earliest monastic foundations bulk more largely in the annals of Irish legend than does our own St. Augustine in English history. It was the missionaries sent out from Ireland who founded the first houses in England. Whitby, among several others in the north, is a conspicuous example. In the south of England their influence extended to one place only—Glastonbury—our sole link in the southern counties between the old and the new monasticism. St. Hilda was the first abbess of Whitby, and Cædmon, the father of English poetry, one of the earliest monks.

Once more religious consciousness received a serious set-back, for, just when the inspired work of the Irish missions bade fair to convert thousands of country folk, a new peril appeared in the persons of the Vikings, and the new seats of religion and learning, where the Saxon monks had begun to write and preach, were swept from the land.

It was not until the country was resettled after the Treaty of Wedmore that an opening was found for a revival of monasticism. Then arose the first of the great orders—the Benedictines—who swore allegiance to the rule of St. Benedict and vowed to observe chastity and poverty. That order, like most of those which followed it, had its origin in Normandy. It was from that source after the Conquest, when the great era of abbey building began, that most of the monks were drawn.

Gradually the wealth of the Benedictines increased to enormous proportions, and with it the temptation to disregard the simplicity which had first bound them together. The abbots ultimately became the richest in the land and travelled from country to country with large

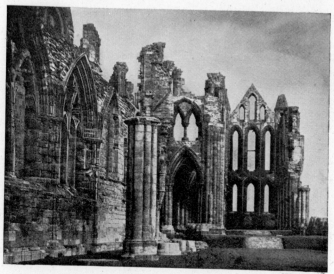

STEPHENSON

PAST BEAUTIES OF WHITBY ABBEY
Overlooking the North Sea the Saxon abbess, Hilda, built an abbey which was sacked by the Danes in A.D. 867. *The existing ruins are those of a Benedictine monastery built in Norman times.*

D. MCLEISH

FAN-VAULTED CLOISTERS, GLOUCESTER CATHEDRAL
These exquisitely vaulted cloisters were part of the abbey which formerly occupied the site of Gloucester Cathedral, and they probably date from 1351. On the left are the carrels, or recesses, used by the monks.

was the focal point of the other orders, and giving to each monk his own cell in which he lived a life of meditation and study in complete asceticism. Although only nine such abbeys were founded in Britain, they retained the ideals for which they were founded until the Dissolution.

The abbey ruins are mainly fragments dating from the Dissolution in the reign of King Henry VIII when the monastic orders had reached the height of their wealth. Consequently their buildings attained an unprecedented magnificence.

The earlier foundations of the Benedictine Order are less ornate than those of the Cistercians or Cluniacs. Without exception, too, they are the only ones which can trace an origin before the Conquest. The cloisters of Norwich stand out as the most extensive monastic cloisters in the country. Nearly 200 feet square, with walks 12 feet broad, they show all the magnificence which we associate with fourteenth-century architecture. The tracery of the windows, the carved bosses (more than four hundred in number) which give added beauty to the vaulted roof, and the columns of the monastic infirmary to the east of the cloisters combine to make this one of the most beautiful and the most living reminders of the monks' life. Tradition relates that in 1272 the citizens of Norwich, incensed by the unjust treatment meted out to them by the abbot as Lord of the Manor, set fire to the church and damaged it extensively, an incident which can be paralleled in the history of many of the abbeys.

A Cradle of Christianity

The ruins of Lindisfarne, in Northumberland, and of Tynemouth are substantial and unusually beautiful. The red sandstone from which the former is built and its romantic situation outweigh for many the superior architecture of the latter, its magnificence dimmed by the grime of nearby industry. The severe lines of the abbey church, its grand Norman doorway, and the unadorned beauty of the claustral ruins make a

retinues of attendants and something of the pomp of kings. Their lives became political as well as religious, and their wealth was reflected in a higher standard of living for the monks and the consequent disappearance of the ideals of simplicity. So new orders were founded by those who deplored the growing indulgence and laxity of the older orders.

Before the end of the eleventh century a number of Benedictine monks founded a new settlement for themselves. This they did at a place called Citeaux in Burgundy, from which is derived the name of the Cistercian order which ultimately rivalled the wealth and influence of the Benedictines. In the course of the next two hundred years more than six hundred Cistercian abbeys were founded in England alone.

The same cause was responsible for the founding of the Cluniac order by Abbot Odo of Cluny, and of the Carthusian order which re-established the principle of the solitary hermit, setting its face against the principles of communal life which

deep and lasting impression even on the casual wayfarer.

Lindisfarne can justly claim to be one of the cradles of Christianity; it was founded in A.D. 635 by St. Aidan who became first abbot and first bishop of the See of Northumberland. The illustrious St. Cuthbert was the sixth abbot; when the abbey was laid waste by the Norsemen the monks took the coffin of St. Cuthbert and moved it from town to town until they founded a new See at Durham, which is thus derived directly from Lindisfarne. It was during this time, before finally settling at Durham, that the bishop's See was set up for more than a hundred years at the village of Chester-le-Street.

St. Albans was a Benedictine House, though only the foundation of the cloisters remains of the conventual buildings. But St. Albans illustrates how great was the influence of monastic life on religious history in the Middle Ages, for the cathedral today is the direct descendant of the original abbey church.

There is a legend that Albanus, a citizen of the Romano-British town of Verulamium, served as was usual in the legions of the emperor, and in his travels on the Continent was converted to the Christian faith. Returning, he tried to convert his fellow citizens, and paid the penalty of so many in advance of their times, and was put to death on a hill overlooking the town. Four hundred years later the Saxon King Offa laid the first stone of an abbey to be the lasting memorial of the martyred Albanus. In the course of time the town of St. Albans grew up around the abbey, and the abbey church became the place of worship for the burgesses. The abbot was one of the wealthiest men of his age, and travelled with a retinue of more than a hundred.

Royal Patronage

Several others of the cathedral churches have their origin in Benedictine abbeys, and, though the ruins seem less spectacular under the more imposing shadow of the cathedral, they are still full of interest. The abbey of Canterbury, where the ruined round arches show the work of the Norman craftsman, had a long history of prosperity and royal patronage, entertaining King Edward I and Richard II, as well as Henry VIII before that merry monarch overthrew the house which had given him shelter. The church which was to become Canterbury Cathedral, the most magnificent example of Gothic architecture in Britain, was originally the church of the monastery. Westminster Abbey and the cathedrals of Peterborough, Rochester, Winchester and Gloucester, Ely, Chester and Worcester, all show more or less of their monastic beginnings. The remains of three of these—Chester, Gloucester and Worcester—are wonderfully preserved, though they have been reconstructed from time to time. At Gloucester we shall see the " carrels,"

DIXON-SCOTT

THE MELLOW BEAUTY OF FOUNTAINS ABBEY
To the valley of the Skell, near Ripon, there came in 1132 a little band of monks from York. In what was then a desolate dale they laid the foundations of Fountains Abbey, which was to become the greatest and richest religious house in the north. In their sylvan setting, these ruins still testify to their original grandeur.

the stone reading-desks at which the monks worked in the cloisters; at Chester the Norman undercroft which adjoins the west walk is the finest of its kind in England. We shall linger, too, over the refectory, a beautiful specimen of the early English style, with its reader's pulpit, where the priest would read lessons and say grace before and after meals. For the rest, the magnificent gateway of Bury St. Edmunds, the fine nave of Blyth and the picturesque ruins of Monk Bretton are all derived from the Benedictines.

Cluniac Houses are fewer in number, but none

of the rich sculpture which distinguished later work—the thirteenth-century choir and refectory which must have been, like that of Chester, typical of the best which that great age of architecture could produce. Fountains is no less impressive. Does the early English elegance of the Chapel of the Nine Altars take pride of place? Certainly its lofty, gracefully pointed arches, its generous windows, its perfect proportions call to the imagination a picture of supreme beauty, even though the glory of its roof has perished. But it is only one of many triumphs. We shall admire the symmetry of the lofty

STEPHENSON

A MONASTERY WITH A TRAGIC STORY

On the banks of the Calder, at Whalley in Lancashire, this Cistercian Abbey was established in 1296. John Paslew, the last abbot, and a leader of the Pilgrimage of Grace, was hanged as a rebel in 1537.

will carp at the artistry and brilliance of Much Wenlock or Castle Acre.

A tour of Yorkshire will demonstrate the wealth and magnificence of the Cistercians. No other county can show such splendour as the combined elegance and interest of Kirkstall, Jervaulx, Fountains, Byland, Rievaulx, Roche and Sawley. Yet all these are within the one county and all belong to the same order. The ruins of Fountains are the most complete of their kind; those of Rievaulx the most picturesque in architecture and situation alike. Rievaulx was the first of the Cistercian abbeys to be founded in the north—it survived to become the wealthiest in the whole country. That perhaps explains the splendour of the ruins, the late Norman nave and cloister, already showing traces

square tower, added a century after the rest of the buildings were complete. We shall pause at the noble piers which support the vaulted roof of the warming room, and at the serene and dignified outline of the refectory. We shall carry away the impression of a unique experience.

When we visit Fountains we shall be at once impressed by the beauty of the abbey's surroundings, for it is set in park-like undulating country, well wooded and fertile. It was not always so. When twelve monks set out in 1132 to found a cell from the abbey of York, they found a desolate wilderness covered in tangled forest and rank undergrowth wherein they had to make a small clearing in which to build their first wooden church. The handiwork of the monks was the first step in reclaiming the valley from the harsh hand of Nature.

In the neighbouring county of Lancashire the most splendid ruins are of a Cistercian House—Furness—where the red sandstone has mellowed and become an integral part of the landscape. Tintern, too, immortalized by Wordsworth's poetry, was built by the same order—the ultimate consummation of Art and Nature combined, taking tone from the horse-shoe bend of the Wye in which it lies, yet, adding as much to its beauty as it derives from it. Curiously, today it looks as much a work of Nature as the other features of an incomparable landscape. Netley and Beaulieu, in Hampshire (in the second of which the monks' refectory is used as a church); Calder Abbey, in Cumberland; Waverley Abbey, in Surrey, which like Tintern is set in a horse-shoe bend of the river; Cleeve Abbey, in Somerset, and Valle Crucis, in Denbighshire, are a few of the others which claim our special notice.

In southern Scotland, Sweetheart or New Abbey was a Cistercian House. Its gaunt beauty is part and parcel of the scene, its weather-beaten ruins toning perfectly with the country's stone walls. Mystery surrounds its foundation. According to popular legend, it was founded in 1275 by Devorguilla, wife of John de Baliol, who also founded Balliol College, Oxford, in memory of her husband. In New Abbey she was buried, and John de Baliol's embalmed heart was buried with her.

Whilst we are in the border country there are several spectacular ruins which invite us to visit them. A mile and a half from Dumfries we shall find Lincluden—in the words of the poet Burns, " an old ruin in a sweet situation "; at Jedburgh an abbey which still shows the full beauty of thirteenth-century art; at Melrose the charming fragments which inspired Scott's *Lay of the Last Minstrel*. Here in the monastery, which was founded by David I, tradition relates that the heart of Robert the Bruce is buried.

Beauty of Cistercian Ruins

Finally, there are Dryburgh and Kelso, both of which were destroyed in the wars between England and Scotland. The church of the former is the last resting place of Sir Walter Scott and of Earl Haig; but of the monastic buildings only insignificant fragments remain, except of the chapter house, which is more richly decorated than any other in Scotland.

It is not surprising that the Cistercian ruins are generally more extensive and more beautifully situated than those of the other orders, for it was the Cistercian custom to build in the countryside, whilst the Benedictines chose places that were already inhabited. Thus, after the dissolution, the ruins which adjoined or formed part of growing townships, were not allowed to stand, but were either pulled down to be replaced by churches or incorporated in modern houses. In the open country, however, when the sites

EDGAR WARD

ROMANTIC RUINS OF FURNESS

In the Furness district of Lancashire, in the " Vale of Deadly Nightshade," Benedictine monks from Normandy settled in 1127 and began the building of a splendid monastery which later adopted the rules of the Cistercians. Built of warm red sandstone, the ruins present a wealth of beauty and architectural detail.

EDGAR WARD

ABBEY OF THE FLOWERY VALLEY

Cleeve Abbey, near Washford, Somerset, founded for Cistercian monks in 1188 by William de Romara was dedicated to " Our Blessed Lady of the Cliff." On the left is the Chapter House with the dormitory above. At right angles to this is the beautiful building with domestic rooms below and the refectory above.

were of less value, the abbey buildings were left to decay, at the mercy only of local road builders who looked upon them as valuable quarries.

It is hard to think of Tintern or Rievaulx being built by unskilled workmen, yet the modern grace of Buckfast will convince the doubtful of what can be achieved by willing, if unpracticed, hands. Medieval chronicles describe the building of several abbeys. Generally a small working party was despatched from one of the powerful abbeys, with a meagre supply of food and water, to found a new house. When they were sent to a town their task was relatively easy, but when, as in the case of the Cistercians, new monasteries were established in the midst of the country, their task was always an Odyssey of toil and patience. We must imagine a party of some twenty or thirty seeking a suitable site for the new foundation, exposed to the dangers of man and Nature alike, for the land was infested with robbers and there was no shelter for the infirm.

How the Abbeys were Built

A valley site was always chosen, for the monks must needs have water. How necessary it was for them to build near the banks of a river is aptly illustrated by the story of William the Conqueror and the Benedictine monks whom he commanded to build a monastery on the site of

the Battle of Hastings. The monks started to build in the valley immediately to the south of Senlac ; but when William heard of it, he commanded them to destroy their work and make a fresh start on the hill where Battle Abbey stands today. So disturbed were the builders that they feared God would visit a curse upon the abbey for the Conqueror's impiousness in daring to build where no water flowed.

When at last the site was found, the monks started to clear the ground and build themselves rude huts of wood for protection, utilizing what shelter they could, and hewing the trees to provide them with timber. Then they would till the ground to provide themselves with the necessities of life, and at the same time started to build a church of timber. When this was completed their own temporary dwelling places were rebuilt, still on a modest scale, and the abbey was truly founded. More and more monks were attracted to the new centre, and a start was made on rebuilding the church in stone, the work proceeding either by the hands of the monks themselves or by hired bands of workmen who travelled the country seeking work where they could find it, generally under a Norman master mason.

After the building of the church had been finished the monks' lodgings and other conventual buildings were rebuilt in stone. But this

DIXON-SCOTT

BEAUTIFUL REMAINS OF BEAULIEU ABBEY

The refectory of this once wealthy Cistercian monastery founded by King John in 1204 now serves as the parish church. Other remains include part of the chapter house, dormitory and cloisters. After the Battle of Barnet, in 1471, Queen Margaret and her son sought refuge in Beaulieu, which had the privilege of sanctuary.

great task was rarely completed without disappointments, or without part of the building collapsing through faulty construction, or through the force of tempest and storm. In the early days funds were often lacking, and it was left to the bounty of the king to complete the building. Eighty years was no long time from the choice of the site to the laying of the last stone of the conventual buildings, and, though the wages paid to the hired workers were often no more than sixpence per day, many thousands of pounds were necessary to complete a building for such an exalted purpose, and to embellish it with the engravings and frescoes which are such a valuable part of Britain's medieval heritage.

The church was the centre of the monastic buildings, and, in its construction, the choir was built before the nave, the former being reserved for the devotions of the monks, the latter being sometimes thrown open to the local people. The monastic buildings were raised round three sides of a square, the fourth side being against the church. Between the buildings and the square were the cloisters which was where the monks walked and talked and studied. At first, after the Italian fashion, the cloisters were left unprotected; but, alas! the monks found the English climate more draughty than that of the Mediterranean countries, so that in all the later monasteries the sides of the cloisters facing the central square were built up and windows provided. Often the cloisters were divided into studies on the side facing south so as to draw warmth from the sun.

In reconstructing the life of the monks we must remember that they were allowed no heating except in the sick room, and that the climate was at least not materially warmer than it is now. Even so, the life of the average citizen in Norman, or even later, times was unprotected in a way that could not be tolerated today. There must have been far fewer invalids if only because the weak rarely survived to man's estate. Perhaps what we regard as undue hardship in the life of the monks was accepted by them without thought. The absence of artificial heating, the stone floors and the abundance of fresh air in which they worked may well have led to greater health and greater vitality.

Well Planned Buildings

Chester, Fountains and Rievaulx show well how the monks' buildings were planned. On the side facing the church was the dining-room or refectory, with the monks' washing-place or lavatory—which had a religious as well as a utilitarian significance, seeing that the washing of hands before and after meals was an integral part of the ritual. On the western side were ranges of store-houses and minor buildings, while on the east was the Chapter House where the officers of the monastery met to transact their daily business, and which, after the church itself, was the most richly ornamented and the most sacred part of the buildings. The rest of the eastern side was occupied by the dormitories and other common rooms of the monks. In the earlier, more austere, days of monastic life the abbots slept with the monks, but, as their wealth and position increased, they had separate lodgings built for them, so that in many ruins the abbot's lodging often rivals the elegance and size of the conventual buildings.

So far we have dealt only with the monkish orders in which the lay brethren outnumbered the priests; but there were also Orders of Canons regular, all of whose members were ordained, and whose chief contribution to the legacy of monasticism consisted in church building. Chief

D. MCLEISH

FAIR MELROSE

Sir Walter Scott wrote eloquently of the beauty of " St. David's ruin'd pile " at Melrose. Like Dryburgh, this monastery suffered in war. Robert Bruce restored it on one occasion, and beneath the window of the stately choir seen above his heart was buried.

STEPHENSON

THE STATELY PILE OF LANERCOST PRIORY

Near Brampton, in Cumberland and eleven miles from Carlisle, this priory for Austin Canons was established by the Norman, Robert de Vaux, in 1169, and is built largely of stones from the Roman Wall.   In 1346 the Priory was plundered by the Scots under David Bruce.   The ruins contain some very old and interesting tombs.

among these were the Augustinians whose first house was founded in this country near the beginning of the twelfth century, and who are better known to posterity as the Black Canons from the black vestments which they adopted. The only Augustinian church which attained cathedral rank was that of Carlisle where we can still observe traces of the monks' life in the refectory. Lanercost Priory in Cumberland, Bolton in Yorkshire, Llanthony in Monmouthshire and Walsingham in Norfolk are a few of the distinguished ruins belonging to this order. The last named became very famous during the late Middle Ages owing to the great number of pilgrims who visited annually the reputed shrine of the Virgin Mary—the Shrine of Our Lady of Walsingham.

Holy Shrine of Walsingham

It is related that in 1661 a widow, praying that she might be able to spread devotion, was transported in a dream to Nazareth where God showed her the Sancta Casa, the home where the Holy Family had lived, and bade her build another like it at Walsingham.   Angels helped her in her task, and when it was finished, its fame and the story of the miracles performed there spread all over England.

Many were the kings and nobles who came to do homage at the shrine in which it was thought

the Holy Virgin herself had taken up her abode. Edward I of England, David of Scotland, and King Henry VIII all made the pilgrimage; but this did not prevent the last-named monarch enriching himself from Walsingham's coffers at the dissolution.   The way these pilgrims travelled was by the Palmers' Way through Newmarket, Brandon and Fakenham; its name means Pilgrims' Way, for it was the custom for pilgrims to Jerusalem to carry palms as a sign of devotion. So the words Palmer and Pilgrim came to have the same meaning.

Bolton, too, which like Tintern owes much to Wordsworth's poetry is rich in legend; for it is related that it was founded in honour of the boy Egremont who was drowned in the Wharfe, near where the famous stepping-stones now span the river.   Cold fact discredits the legend, for the priory was originally founded at Embsay in 1121 and transferred to its present site thirty years later.

Scarcely less powerful than the Augustinians were the Premonstratensians, better known as the White Canons, taking their name, as the Augustinians, from the colour of their vestments. Priories belonging to this order were fewer— Torre Abbey in Devon, Bayham Abbey in Sussex, and Shap Abbey in Westmorland are the only ones of which there are remains.

Finally, we must not overlook the Orders of

and work, though their games seem to have been limited to draughts and skittles. Even the vestments in which they retired for the night were fixed.

The influence of the church builders on architecture is obvious ; the English styles became second to none in the world. Because the monks were almost the only class who could read or write, they kept alive the spirit of literature and made possible the beginnings of learning which never became extinct in the centuries which followed the dissolution. More, they brought education into existence, for the monastic schools were the earliest in the country and set an example of discipline and scholarship which otherwise would have been impossible. They re-established, too, the dignity of the worker on the land by doing themselves the work which the Norman landowner thought fit for inferior classes only, and they set a high standard of hospitality by throwing open the convent to the wayfarer in search of a night's lodging.

As the orders became more and more powerful they too became great landowners and shared in the faults of the barons. They began to employ outside labour and rewarded their workers with no better treatment than they received from the squires ; nor did they use their wealth always to alleviate distress among the people who dwelt under the protection of their goodwill. So they displeased

STEPHENSON

AN IMPOSING FRAGMENT AT GUISBOROUGH

Robert Bruce, of Skelton, an ancestor of the more famous Bruce, endowed this Augustinian priory in 1119. The lofty east window is a beautiful example of Decorated architecture and still bears the lion of Bruce and arms of other local families. In front of the window are bases of pillars of the nave arcades.

Friars who were trained to become wandering preachers, and did more than other orders to spread the Gospel through the countryside. They were introduced into England in the thirteenth century, and for two hundred years acted as missionaries in a still unfriendly land, earning high praise for their care of the sick as well as for their preaching of the Gospel. Like the canons they too were generally known by the colour of their vestments. So the Dominicans are better known as Black Friars, and the Carmelites as White Friars.

The monks' life started at midnight when they were roused and filed into the church for the longest service of the day. After a second sleep they arose at daybreak and literally spent the time until sundown in devotion, study and eating. Almost every movement was governed by order—the manner in which they took their food, the order of the services, the pews in which they worshipped. There were breaks for talk in the cloisters and in the afternoon for recreation

the countrymen, and the villages which had sprung up around the monasteries, now grown into towns, rebelled against their pride and prejudice. Instead of a home of peace and learning they became a centre of strife, so that when Henry VIII enriched himself at their expense and dissolved all the monasteries, they had long ceased to be useful institutions.

Founded by Canute

Even after the dissolution the ideal of monastic life survived. The history of Buckfast Abbey is proof enough of that. We know that it was founded in the reign of Canute ; then it disappears from the annals of history. In the twelfth century it was refounded by the Cistercians. Dissolved by Henry VIII its ruins were turned into a Gothic mansion, then in 1882 the site was purchased by the Benedictines who in the course of forty years have raised the immortal structure which stands today as a wonderful monument to their devotion.

W. F. TAYLOR

MONASTIC SPLENDOUR IN A YORKSHIRE DALE

Wordsworth and Ruskin wrote of Bolton and its romantic situation by the banks of the Wharfe. The Priory Church, built in 1170, escaped destruction during the dissolution of the monasteries and is still is use.

EDGAR WARD

TREE-CLAD WALLS OF BUILDWAS ABBEY

The ruins of this Shropshire monastery founded in the twelfth century consist mainly of remains of the chapter house and the nave and chancel of the church. The Abbot's House, dating from the following century, has been restored. The seven massive pillars of the nave were said to represent the Seven Pillars of Wisdom.

D. MCLEISH

WESTERN TOWERS OF ENGLAND'S PREMIER CATHEDRAL

Canterbury, England's premier cathedral, takes us back to the days of St. Augustine, the Roman missionary who converted Ethelbert, King of Kent, and who was the first " bishop of the English." The oldest remaining fragments date from Archbishop Lanfranc (1070-1089), but most of the structure is due to subsequent builders, including William of Sens the famous French master mason, who began building in 1175.

THE CATHEDRALS OF ENGLAND

by CHARLES FRY

THE history, if not the fabric, of most of our cathedrals has its origin towards the close of the Dark Ages. Its background is that half-primeval England of the swamps and forests, in which a scattered population was settling down to husbandry in huddled little hamlets and clearings, still much at the mercy of warring chiefs and raiders, while the weeds grew thick over the foundations of the Roman settlements. It was a shaggy England still, brooding, as it were, in a dangerous early light, to which Christianity was to bring the first promise of a dawn.

The story of St. Augustine's great mission has often been recounted. We owe to it our three earliest cathedral foundations, Rochester, London and Canterbury; while three more, Lincoln, Southwell and York, in part or in whole owe their inception to the greatest of his followers, Paulinus, one of that eager band sent out from Rome by St. Gregory to further Augustine's task. While Augustine, with his English converts and Roman followers, spread the doctrine of Christ through the southern provinces, to Paulinus and his successors belonged the task of gathering the wilder north into the Catholic fold.

It was a task made delicate at first by the labours of another missionary group, simple men who had already in these parts made many converts to a primitive Celtic Church. The influence of this church had spread from Ireland to Iona, a little island off the west coast of Scotland, a forcing-house of faith, whence a devoted band had set forth to preach and baptize in the wilds of Scotland and Northumbria.

Chief among the Celtic missionaries was St. Cuthbert, who, after a youth spent as a shepherd boy near Melrose, joined the fraternity of Iona and made his way to Lindisfarne, the Holy Island off the Northumberland coast from which this evangelization of Northern England was largely effected. Here he died and was buried in A.D. 687. But with the growing terror of the Danish and Norse raids, it soon became necessary to remove his relics, with the treasure of the little church, to more secure surroundings, and so the Lindisfarne brotherhood set out on a remarkable pilgrimage of several hundred years' duration. Each place of halt was commemorated by a church dedicated to the saint, but it was not until A.D. 997 that the brothers "with great joy arrived with his body at Dunholme," where, attracted by the security of that hill-fortress surrounded on three sides by the Wear, they built "a little church of wands and branches" on the site where Durham Cathedral now stands.

Such was the origin of one of the most splendid of our cathedral churches. Many another can tell a story equally fraught with danger and devotion. Some owe their inception to Saxon or Roman missionary bishops, as Lichfield to St. Chad, Winchester to St. Swithun, Ripon to St. Wilfred—men whose tombs were to develop into some of the most popular shrines of the Middle Ages, the offerings at which went largely to endow the costly fabrics and fitments of later cathedrals. Some again were due to the piety of Saxon rulers; the first cathedral of Peterborough commemorated the conversion of Peada, King of the Mercians, about A.D. 665; that at Hereford

W. F. TAYLOR

NORWICH CATHEDRAL

Norwich became a cathedral city in 1094, and the Norman tower surmounted by a fifteenth-century spire makes a landmark, rising above the historic town.

DIXON-SCOTT

THE LOVELY WESTERN TOWER OF ELY CATHEDRAL

On the site of a Benedictine abbey, established by a seventh-century Queen of Northumbria, stands the magnificent Cathedral of Ely. The building of the present structure was begun in 1083 by Abbot Simeon, and after the collapse of the tower in 1322 was completed with a wealth of fourteenth-century carving by William of Walsingham. Far and wide across the low levels of the fens its lofty towers are seen soaring heavenwards.

was originally raised about A.D. 825 over the tomb of Ethelbert, King of the East Angles, who was lured to his death by the great Offa of Mercia ; while that at Ely was founded in A.D. 673 by Ethelreda, princess of East Anglia, who built a religious house on her own lands and assigned to it her absolute principality of the surrounding " Isle of Ely "—a bequest that was to form the nucleus of the wealth accruing to one of the proudest monasteries of the Middle Ages.

The early days of some of these rude little churches were often stormy. The establishment at Ely, for instance, was sacked and gutted by the Danes less than a hundred years after its foundation. But a handful of survivors escaped, creeping back a few years later to effect a partial restoration of the church, which, surviving the fury of Hereward's last stand at the nearby " Camp of Refuge," was to continue in active use until 1080, when its rebuilding was begun in the present form. The church at Peterborough suffered a rather similar fate, having been sacked by the Danes in A.D. 870 and rehabilitated, very sumptuously for the time, a hundred years later. At the Conquest the abbey passed into Norman hands, but was stormed by Hereward, who destroyed all but the church where he himself had taken the vows of knighthood.

W. F. TAYLOR

WEST FRONT, PETERBOROUGH CATHEDRAL
Peada, a Saxon King of Mercia, founded a monastery at Peterborough in the seventh century. This suffered many vicissitudes, being destroyed by the Danes in A.D. 870 and after rebuilding being burnt down in 1116.

Danish Plunders

Even in the west the sacred places were not immune from the Danish terror, and we find the church built by St. Oswald for the Worcester Benedictines plundered and burnt as late as 1041, though only a few years were to elapse before a greater building rose from the ashes at the hands of the famous Wulstan, who alone among English prelates retained his position after the Conquest.

The earlier churches were, for the most part, rough and ready affairs of timber, easy to destroy and not so difficult to rebuild. But with the more settled conditions of the tenth century, and the establishment of rudimentary connections with the Continent, came a wave of rebuilding in stone, in a style that may be recognized as a primitive but none the less effective version of the Anglo-Norman Romanesque that was to succeed it. These churches and their surrounding buildings formed little oases of thought and devotion in the crude life of a barely united people. They might be served by colleges of secular canons, as was the case with nine of the pre-Conquest sees—Chichester, Exeter, Hereford, Lichfield, Lincoln, London, Sarum, Wells and York—or by communities of monks or nuns, communities who were just beginning to sort

DIXON-SCOTT

WORCESTER CATHEDRAL

From Saxon times Worcester has been the seat of a bishop. St. Oswald rebuilt the original church in A.D. 964.
His work was destroyed by the Danes to be built again on a grander scale by Wulstan, the only Saxon bishop
to retain his seat after the Conquest. Today the Cathedral makes a fine picture with the Severn in the foreground.

themselves out among newly rising monastic orders. Chief among these orders was the Benedictines, whose growing prestige and wealth did much to enhance the progress of the Romanesque style, and had by the time of the Conquest clothed Northern France in its "white robe of churches."

Norman Builders

But it is from the Conquest that the history of the English cathedrals as we know them today begins. With the consolidation of Norman rule began that remarkable outburst of building vigour—*furor Normanorum* it has been called—that has left its permanent mark upon so many of our cathedral churches.

To the pre-Conquest sees were added at this time the abbey churches of Canterbury, Durham, Ely, Norwich, Rochester, Winchester and Worcester, each still with its establishment of Benedictine monks, but containing, by an arrangement little known outside England, the throne of a bishop. They were bishops of a new type, these Norman prelate-princes—active, ambitious men who competed with one another in the grandeur of their building schemes, the speed of their realization.

De St. Carileph at Durham, De Losinga at Norwich, Walkelin at Winchester, and many others, filled the little cities where they ruled with swarms of untrained workmen, and scoured the country for that rare phenomenon of those

days, the skilled craftsman. Considering the speed at which they arose, and the frequent haphazardness of the methods employed, it is indeed a wonder that some of these buildings have endured at all.

But what splendid churches they were ! Norwich, Ely, Peterborough, Rochester, and, in supreme measure, Durham, furnish unforgettable instances of the solid strength and dignity of the Anglo-Norman manner at its best, though now stripped of the external covering of thin, white plaster that must have given them a radiance that their present severity belies.

Similarly, within, one can only visualize from the worn traces that survive here and there upon their walls the former richness of their frescoed decorations, forming a glowing background to the glitter of myriad candles. But deeply impressive as are the ranges of vast internal piers, their appearance is often deceptive, for in many cases they constitute no more than a casing of ashlar masonry filled with loose rubble, occasionally in itself insufficient to support the weight of the squat central towers that crowned the crossings. Thus it was at Norwich, where the collapse of part of the tower, necessitated the building of the beautiful fourteenth-century substitute surviving today, and the reconstruction of the quire clerestory to form one of the most perfect eastern terminations of any English church.

Impressive, too, are the cavernous triforium arcades of round-headed arches, the tiers of interwoven arcading such as adorn the great tower at Ely, and the sculptured portals that may be seen at the same cathedral, at Rochester, and elsewhere. If there is sometimes an almost cliff-like severity in the external elevations, with their successive strata-bands of arches, arcading and windows, the whole style breathes a virility and grandeur which, I think, expresses itself as well in a very concise manner in a handful of English cathedrals as in any contemporary productions to be found on the Continent.

Cruciform Churches

Planned and arranged on remarkably consistent lines, each of these churches took the form of a vast cross—though the theory that this was ever based symbolically upon the Cross of Christ has proved a fallacy. In the case of those that also served a monastic purpose, the quire that formed the eastern limb contained the stalls of the monks and the sanctuary of the high altar, ending eastward either in a trio of chapel-apses or a continuous semi-circular processional path with small chapels radiating from it. Beneath the quire was usually a vaulted crypt to house the sacred relics in the possession of the community. Quire and transept were separated from the nave by a stone *pulpitum* or screen. East of this screen was the domain of the community, who served the church in a ceaseless rotation of ritual and worship, while the nave west of it was reserved for the services of the lay congregation.

The subject of the conventual buildings attached to these churches is beyond the scope of this chapter. Nevertheless, two outstanding features demand brief mention, for throughout the Middle Ages they were often to persist in cathedral churches of non-monastic foundation. They were the cloister, or vaulted quadrangular walk which formed the centre of communal life and activity in every monastery, and was usually placed on the south side of the church between nave and transept, and the Chapter House, where the brethren met in conference and for the administration of justice. It is certainly cause for rejoicing that their appearance became almost a convention of later cathedral architecture, for the vaults and open arcades of the cloisters, giving on to the green lawns of their garths, were to see the development of some of the loveliest stonework of English Gothic, while the Chapter House, taking as its prototype the decagonal thirteenth-century structure at Lincoln, with its great areas of glazing and intricate scheme of vaulting from a central pier, was to develop into a rich and individual national feature, and produce the superb examples at Wells, Salisbury, Southwell, York and elsewhere.

If the eleventh and twelfth centuries were *par excellence* the period of monastic building in this country, with the thirteenth came a change of heart. The population was growing and the lay congregation beginning to assert itself. The flow of subscriptions and bequests from the faithful now began to be diverted to other ends, and the new century witnessed what was perhaps

HUMPHREY AND VERA JOEL

TRIPLE SPIRES AND WEST FRONT OF LICHFIELD
St. Chad moved the Saxon bishopric of Mercia from Repton to Lichfield, but the first church was built by Bishop Hedda (A.D. 700). The oldest portions of the existing structure date from about 1200.

the most spectacular wave of cathedral building in our history—one that was to produce in their original entirety the great fabrics of Salisbury, Lincoln and Wells, and leave its mark upon many another of our cathedrals.

Perhaps this tendency was due in part to the growing arrogance and unpopularity of the monastic houses. Thirteenth-century records contain many accounts of clashes between monks and townsmen, clashes which must have reached a climax in the pitched battle fought out at Norwich in 1271, lasting for several days, in which many were killed and the cathedral gutted down to its walls.

But the new period, like the old, owed its measure to its " building bishops." Grosseteste, who carried on the work begun by St. Hugh at Lincoln ; Poore, who transferred the see of Sarum from the little hill-fortress to its present Salisbury site, and was afterwards to add the splendid Chapel of the Nine Altars to the east end of Durham ; and Jocelyn, who at Wells completed the great task begun by Reginald de Bohun as early as 1174—to these men, and there were others, belongs credit for fostering the enterprises of a school of masoncraft that was to produce the first achievements of a dawning national Gothic.

William of Sens

We know that a French master mason, William of Sens, was employed by the Canterbury monks for the rebuilding of their quire, one of its earliest experiments ; but we know, too, that after the fall from the scaffolding that incapacitated him from further work the task was taken over by one William the Englishman, while at Wells, at least, west country masons had already begun to formulate, in the new nave, a precocious and highly successful experiment in Gothic before its time.

We know that at Durham, by 1133, English masons had completed the task of roofing the entire cathedral with ribbed stone vaulting—

EDGAR WARD

GLOUCESTER CATHEDRAL

Founded in A.D. 681 as an abbey for monks and nuns, Gloucester later became a college for secular priests. These were expelled by Canute in 1022 for evil living and their place was taken by Benedictine monks. The Norman work dates from Abbot Serlo 1089. The beautiful Central Tower was erected in 1450.

DIXON-SCOTT

THE NOBLE BEAUTY OF WELLS

This beautiful cathedral at the foot of the Mendips has been described as " the best example to be found in the whole world of a secular church with its subordinate buildings." According to tradition, the first church was founded by King Ine in A.D. 705. The present structure dates from the days of Bishop Reginald de Bohun.

possibly the first achievement of its kind in Europe—and how largely it was from this constructional innovation that the pointed fashion emerged. It would, of course, be absurd to suggest that the first phase of English Gothic—" Early English," to use the time-honoured, if rather unsatisfactory, label—did not originate in the main from the experiment that had already filled the Ile de France with its cathedral constellation. It may even be admitted that such a cathedral as Salisbury represents little more than a minor provincial variation on that prodigious theme. Nevertheless, there is much in the development of this style, and in its ornament, that breathes an English air, and that, to me at least, makes these great churches of the thirteenth century a dearer possession than the mightier achievement of France.

Their planning marked a definite innovation on English precedent, involving a considerable enlargement of the eastern limb to provide more altar accommodation for the canons who now swarmed the cathedral precincts. Beyond the high altar, a processional path generally gave access to an eastern extension, or retro-quire, often with its own eastern transept, sumptuously built to contain the relics and treasure brought above ground from the crypt.

Lady Chapels

With the rising cult of Our Lady, a Lady Chapel of lower elevation came to be considered the most fitting eastern termination to these *congeries*, with the effect of largely abolishing the original apse-scheme and substituting the square ends always so characteristic of English Gothic. These innovations were not only applied to new buildings ; in varying degrees they were carried out, now and hereafter, on existing structures. Thus it was at Canterbury, Ely, Beverley, to name only three ; while as a compromise to the lay congregation, the nave might be lengthened westward by a few bays, and one of those majestically sculptured screen-fronts in which the thirteenth century delighted added as a frontispiece, as at Peterborough, Wells and Lincoln.

W. F. TAYLOR

SALISBURY'S SPLENDID NAVE

This cathedral was begun in 1220 by Bishop Poore and was consecrated thirty-eight years later in the presence of Henry III. It was ruthlessly restored in 1798 and later, and many fine features were destroyed. The long narrow and lofty nave is divided into ten bays by smooth grey piers and slender pillars of Purbeck marble.

This last great church, crowning its steep little hill above the Witham, does, in fact, represent an almost complete epitome of the progress of the thirteenth-century style in this country. The severity of St. Hugh's own quire (1186-1200) shades into the solemn beauty of Grosseteste's nave and transept (1209-1235), with their tall clustered piers and ranges of lancet windows and arcading, just rescued from sternness by the sculptural relief of mouldings and foliated capitals. From here one must move eastward to realize the rich culmination of this art during the later years of the century. The so-called "Angel Choir" was built as a presbytery to contain the relics of the canonized builder-bishop, St. Hugh, and its consecration about 1280, attended by most of the crowned heads of Europe, was one of the most glittering ceremonies in the history of our cathedrals. It is a work exquisite in proportion and rich in sculptured detail, culminating in the carved angel orchestra from which it takes its name, filling the spandrels of a sumptuous triforium arcade which displays the stone cuspings and circles of the "geometrical" tracery on which the transition from Early English to the "Decorated" of the next century so largely centred.

Just as Lincoln forms an

W. F. TAYLOR

ANGEL CHOIR, LINCOLN

Magnificently placed on a hill above the city, Lincoln Cathedral is a landmark. The exquisite Angel Choir was built in the thirteenth century and takes its name from the thirty figures of angels carved on the spandrels.

epitome of thirteenth-century development, so Exeter, in supreme measure, exemplifies the transient beauty of the style that succeeded it during the earlier part of the next century, to receive its quietus from the epidemic of the Black Death which was to paralyse church building for over a generation. The Cathedral of the West owes much of its peculiar radiance to a line of bishops with whom the work of enlargement and adornment was nearer to a passion than a duty. The earlier work of

Bronscombe, Quivil and Bytton was brought to a conclusion under Stapledon and Grandison, from whom the quire received its furnishing and the whole church its rich covering of vaulting. It is hard to give any impression in words of the warmth and exuberance of the finished effect. "A luxurious, spendthrift art," Professor Prior characterized the almost pagan profusion of its close-clustered shafting and restless curvilinear tracery, its elaborate screenwork and soaring bishop's throne.

EDGAR WARD

YORK MINSTER'S SPLENDOUR IN STONE

York's great and glorious minster had its humble beginnings in a little wooden church where Paulinus, first Bishop of York, baptised Edwin, the Northumbrian king, in A.D. 627. *The present structure was begun about* 1227 *while the massive central tower, the largest in England, was completed early in the fifteenth century.*

It was an art that found similar expression among the cathedrals in the perhaps slightly overloaded west front of York Minster, in the splendid free carving of the Southwell Chapter House and the Ely Lady Chapel, in the tower and slender spire of St. Mary's at Salisbury, and in great curvilinear windows at Carlisle and York, with their movement " as of a flickering of wings."

Pilgrims' Shrines

This period marks the culmination of perhaps the most lavish phase of English cathedral building. The church was now at the summit of its power and activity. The cathedral shrines were flocked with pilgrims, each bearing his offering, however modest, to add to the sums expended on the developing fabrics. It was not only to the older shrines that the pilgrims journeyed; the cult of some latter-day saints had grown to prodigious proportions, and Chaucer, in *The Canterbury Tales*, which dates from about this time, has left a picture of the varied companies, drawn from all classes, that would wend their way, on horseback or on foot, over the green Kentish country, to sink one and all to their knees on first sight of the gilded " Angel Steeple " from the crest of Harbledown Hill.

A steady stream of bequests also went to the building of the chantry chapels that so enrich our cathedrals, each with its resident priest and endowment for the saying of masses " in perpetuity " for the soul of the faithful departed. Some of the finest craftsmanship was bestowed on these little chapels, and on the costly tombs of nobles, bishops and burgesses that crowded the available spaces. Masoncraft had by now reached its highest peak of skill and organization. It had travelled far from the haphazard, speculative days of Anglo-Norman construction, and represented a mature guild of artisans, working under masters in collaboration with a variety of dependent crafts such as those of the carpenters, glaziers and metalworkers, supplemented by local supplies of labourers, hewers and carriers.

Here it may be mentioned that the theory that the religious themselves were ever responsible in any large degree for the fabrics of their churches has been discarded. The bishops, priors and sacrists to whom so many famous works have been loosely attributed acted in the majority of cases as little more than " business organizers " of the projects, though they were often responsible for the provision of building materials—no light task when one remembers the appalling state of communications throughout the Middle

Ages. If the famous sacrist, Alan of Walsingham, can no longer be credited with the design of that unique and lovely fourteenth-century feature, the Ely Octagon, it is at least to be remembered that its great timbers, of a scantling prodigious for modern times, were transported under his direction over the soggy marshes that surrounded the cathedral by roads and bridges specially built for their carriage.

It was to the cult of pilgrimages that, in some degree at least, we owe the last and greatest revolution in English medieval building. After the murder of Edward II at Berkeley Castle in 1327, none of the great churches of the West had been willing to receive his body until it was brought to Gloucester, whose monks gave it a fitting burial and later set up a shrine to the newly-canonized martyr which began to attract pilgrims from all over England.

So greatly did the flow of offerings increase into the Gloucester coffers that it was decided, with the proceeds, to reconstruct the old Norman choir as a splendid mortuary chapel to the profitable saint. To this end Abbot Wygmore, a man of singular artistic perception, employed the "clever and rather eccentric" masons who had formed a school in the Severn Valley which had already devised the curious open-work vaulting in the Bristol aisles. Their work at Gloucester, begun less than halfway through the fourteenth century, brought about an almost overnight revolution in building methods, a revolution that was to be perpetuated through the remaining Middle Ages and beyond in the so-called "Perpendicular" style—the last, the most enduring and perhaps the greatest of the phases of our national Gothic.

Fan-vaulted Roofs

Broadly speaking, it was a style of open, airy spaces, lighted by sheets of radiant "silverstain" glazing; a style of light rectilinear stone panelling and lofty slender shafting, that was to evolve as a covering the most individual of our forms of stone roofing, the fan vault. It was a style that, for its economy and effectiveness in those depleted days, found almost instant acceptation; already, by 1379, the Canterbury monks had adopted it for their new nave, while under William of Wykeham the immense Norman nave of Winchester was recased with brilliant effect in the same manner.

It was a style that went hand in hand with the remarkable reflorescence of woodwork in stalls, roofs and screens, during the fifteenth century, when English carpenters first adopted to their uses the slender pinnacled conceptions of mason-craft, and was to evolve in its time the lofty aisleless fabrics of a great preaching age, best exemplified in the chapels of St. George at

DIXON-SCOTT

WINCHESTER FROM THE CLOSE

Winchester, the ancient capital of Saxon kings, became a bishopric about A.D. 670, *and St. Swithun of the rain legend was bishop* A.D. 852-862. *Alfred, Canute and others were crowned in the old minster. The present cathedral was begun by Bishop Walkelin in 1079, additions and alterations being made later.*

Windsor, King's College at Cambridge and Henry VII at Westminster. And lastly it was a style to which we owe some of the stateliest of our cathedral towers—splendid structures such as arose over the central spaces at York, Gloucester, Worcester, and, perhaps most strikingly, Canterbury, to fill England with the music of bells and form the focal points of what are still some of our loveliest landscapes.

The events of the Reformation belong as much to political as to cathedral history, but it is perhaps not always realized what a spoil awaited the fingers of Henry's commissioners as they

gifts, for at this time the great Benedictine churches of Peterborough, Gloucester and Chester were saved from otherwise inevitable decay or destruction by their conversion into cathedrals, as was also the case with the Augustinian churches of Bristol and Oxford.

The seventeenth century marked the leanest and saddest years in our cathedral history. Those of the greater churches that had been afforded a status in the post-Reformation scheme had remained largely intact in fabric and fitting, and it was left to the factional zeal of extreme parties at this later time to work a thoroughgoing vengeance on all vestiges of the old ecclesiastical dignity. Much of the glories of English stained glass, for instance, that had survived the Reformation, was destroyed by Puritan fanaticism at the time of the Civil War. Certain fabrics were singled out for particular violence, as Peterborough, where every interior fitment was smashed to pieces by Cromwell's troops and even the walls shaken to their foundations, and Rochester, where Puritan soldiers "so far profaned this place as to make use of it in the quality of a tippling place, as well as dug several saw-pits, and the chief joyners made frames for houses in it." The embattled close at Lichfield was subjected to a fierce siege, and the cathedral shelled by artillery; at Exeter the cathedral was divided into two preaching-houses,

W. F. TAYLOR

ST. DAVID'S FROM THE NORTH-WEST

St. David's, in Pembrokeshire, is the smallest of our cathedral cities. Traditionally the see was founded by the patron saint of Wales about A.D. 550. Peter de Leia, the third Norman bishop, began the present edifice in 1180.

went about their task of suppression and eradication. The cathedrals were by now treasure houses of craftsmanship of every kind, and the riches of their shrines, despite a slowly waning popularity, were enough to dazzle the eyes of the stranger privileged to inspect them in their completeness, as the eyes of Erasmus were dazzled by the jewelled hoard of St. Thomas.

These national shrines were accorded the same ruthless treatment as the conventual riches. In 1538 Henry issued his posthumous writ against Thomas Becket for "treason, contumacy and rebellion," which was in due course read at Canterbury before the saint's tomb. The suit was tried at Westminster and had its sequel in the removal of twenty-six cartloads of gold and jewels into the royal treasury. But at least this bleak ecclesiastical reorganization made its public

the "East and West Peters," while at St. Albans a public passageway was driven through the exquisite little Saint's Chapel of the immense and mouldering abbey church, since restored as a cathedral. Many another case of violation could be instanced. It is little wonder that, after the long laxity and neglect of the eighteenth century, the cathedrals presented a shameful and woebegone spectacle that roused a fury in the younger Pugin. "I have been at the Cathedral all the morning," he wrote from Ely in 1834. "How I am delighted! How I am pained! Here is a church, magnificent in every respect, falling into decay through gross neglect. Would you believe it possible? There is no person appointed to attend to the repairs of the building, and the only person who has been employed during the last sixty years is a bricklayer. Not even common precautions are taken to keep the building dry," While at another cathedral the bishop, who had refused to subscribe to the re-erection of his own throne, had lost £7,000 on the Derby!

It is easy to be over critical of the hand of the nineteenth century on the cathedrals. It is true that Wyatt, the first and therefore the least informed of the restorers, worked much havoc on the ancient fabrics, such as the demolition of the splendid Beauchamp and Hungerford chantries at Salisbury, though he was fortunately thwarted in his attempt to demolish the unique late-Norman "Galilee" at Durham to make a carriage-drive to the west front.

Nevertheless, though they sometimes over-stepped their powers, it must be conceded that the Victorian church architects accomplished a magnificent structural feat in saving many crumbling edifices from otherwise inevitable decay. If such buildings as Worcester and Chester now represent little more than mid-Victorian reconstructions, it is doubtful whether any less drastic treatment would have been efficacious, for long years of neglect of their soft friable stonework had probably left them past repair. But in their work on the interiors the Victorians were guilty of some appalling lapses. It would be hard to envisage a more hideous object than Scott's screen at Hereford—the last touch of humiliation to that humiliated fabric—or a more unhappy scheme of decoration than that which left Salisbury in its present state of "encaustic floors, varnished marble and a quire bepainted and bedizened."

Only three new cathedrals have been built on English soil since the Reformation, though a number of churches intended for collegiate or parochial uses have, with the growth of the population and the multiplication of its centres, been of recent years raised to cathedral status. St. Paul's, Wren's great monument to Renaissance craftsmanship, humanism and churchmanship, stands in a class by itself. Truro Cathedral, completed almost a couple of centuries later to Pearson's designs, incorporate some of the structure of the old Perpendicular parish church on the south-east and so add a third aisle to the choir. Like the half-completed Liverpool Cathedral, it marks successful if somewhat over-literal essays in revived Gothic, though almost as I write the foundation stone has been laid of a new cathedral at Guildford which will unite modern structural developments with traditional English forms.

It is clear, therefore, that the cathedral achievement in this country is almost overwhelmingly a medieval one. It was an achievement so fertile, so various and withal so characteristically English that it is almost impossible to condense its

W. F. TAYLOR

TRURO CATHEDRAL
This beautiful modern cathedral begun in 1880, was the first one to be built in England after the Reformation. Cruciform in structure and built in the Early English style, it has a handsome central tower.

appreciation into a brief preroration. Serenity, I think, is the most befitting word for the sum effect of these great churches, despite the grandeur of a Durham, the glory of a Lincoln. Their very inconsistency—that patchwork quality that is the despair of the foreign purist—lend them an intimate and English quality that is enhanced by the almost invariable beauty of their settings among smooth lawns and quiet old houses. Their piecemeal evolution seems, in fact, almost one with that of the English people, striving through splendour, humiliation and danger towards that peaceful maturity that has always been their better goal. To the aura of dignity and veneration that surrounds them has been added a gentleness that seems to emanate from the affection of Englishmen through many centuries. It is not the least part of our national duty to preserve them, reverently and solicitously, in the twilight beauty of their last phase.

114

EDGAR WARD

AN ANCIENT STREET IN YORK

This delightful city has many fascinating reminders of its long and varied past.   There is a remarkable suggestion of the Middle Ages in the Shambles, a narrow winding street flanked with old houses and shops and overhanging upper storeys from which one may shake hands with a neighbour across the street.   Formerly known as High Mangergate it takes its present name from the fact that in olden days cattle were slaughtered there.

SOME MEDIEVAL TOWNS

by HAROLD SHELTON

TO the Romans belongs the distinction of introducing the walled town to Britain. It was they who encircled cities such as Canterbury, Rochester and York many years before the first castle was built. The medieval walled town is in the same tradition, for in many cases the medieval walls were constructed in the form of, and from the fragments of, the Roman defences.

Only Colchester, Chester, York and Southampton retain their walled girdle in any degree of perfection. But there are very many others where parts of the wall, or perhaps a gate-house remains, and in which we can trace the narrow, crooked streets of the medieval, or like as at Wareham, the straight intersecting thoroughfares of the Roman town. It is, in fact, surprising how often the ancient town survives as the core of the modern city, sometimes being characteristically raised above its surroundings, and generally lying within a circumference of between one and two miles. At Bristol the course of the old wall is marked by a lane which was originally the alley-way between the wall and the houses. It encloses a space less than nineteen acres in extent, but the circuit of the walls of York is nearly three miles. Most of the existing walls are derived from the Norman builders, though they were reconstructed as occasion arose down to the fourteenth and fifteenth centuries. Walled towns like Conway and Caernarvon, and others in Wales and the Welsh Marches owe their mural defences to Edward I.

We can trace in nearly every case the reasons which led to the growth of a town. A frequent cause was the existence of a ford or bridge where an important road crossed a wide river. Again, many towns arose round the castles and the abbeys when these began to offer an assured market, bringing trade and employment with them. A good natural harbour was reason enough for the rise of a port. The place where two roads intersected naturally drew an increasing population as men travelled more and trade became greater. In fact, a moment's reflection will show that all the towns which we shall describe

sprang from economic or military causes except those which were founded again and again on the site of previous centres of population.

Canterbury is perhaps the most interesting of all the cities of England. In turn an early British settlement, Roman walled city, the capital of the Saxon kingdom of Kent, it became the See of St. Augustine whom Ethelbert, King of Kent, invited to the English shore. St. Augustine's Abbey, where the saint was buried, was founded in A.D. 613. Thereafter the history of the cathedral became the history of the town. Burnt by the Danes it was rebuilt by King Canute. It was burnt again in a great fire which destroyed

W. F. TAYLOR

BRISTOL'S BEAUTIFUL ABBEY GATE

This structure which now serves as an entrance to the Cathedral Close was the gateway of the abbey which was founded in 1142 and which flourished through medieval times. After the Reformation the abbey church became the cathedral of Bristol.

grown from a Saxon church where King Edwin was baptized in the seventh century. Like Canterbury Cathedral, too, the Minster dominates the town, with its great central tower which is more massive than any other in England. The Roman walls and the multangular tower stand cheek by jowl with the later walls, and four of the main gateways are standing, so making York unique among English cities. But it is the ancient gabled houses of the Shambles, where the upper storeys almost meet each other across the narrow lane which lend the city its chief enchantment.

York was the Roman outpost city of the north-east, Chester of the north-west, and, like York, Chester has the air of a walled town within the modern city. If we enter by the East Gate we are confronted by dozens of half-timbered houses with overhanging fronts. A medley of ancient dwellings reaches its greatest distinction in The Rows—a double row of shops, one above the other, the upper ones being fronted by a covered footway to which access is gained by steps leading up at frequent intervals from the ground

PHOTOCHROM

CHEPSTOW'S CRUMBLING RUINS
On the high ground by the banks of the Wye, William Fitzosbern raised a fortress in Norman days which was known as the Castle of Striguil. Except for the keep, the structure dates from the fourteenth century.

half the town, but a new cathedral was consecrated by the Normans in 1130, destined to become the perfect example of Gothic architecture in England, and dominating the city from whatever angle it is approached. The martyrdom of St. Thomas made Canterbury the mecca of countless pilgrims who brought prosperity and trade to the medieval city, increased by the migration of the Flemish weavers whose quaint houses overhang the Stour. The fourteenth-century walls are about half intact, and contain within them not only the cathedral and the abbey ruins, but the great Dane John also, the mound which may well be a prehistoric fortress, the church of St. Martin which is certainly of Saxon foundation, and was probably the church from which St. Augustine first preached, and the ruins of the Norman castle. One gate only survives—the West Gate—though this barely escaped demolition at the end of the last century when rumour has it that the City Fathers decided by a single vote against removing it as an obstruction to traffic.

York has much in common with Canterbury. Like Canterbury Cathedral, York Minster has

HUMPHREY AND VERA JOEL

THE LANDGATE, RYE
Rye, now two miles from the sea, became one of the Cinque Ports in the twelfth century. Despite its mural defences dating from Edward III, the town was burnt by French invaders in 1377 and in 1448.

VALENTINE

CITY WALLS OF SOUTHAMPTON

Southampton is said to have been surrounded by a defensive wall in Saxon times. The Normans shortly after the Conquest enclosed it with ramparts of masonry thirty to forty feet high, and making a circuit of one and a quarter miles. Three gates remain. On two sides the River Test was utilized as a moat.

PHOTOCHROM

POTTERGATE, LINCOLN

Lincoln had its beginnings in Roman times, if not earlier, and in the thirteenth century was the fourth seaport in Britain. This fourteenth-century gateway of the medieval defences is said to take its name from the supposed existence of a Roman pottery near the spot. In the background are the imposing towers of the cathedral.

FELTON

A PICTURESQUE STREET IN HISTORIC CHESTER

In Eastgate Street, Chester's principal thoroughfare, are some of the famous Rows. These galleries or arcades along the first floor level are a unique feature of the city. They are possibly built over the ruins of Roman Chester, and had the advantage of being above the ill-kept streets. Shops were later opened on the ground level, thus giving the double tiers. In the basement of No. 28 is a finely preserved medieval crypt.

level. The seventeenth-century "God's Providence House" and the "Bear and Billet" are two of many black and white houses which are so characteristic of the Marcher country. Side by side with the red brick of many of the other houses, toned to a depth of mellowness almost unbelievable, they stand out in startling but wonderfully effective contrast. Though the exterior of the cathedral is not so impressive as those of Canterbury and York, the early English architecture of the choir and the carved woodwork of the choir screen contain beauty enough to make a journey to Chester well worth while if only on that account.

As at York the best views of the town are obtained from the parapet walk along the wall. The Phoenix Tower, which we reach at the northern corner, is a reminder of the troublous times of the seventeenth century ; for it was here that Charles I watched the dwindling of his hopes as his troops were defeated at Rowton Moor. On the opposite side of the circuit in the south-east corner we shall find the wishing steps where, in order to have our wish fulfilled, we must run up and down seven times with one breath. It is from the parapet, too, that the red sandstone of the cathedral walls gives such a warm colouring to the whole city.

Border Cockpit

Berwick-on-Tweed is another northern town which has lived through many wars and rumours of wars. It was the cockpit of all the fighting between England and Scotland, and was in the hands of first one and then the other country, a problem which was solved in 1551 by declaring it a neutral town after it had changed hands, it is said, no less than thirteen times. Here, too, no inconsiderable fragments of the walls survive, more than usually interesting because the fortifications, dating only from the sixteenth century, show the modifications in design which were thought necessary to combat the invention of artillery. Perhaps it is by its three noble bridges that Berwick impresses itself most upon the imagination, where the medieval stands side by side with the modern. The most recent is a three-span bridge opened in 1928, designed to take the place of the seventeenth-century stone bridge of fifteen arches, whilst the

third is the high railway viaduct designed by Stephenson in the middle of the last century.

It has been said by one shrewd observer that the more turbulent the history of a town, the quieter the dignity which it presents to the modern world. Certainly Chichester bears out that statement, for this is a city which has been British settlement, Roman town, Saxon capital and cathedral city. It was destroyed in turn by the Romans, the Saxons and the Norsemen, yet, when once the Saxon bishopric had been transferred from Selsey in the eleventh century, it led a life of peace and quietness. Apart from the cathedral there is the medieval hospital of St. Mary and the sixteenth-century market cross to remind us of past times— the only cross remaining in Sussex apart from the

W. A. CALL

MEDIEVAL GATE AT MONMOUTH
On the bridge spanning the River Monnow stands this thirteenth-century gateway, the only instance in England of a defensive gateway situated on a bridge. Formerly known as Welsh Gate it was one of the five gates in the town walls of Monmouth.

FELTON

GATEWAY OF A CORNISH TOWN

Launceston has a long historic past, and became a royal borough in the days of William the Conqueror who built a castle there. In the Middle Ages it was a walled city, and some fragments of the walls are still standing. The photograph shows the South Gate of the city wall, a solidly built fourteenth-century structure. Above the town stands the ruined Norman castle where the Quaker, George Fox, was imprisoned in 1655.

stump at Alfriston. A legend is remembered in Chichester that if the church steeple were to fall, there would be no king in England—a legend which was given the stamp of truth when the steeple fell in 1861 when there was no king, but a queen on the throne of England.

Although Chichester has exchanged turbulence for peace its near neighbour, Southampton, belies the statement. As the most strategic point along the Channel coast, it has through history been a place which invading forces have tried to capture, but in the modern era it has increased rather than diminished in activity, and is today a bustling centre of trade. Its medieval character is almost lost except in the walls which are almost as complete as those of York and Chester, and at least as impressive as either. Its three gates, the North, the West and the Spur are intact. Near the West Gate the *Mayflower* memorial was raised to the memory of the Pilgrim Fathers who sailed from the port in 1620, and the High Street, which runs to the Bar Gate, surmounted by the Guildhall, still retains the aspect of a very ancient thoroughfare.

Border Castles

Chepstow is another walled town which was an important medieval port. In the struggles with Wales it played almost as great a part as Berwick in the struggles with Scotland. Indeed the whole of the Marcher country is rich in medieval fortified towns. Monmouth is unique in that its ancient bridge of stone which spans the Monnow is surmounted by a stone gateway which was the main entrance to the town, and withstood for some time the siege of Simon de Montfort in the reign of Henry III, and another siege in the Civil Wars when Cromwell in person marched to subdue it.

Ludlow, too, was a border town which was often attacked, but protected as it was by its two rivers on three sides its position was well nigh impregnable. On the north, by the church, the wall rises nearly twenty feet above the ground. The Edwardian Broad Gate, the Elizabethan Feathers Inn, the timbered houses which rival those of Chester, and the dignified Georgian dwelling-places combine to make it in appearance the perfect ancient town. Aptly was the manuscript of " Comus," first produced in the castle

VALENTINE

QUAINT OLD SHREWSBURY

This attractive city almost encircled by the Severn, and from its situation near the Welsh border a place of historical importance, has many interesting old streets with quaint names. One of these is Fish Street, seen above, with its ancient timbered houses.

which is the ancestral home of the Mortimer family.

Hereford is another picturesque and historical city with remains of its old walls and a few scanty fragments of its Norman castle which was of old "high and stronge and full of great towres." Within the cathedral which had its beginnings in the days of Offa, the seventh-century Mercian king, there is preserved the famous " Mappa Mundi." This map of the world, one of the earliest attempts of its kind, was drawn on vellum by a monk about 1300, and illustrates the medieval conception of geography. Jerusalem occupies the centre of the map, and Paradise is located at the top. Today a peaceful old town, Hereford has known turbulence and tumult. That fierce Welsh chieftain Owen Glyndwr seized the city on one occasion, and it was there, after the battle of Mortimer Cross, that Owen Tudor was beheaded.

have an ancient and outlandish ring. Castle Street, Pride Hill and Shoplatch may not be unusual, but what of Mardol and Dogpole, of Wyle Cop and Murivance, of Grope Lane and Leopard Passage?

Hidden in these narrow streets and medieval alleys are many strikingly antique buildings including the Old House which lodged Mary Tudor; the house, now a shop, where Henry VII stayed on his way to Bosworth Field, and the Council House, partly modernized, which served as a meeting place for the Council of the Welsh Marches.

Royal Saxon City

Gloucester, seat of the Norman Earl Fitzhamon, like Shrewsbury, stands guard over the Severn. Its traditions of independence date from the time when Glevum was a self-governing Roman town, and from the Saxon days when the kings of Mercia had a royal palace there. Henry III was crowned in the cathedral and two kings, Richard II and Henry IV held parliament in the city. Apart from the cathedral, whose cloisters are the most magnificent in the country, there is little of the medieval left except the " New Inn " (what an anachronism!) which boasts timber work of the fifteenth century.

W. F. TAYLOR

A FIFTEENTH-CENTURY INN
This interesting old hostelry most inappropriately named, was probably built about 1450, and may have served as a hostel for pilgrims. In its fascinating galleried courtyard seen in the photograph, the ill-fated Lady Jane Grey was proclaimed queen in 1553.

Among the ancient and attractive towns of England, Shrewsbury must be given honourable mention. In the ground almost encircled by the Severn there stood the British town of Pengwern. On the same site grew the Saxon Scrobbesbyrig. The Normans saw the advantages of the place, and the Conqueror made Roger de Montgomery overlord of the surrounding country. Roger added to the natural strength of the place by erecting a castle on the narrow neck of land, thus guarding the only dry approach.

In subsequent centuries the town developed, and much of its old architecture still stands as evidence of the past. The very street names

FELTON

MEDIEVAL HOUSE AT COLCHESTER
This well preserved fifteenth-century, timbered dwelling is an interesting relic of ancient Colchester. It is known as the Siege House, and its woodwork bears many bullet marks received during the Civil War when the Royalist forces held out for twelve weeks against Fairfax's soldiers.

East Anglia is almost as rich in ancient towns as the border country of Wales. Like the Welsh Marches too it is singularly apart from the rest of England, in history and tradition alike. Until a comparatively recent date it was to all intents and purposes cut off from communication with central England, and has the history of an island within an island. The Wash, the North Sea and the estuary of the Thames formed effective barriers on three sides, and on the fourth, Fenland, before it was drained, acted as a complete barrier between Norfolk and the country to the west. The cities even now reflect this insular position. They have a character akin to the independence of outlook which the typical East Anglian retains in the face of growing uniformity.

Norwich is the true capital of East Anglia. The Boom Towers and St. Martin's Gate belong to that period in the city's history when it was one of the largest of the walled towns. The Norman cathedral with its magnificent tapering spire, the castle of Robert Bigod, the Strangers' Hall (a fifteenth-century house which is now used as a museum), the Erpingham Gate which is nearly a century later than the walls, and the queerly-named Sampson and Hercules House, which is a perfect example of sixteenth-century architecture, are a few of the other links with the past which the wayfarer will find in modern Norwich.

Two other towns in Norfolk—Yarmouth and King's Lynn—were illustrious in the Middle Ages, both ports of the first magnitude, though they have suffered unequal fates in the intervening centuries. Yarmouth has grown apace, and, in its growing, has lost its former charm, whilst Lynn has declined, but testifies by its many fine seventeenth-century merchants' houses how great was its former prosperity.

Colchester is another city of East Anglia which allies historic interest with modern prosperity. Here, as at Canterbury and Norwich, the Flemish established a weaving industry perpetuated in the cloth manufacture of today. There are records that flour-milling, another staple industry, has been carried on since Saxon days. The Normans have bequeathed the ruins of the Priory of St. Botolph, and the castle which is on the lines of

EDGAR WARD

A BEAUTIFUL RELIC OF THE OLD GUILDS

The Merchant Guilds arose in the eleventh century and developed during the Middle Ages, playing a prominent part in the development of the town. Royal Charters were granted to the guilds, and Guildhalls were created to conduct their business. This example at Lavenham, in Suffolk, served a Cloth Guild.

FELTON

A MONASTIC FRAGMENT

The Dorset town of Sherborne had its beginnings in Saxon times.   A Benedictine monastery was founded there in A.D. 998.   Parts of the abbey, which was rebuilt in the thirteenth and fourteenth centuries, now serve as Sherborne School.   The photograph shows the Conduit which once stood in the cloisters.   Behind it are some beautiful timber framed houses, and in the background the tower of the abbey church.

those at Rochester and London. It has much in common with Bath, which, though its chief claim to interest is its Roman remains, and in appearance is a typical nineteenth-century town, yet was an important walled city in the Middle Ages.

The cathedral cities of the older foundation were without exception towns of antiquity. Six of these, Exeter, Durham, Salisbury, Winchester, Carlisle and Lincoln, have not so far been mentioned. All except Salisbury were walled cities; all have become the county towns of their respective counties. Exeter has flourished under every civilization. The castle of Rougemont was built by the Normans, besieged by Perkin Warbeck, by the religious insurgents of the Western Rebellion, and again by Prince Maurice. Its ruins are small but picturesque, whilst the Elizabethan Guildhall is a reminder of the town's later wealth. Durham is best seen from the hills to the south. The square block of the cathedral looms over the whole town, and the three bridges that span the Wear give it added grace.

Carlisle, like Berwick, is still essentially a border town as it has been since Hadrian's Wall was built where its northern suburbs now stand. Lincoln has many ancient monuments. The High Bridge is one of the very few in England which still bears houses, as did the Old London Bridge. The Jew's House, a Norman dwelling-place, is claimed to be the oldest in the country. The bishop's chair in the cathedral Chapter House is the throne on which Edward I sat when he convened his parliament in Durham.

City of Peace

Salisbury, dominated by the four hundred feet of the cathedral spire, is rather Georgian in appearance, though the Hall of John Halle, and the Poultry Cross are of the fifteenth century, and there is the Joiners' Hall, a very ancient house which is now the property of the National Trust. Unlike so many towns we have described, the history of Salisbury has been one of peace. It always has been, and probably always will be a cathedral city and little else. Not so Winchester, which was the Venta Belgarum of the Romans, the capital of United England under King Canute and, with London, joint capital of William the Conqueror. Yet here, too, after the cathedral was founded, peace reigned.

Our search for Britain's medieval towns must end with a passing reference to the Cinque Ports —Hastings, Romney, Hythe, Dover and Sandwich, to which were added Winchelsea and Rye, all of which throughout the Middle Ages enjoyed many privileges of independence in return for supplying ships for the navy. The latter three retain much of their medieval appearance. Sandwich, with its barbican; Winchelsea, with one gate a full half mile from the present village; and Rye, with its cobbled streets, live more really in the past than any of the great cities.

DIXON-SCOTT

A CORNER OF ANCIENT NORWICH
This old dwelling stands in Tombland Alley, a passage taking its name from a piece of open ground long known as Tombland. There medieval fairs were held, and often proved occasions for conflict between the citizens and the monks of the adjacent monastery.

STEPHENSON

EVENTIDE IN A HIGHLAND GLEN

Glen Affric in western Ross is perhaps the wildest and most beautiful of Scottish glens. In the lower portions of the glen ancient pine forests fringe the dark flowing stream and the lonely lochs, but these are eventually left behind and the glen leads into the scarcely tenanted and little frequented mountainous country between the heights of Mam Soul and Ben Attow, through which a right of way leads to the sea at the head of Loch Duich.

SCOTLAND, LAND OF ROMANCE

by A. A. THOMSON

SCOTLAND is a land steeped in beauty and drenched in romance. This romance lies deeper than what is called scenery—a rather theatrical word which suggests " set pieces " and perfunctorily praised views. It is something that breathes in Scotland's caller air and is impregnated in the very soil itself. It is a romance of sharp-edged contrast and bewildering variety, of grim peaks and smiling green straths, of foaming mountain torrents and rippling silver streams, of gently sloping meadows and rolling moorlands where the wild wind skirls like a pibroch.

It is a romance of history, of a people battling fiercely for liberty and independence. The Scots, true to their emblem of the thistle, have always been a turbulent race. Even from the days of the fierce Picts who surged round Hadrian's Wall, they have had in their veins the fighting blood of mountain men. Under Wallace and Bruce they struggled indomitably to national freedom against the English invader. But they never fought in a mean cause. The story of the Jacobite rebellions is a tale of deathless heroism and unstinted loyalty for a cause that could not succeed. And even now, wherever a Scot plants his foot at the uttermost bounds of empire, there stands something of the old Scotland. He carries its spirit with him to the ends of the earth.

It is a romance of character—character that comes from the land; the free winds of the mountains, the salty tang of the rugged east coast, the misty airs of the rainbow west, the breezes that blow over the sturdy lowland hills— all these things have gone to weld the character of the Scots. Dreamy Celt and sturdy Lowlander alike owe their character to the land they live in. Romance is Scotland and Scotland is romance, but you cannot tell why this should be so, unless you see the country for yourself.

W. F. TAYLOR

" TANTALLON'S DIZZY STEEP "
This fourteenth-century stronghold overlooking the North Sea, figures in Scott's classic " Marmion."

To cross the border at Carter Bar amid the Cheviots is to plunge headlong into history. By that road the old freebooters—steel-capped, bearded men on shaggy horses—rode down under a misty moon to rob the English of their cattle. The Border rievers were a fierce race, and found raiding easier than farming. All the old stories and ballads tell of their wild exploits, sometimes with a grim humour and sometimes with moving and tragic pathos. There is the story of the lady of Yarrow, who placed a pair of spurs upon the great meat-dish, as a hint to her husband that cattle were needed (from English farms) to replenish honest Scots larders ; there is the rattling tale of Kinmont Willie's escape from Carlisle Castle ; and there are exquisite fairy stories, such as those of Thomas the Rhymer, or of Janet of Carterhaugh. But most moving of all are the tales of stark tragedy, like that of the *Border Widow's Lament* or the *Dowie Dens of Yarrow.*
" Nae living man I'll
    love again,
Since that my lovely
    Knight was slain,
Wi' ae lock of his
    yellow hair
I'll chain my heart for
    evermair."
Women must weep.
. . . That is the burden of many a song of those wild days, and even now something of that air of pensive sadness hangs over the Borderland, by the streams of Yarrow and Ettrick, and along the moorland, still dotted with grim grey peel towers, sentinels that kept silent ward against the raider.

Men, alas, were harsh and cruel, but, oh, they were brave. The Border is rich in ruined castles, the skeletons of far-off feuds and battles long ago—Hermitage, home of the ruthless Bothwell, Lochmaben, reputed home of Robert Bruce, Newark, where the last minstrel sang his lay, and red Tantallon, where Marmion bearded
    " the lion in his den,
    The Douglas in his hall."

There are peaceful fields, too, where once swords flashed and musketry rattled ; Dunbar, where "the Lord delivered the Scottish army into Cromwell's hands," and red Philiphaugh, where Leslie defeated the gallant Montrose.

The Border was wealthier in lovely abbeys than any other part of Scotland—Jedburgh, Kelso, Melrose, where the heart of Robert Bruce lies buried, and Dryburgh looped in a silver bend of the chiming Tweed, where sleep Sir Walter Scott and Earl Haig. The abbeys tell their own tale, first of the piety of the kindly monks, then of the ferocity of English harryings and then of the still crueller hands of decay and neglect. But now, in happier times, their ruins are preserved and carefully tended, and the tranquil peace of the old monastic life in some measure returns.

Nor are all the tales of Border history shadowed by the wastage of strife. Great poets have sung to the ripple of the Tweed. The Vale of Ettrick enshrines the life and exquisite lyrics of James Hogg, the shepherd-poet, who sang of the birds and trees of his own sweet valley, and rollicked by the ingle of Tibbie Shiels' Inn. But if one spirit more than another can be said to call the Border its home, it is the serene and gallant spirit of Sir Walter Scott. The Border saw his boyhood, it inspired his grandest work. It watched his success, his financial disaster through another's fault and his ultimate triumph through Herculean labours and strength of spirit.

Many places are rich in memories of him : Sandy Knowe, Smailholm Tower, Selkirk with its memorial to the men of Flodden and to Scott's brave explorer-friend, Mungo Park, Eildon, Bemersyde, Ashiestiel and Abbotsford, the home he loved, and which he built as part of the romance of his eager life, and Dryburgh, where he now lies sleeping. All these names are enshrined in the one name, Tweed, that silver river which rippled past his home, where he fished with the devoted, cantankerous Tam Purdie, and where his footsteps ever strayed, in sickness and health, in sorrow or contentment.

Gaunt Peel Towers

Many are the romantic pictures which the traveller may carry away from the Border : the soft green of low hills where the curlew pipes and the sheep wander at will, leafy woods of birch and beech that run down to wimpling streams ; grey abbey ruins and gaunt peel towers, the silent waters of Our Lady's Lake. These are such stuff that dreams are made of ; the warp and woof of Border history, tragedy and life. Yet there is one more picture which the traveller must not miss. Before the War Memorial in Galashiels, that little grey town which lies at the foot of sturdy green hills, where Tweed and

R. M. ADAM

LONELY BORDER COUNTRY

Out of Redesdale, in Northumberland, a road climbs to the border at Carter Bar, 1371 feet above the sea level. On the Scottish side there is a splendid prospect including the Cheviots, the vales of Tweed and Teviot, and the fine upstanding Eildon Hills. The Cheviot, 2676 feet, is seen in the background.

R. M. ADAM

A POET'S STREAM

Many of the old Border Ballads mention the River Yarrow, here seen near St. Mary's Loch. Later poets, including Wordsworth and Scott, also sung its charms. From the banks of Yarrow came James Hogg, the "Ettrick Shepherd," "after Burns the greatest poet that ever sprang from the bosom of the common people."

Gala meet, stands the figure of the Border Horse-man, a bearded warrior, morion on head and lance at saddle-bow. Here is the true spirit of the Border, the epitome of Border story—a long tale of not ignoble strife, of eternal vigilance and, above all, of matchless courage.

The country of the western Border may not, at first sight, have the same romantic appeal as the immediate east, but the hurrying traveller, did he but know it, would find in Galloway, lochs as enchanting and mountains as wild as ever he would hope to find in the Highlands. Grey Galloway . . . So runs the ancient name, but the grey is neither dull nor drab.

Galloway, like Fife, is an ancient kingdom, and it preserves all that craggy individuality of scenery and character which is an ancient king-dom's right. It has a widely varied coast; the long low line of the Solway and the western sea-board with its myriad caves and inlets, and these two stretches culminate where wild seas roll around the mighty cliffs of the Mull of Galloway. Away from the sea, the land rises, sometimes gently and sometimes sharply, towards highlands of almost incredible wildness.

Many are the enchanted corners of Galloway, and better roads have made them less inacces-sible than once they were. The coast roads are full of fascination; either along the south by Heston Island (the Isle Rathon of Crockett's *The Raiders*), and the ruined abbey of Dundrennan, where Mary, tragic Queen of Scots, said her last farewell to Scotland; or by the west, past Turn-berry, early home of the Bruce, and Gamesloup, scene of the ancient ballad of May Collean.

If you take the hill-road inland from Newton Stewart—the road where the old Free Traders drove their pack-horses—you will come to one of the fairest lochs in all Scotland, Loch Trool. Here is a mirror of cool, clear water, encircled by silent hills and wooded to the shore. Even now, he is an intrepid traveller who penetrates to the inmost recesses of the Gallovidian hinter-land; towards the Wolf's Slock and the Dungeon of Buchan and dark Loch Neldricken, with its legendary Murder Hole. There lies the real secret of Grey Galloway.

Galloway lives in literature by the extraordinary grip which it has always held on the imaginations of great writers. R. L. Stevenson wrote of the grim cliffs of the Mull in his rousing ballad, *The Secret of the Heather Ale.*

" The King in the red moorland
　　Rode on a summer's day;
　And the bees hummed, and the curlews
　　Cried beside the way. . . ."

A. DURRANT

ABBEY OF THE SWEET HEART

This abbey, near Dumfries, was built in the thirteenth century by Devorgilla, who ordered that the heart of her husband, John Baliol, founder of Balliol College, Oxford, should be buried in her tomb; hence the name. Only the south transept has a roof, but the central tower and arches of the nave are well preserved.

Borgue, that home of ancient smugglers, is the original setting of that gripping romance *The Master of Ballantrae*, with its sinister, but enthralling hero-villain.

Scott, too, found romance here. Much of the action of Redgauntlet takes place upon the Solway coast, while near Gatehouse of Fleet, which Scott in *Guy Mannering* calls Kippletringan, you may still see the reputed cave of Dirck Hatteraick, the book's doughty smuggler-villain.

Rugged Galloway

But of all the names in Gallovidian literature that of S. R. Crockett shines the brightest. He knew every inch of Galloway, and in many romantic novels has vividly painted both its ruggedness and its gentler charms. If you want a breathless story of the old smuggling days, read *The Raiders*, and take it with you on your journey, for it pictures this wild countryside as no other book has ever done.

The history of this south-western corner of Scotland is a stormy chronicle of civil and religious strife. It has at least one lovely abbey—red Sweetheart—which lies under the shadow of blue Criffel—and its many castles—among them, Caerlaverock, Lochmaben and the grim keep of Thrieve—tell of desperate fights and fierce

encounters. The old free-traders haunted the caves and sea-roads of the Solway, singing their rough song :

" There's brandy at the Abbeyburn, there's rum
    at Heston Bay,
    And we will go a-smuggling afore the break
    o'day."

The darkest and yet the bravest page in this land's story concerns the religious persecutions of "the killing time." The Scottish Covenanters were the bravest of the brave ; in the rocky glens they held their conventicles in defiance of cruel laws. Hundreds died for their faith ; their blood stained the heather and the moss-hags. At Wigtown you will see the spot where two brave women suffered for the Covenant,

" Within the sea, tied to a stake,
    They suffered for Christ Jesus' sake."

The rough stones that are found in the heather mark the graves of the martyrs who were shot for their faith by Claverhouse's dragoons, and it was the man whom Scott calls " Old Mortality " who sought out and restored as many as he could find, wandering among the lonely moors, " where about the graves of the martyrs the whaups are crying . . ."

Moving northward on this western side we come to the gentler shires of Dumfries and Ayr.

Less wild than Galloway they may be but they are not without their romance, for they hold within their borders the life-story of Robert Burns. It is no great distance from the auld clay biggin at Alloway, near the banks of bonnie Doon, where he was born, to Dumfries, where he died young. Place-name after place-name in this district tells of his brave, tragic life; Kirkoswald, where he went to learn surveying, Mauchline, where the flower of his genius blossomed, Ayr, where the Tam o' Shanter's Inn still stands, Kilmarnock, where his "little beuk for Scotland's sake" was first published, Ellisland on the banks of lovely Nith, and Dumfries, douce country town, with its old inns and sturdy Mid-Steeple, where he lies sleeping in St. Michael's Kirkyard.

This is a pleasant countryside, greenly meadowed and wooded, and watered by the streams he loved so well : the Doon, of which he wrote one of his saddest love songs ; the Ayr, where he wandered, singing his song of farewell to Scotland and the Nith, which ran behind his little farm at Ellisland and on whose bank he strode up and down, joyously shouting aloud the immortal couplets of "Tam o' Shanter."

To see this land as he saw it, with its fields and woods and rippling streams, is to see Burns as he himself was, ploughman, patriot and immortal singer of life's simpler joys and sorrows. Nor must you miss, in this south-western section the enchanting village of Moniaive, with its white cottages and rambler roses, nor Maxwelton House, near Dunscore, where dwelt Bonnie Annie Laurie of the song, nor Craigenputtock, where Carlyle wrote *Sartor Resartus*, nor Irongray, where in the old churchyard, sleeps Helen Walker, real-life prototype of Scott's sweetest heroine, Jeanie Deans. Almost every cottage and every by-road is alive with romantic history.

The Busy Clyde

Central Scotland is almost cut in half by two deep river valleys, the Clyde on the west and the Forth on the east. The Clyde flows through the most thickly-populated industrial districts of Scotland. On its banks lies Glasgow, second city of the Empire, and from its clanging yards the great ships go out to the seven seas. The building and launching of the mighty ship, the *Queen Mary*, in times of industrial depression, is one of the most romantic episodes of our time. No tale of ancient chivalry can match the gallant hope and dauntless courage that went to the making of that brave ship.

But the Clyde is not wholly shrouded by chimney smoke or deafened by the clang of riveters' hammers ; you may sail down past the yards of Greenock towards the open waters of

R. M. ADAM

A GALLOWAY GLEN
Amid the desolation of the Galloway Hills lies Glen Trool with its beautiful loch reaching almost to the head of the glen. It was in this glen that Robert the Bruce overcame an English force in 1307, and began the campaign of independence which was brought to a decisive close at Bannockburn seven years later.

A. A. MACGREGOR

BY THE BANKS OF LOCH LOMOND

Loch Lomond is the largest, and to many people also the most beautiful of Scottish lochs. Its surroundings have not the rugged grandeur of Loch Coruisk, and it depends rather for its charm on the harmonious combination of green curving shores, picturesque isles and mountains sweeping rather than soaring upwards. The photograph shows the loch at Rowardennan, near where the track starts to climb the famous Ben Lomond.

A. A. MACGREGOR

SNOW-CLAD HILLS

Winter at the base of Rest-and-be-Thankful, the name given by General Wade and his road-making soldiers to the highest point attained by their military road running westward up Glen Croe, from the shores of Loch Long, and then descending through Glen Kinglass to Loch Fyne, at Cairndow, on its way to Inveraray, the ancestral home of MacCallum Mhor, the Duke of Argyll and chief of the Campbell Clan.

the Firth, where sunshine and dappled shadow play among the fairy islands of the Kyles of Bute. And not very far to the north-west of Glasgow lie the bonnie, bonnie banks of Loch Lomond. Here you may see not merely one of the world's most dazzling beauty spots, but one which has survived the handicap of a hundred years' praise. The beauty of Loch Lomond captures the imagination of even the most hardened sightseer; its wooded banks, its gleaming waters and its jewelled islands blend in a picture of unforgettable colour and charm. You feel that you are in a fairy world. And above the north-eastern corner towers the mighty shadow of Ben Lomond, the mountain-guardian of the lake.

Westward you might go, in sunshine or shadow, by Inversnaid, where Wordsworth saw his "Highland Girl," towards wilder country by the shores of Loch Long, where Magnus, the Manx pirate king, once rowed his raiding galleys, and over the pass of Rest-and-be-Thankful to Inveraray, ancient home of the great Clan Campbell.

In Inveraray you may consider the living romance of the brave fisher folk who bring the "Caller Herrin'" from Loch Fyne, or you may ponder on the ancient feuds and fights of the Campbells, who gained an undeservedly evil reputation for treachery and cowardice, because their chiefs were sometimes on the side of the English. The most delightful portrayer of this wild west country was Neil Munro, who, in such novels as *Doom Castle* and *John Splendid* depicted scenes and doughty deeds.

Rob Roy's Country

If you go eastward from Loch Lomond, you come to the Trossachs and the enchanted country which Scott has immortalized in *The Lady of the Lake* and *Rob Roy*; Loch Katrine from whose clear waters rises Ellen's Isle, home of The Lady of the Lake; the gorge of the Trossachs, where Fitz-James fell with his "gallant grey" under him; Loch Achray, with its thickly-wooded shores—all these are part of what Scott called "the scenery of a fairy dream." Everywhere

A. A. MACGREGOR

DOOM CASTLE
Near the shores of Loch Fyne in Argyll stands the tall, grey, turreted Dundarave Castle, the Doom Castle of Neil Munro's book, "John Splendid."

you will find pictures, which your mind's eye can carry away to typify this magical land; stretches of glittering water, fringed with larch and silvery birch; guardian hills whose slopes are stained wine red with heather, and fairy glens where the wild hyacinths, the purple foxglove and the scarlet rowanberry colour the seasons as they come and go. And over all these beauties lies a kind of luminous haze, as though this land were under a magic spell. A fairy dream indeed.

The eastern side has less of this purely enchanted quality, but it is none the less alive with beauty and interest. In whichever direction you go from Edinburgh, with its castled rock and quiet Georgian squares, you are never far from romance. The short road down from Edinburgh to Queensferry, where the great Forth Bridge spans a mile and a quarter of water, tells us many tales: of Margaret, gracious Queen of Malcolm Canmore, who encouraged the peaceful arts among a turbulent people, and of the famous Jock Howieson who saved his king's life from robbers at Cramond Bridge. Pict and Roman, Saxon and Norman, Whig and Jacobite have trodden this road, from ship to capital and capital to ship.

If you cross the Firth by railway bridge or ferry boat, you are in the ancient kingdom of Fife, that compact peninsula which lies between the long arms of Forth and Tay. A king once described Fife as a "grey cloth mantle with a fringe of gold." The grey mantle is now represented by the smoke of modern factory and mine, but the golden fringe remains as bright and shining as in the old days. All along the Fife coast you will find little sandy bays of the purest gold, and here the "grey" North Sea is, as often as not, a beautiful blue.

The fishing villages of the Fife coast are among the most fascinating little places in the whole of these islands: Elie, St. Monans, Crail—these make a series of unforgettable pictures, with their rocky harbours, their winding streets and their gaily-painted fishing boats. There is hardly a village on this coast which does not preserve some link with the past: Kirkcaldy, where

VIOLET BANKS

LOCH KATRINE AND ELLEN'S ISLE
Loch Katrine owes much of its fame to Sir Walter Scott who called it Loch Cateran, or the Lake of the Robbers, and is part of the famous Trossachs country, once a wild and inaccessible region but now one of the most frequented of Highland beauty spots. Ellen's Isle, mentioned in " The Lady of the Lake," was the refuge of the banished Douglas, and still retains the " blighted tree " against which the harper reclined.

Carlyle was a schoolmaster, Largo where lived Alexander Selkirk, from whose real adventures the story of Robinson Crusoe was taken, and Anstruther, where certain ships of the Spanish Armada drifted to destruction. And so, by many a quaint " auldfarrant " fishing town, and many a tiny golden bay, the coast winds round to the venerable university city,
" . . . the little town,
　　The drifting surf, the wintry sea,
　　The college of the scarlet gown,
　　St. Andrews by the Northern
　　　　Sea. . . ."

Inland, where the conformation of the country is so deeply indented, the traffic of history has passed, perforce, through a narrow channel. Linlithgow, Falkirk, Stirling. Here are names that, by battle, siege and sortie, live in history's page. Stirling, with its castle set on a high rock, has been from time immemorial " the gateway of the south, the bulwark of the north," and it has looked down on battles from Wallace to Prince Charlie.

To the Highlands

But now the traveller is impatient to be away to the Highlands, to the land of the mountain and glen. Shall he go eastward from the fair city of Perth, by the rich Carse of Gowrie and over the Devil's Elbow to Braemar, whence the road winds onward through our greatest queen's own Balmoral country toward Aberdeen, city of granite and of " Bon Accord "?

W. F. TAYLOR

A NOBLE NORMAN NAVE
Dunfermline Abbey, among later and less worthy features, retains its impressive nave, one of the finest illustrations of Norman architecture in Scotland.　Robert Bruce is buried in the church.

Shall he take the middle road, that magnificent highway, which pierces the heart of the Highlands, and sweeps up under the shadow of the towering mountains, by Pitlochry and Blair Athol toward Inverness? Or again, shall he follow a westward route over the sinister pass of Glencoe to Fort William and thence farther westward still, to the misty sea-lochs, whose outer waters wash the islands of the Hebrides?

He can go farther ; by the east coast road to Scotland's most northerly point, where John o' Groat's eight-sided house looks out towards the Orkneys, or, westward, by rough roads, to where the Atlantic breakers lash and roar around the lighthouse of Cape Wrath.

The soul of the Highlands lies in the mist-capped mountains, high above the ordinary haunts of men. The very names of some of them have a quality of godlike mystery and grandeur, even of terror. Schiehallion, Stobinian,

dark Lochnagar. . . . No wonder some mountain legends are tales of witches and warlocks, of nameless spectres that haunt the dark rocky glens. But not all the Highland legends are dark and fearful ; many of them concern the *sith*, or fairy folk, who live underground, in green knowes or in the pleasant hollows of the hills. These fairies were fairly friendly people, and would do no more harm than a puckish trick or two or, perhaps, the stealing of a crofter's cow. But if, in a Highland valley, you should see a patch of a vivider green than the surrounding grass, you must walk softly, for the fairies dwell below. Or so the old Highland folk will tell you.

There is no beauty like the beauty of a Highland loch, hemmed in by immemorial hills. Sunlight glints on the water, which is clear as a mirror, except where the mountain shadow falls darkly across it. Green woods, starry with

VIOLET BANKS

A PICTURESQUE FISHING VILLAGE

On the Fife coast, at the mouth of the Firth of Forth, and about ten miles south of St. Andrews is the village of St. Monans, or St. Monance as it was originally known. In addition to its quaint charm St. Monans is also of historical interest. It possesses a little church founded by the Scottish king, David II, about 1362.

wild anemones, roll down to the water's edge, and over all silence and tranquillity lie, like the mantle of peace.
" By Tummel and Loch Rannoch and Lochaber
    I will go
  By heather-hills with heaven in their wiles. . . ."
Loch Rannoch is lovely, but Loch Tummel is lovelier still. High above its waters, you can stand upon a little wooded eminence and see the view which Queen Victoria so often delighted to look upon : richly wooded slopes, purple hills melting into blue sky, river-loop glittering like

treacherously slain ; the Great Glen, Wade's men stolidly toiling on the new road that was to conquer the Highlands more surely than English muskets ; Glenmoriston, a fugitive prince, hiding among the heather ; Balmoral, the tiny figure of a great queen, riding in her carriage, attended by the stalwart John Brown.
  Mountains, tumbling torrents, silent moorlands.
" Lo ! for there, among the flowers and grasses,
  Only the mightier movement sounds and passes ;
  Only winds and rivers,
  Life and death. . . ."

R. M. ADAM

RIVER TUMMEL AND SCHIEHALLION'S GRACEFUL CREST
Above the River Tummel, in Perthshire, rises the splendid pyramid of Schiehallion (3,547 feet), one of the most beautiful of Scottish mountains. From the summit the view extends westwards across the desolate Moor of Rannoch to the peaks at the head of Glencoe. The name is said to mean a dwelling-place of fairies.

a diamond necklace, and the still sheen upon the bosom of the loch. Truly a view for a queen.
  The romantic names of the Highlands are legion. They recall the rushing rivers, where the salmon leaps—Garry, Spey, Don and Dee ; they tell of magic glens where the wild deer roams—Shirra, Cannich and Affric, loveliest glen of all ; of Glengarry and Glen Quoich, of Glen Moriston and the lonely Glen Shiel reaching down to the sea.
  You have only to close your eyes to see the pictures that a few Highland names, taken at random, may evoke : Killiecrankie, the cataract-charge of kilted clansmen, hurtling down the gorge ; Glencoe, the glen of weeping—weeping amid desolate snows for sons and fathers,

There are a dozen ways in which the traveller may drink delight from the glamour of Scotland. Book in hand, he may study the romantic topography of his favourite authors : the Scotland of Sir Walter Scott, not merely the beloved borderland that was his home, but the ancient city of *The Fair Maid of Perth*, the Arbroath of *The Antiquary*, the Covenanting country of *Old Mortality*, the southern Highlands of *Rob Roy* and many another real place which gave pleasure under fictional guise. He may seek out the Ayrshire farmsteads and Dumfriesshire streams of Robert Burns, or wander round the little Angus town of Kirriemuir that was Barrie's *Thrums.*
  He may follow, in the Appin country, near the

shores of Loch Linnhe, all the thrilling adventures of the hero of Stevenson's *Kidnapped*, with his friend, the " bonnie fechter," Alan Breck, and, in the western highlands and along the Great Glen, he may see the places he has read of in the breathless tales of Neil Munro and the exquisite Jacobite romances of D. K. Broster. And if he is one of those happy old-fashioned folk who once revelled in *Beside the Bonnie Brier Bush*, he will find the original Drumtochty, which is really the Perthshire village of Logiealmond.

defended Dunbar Castle against the English, Catherine Douglas who, in the old Blackfriars Monastery at Perth, thrust her arm through the bolt-staples of the door in a vain attempt to save her king from the assassin's dagger, and Flora Macdonald, more lovable heroine than any other. Everywhere he will find places and memories connected with these great names ; and he will learn, too, how it was something in the spirit of the land itself which inspired great deeds and high endeavours. He will feel in his

R. M. ADAM

THE GLEN OF WEEPING

For Macaulay, Glencoe was the most dreary and melancholy of all the Scottish passes—the very valley of the Shadow of Death. As the valley of historic tragedy it is still remembered, but the visitor today sees in it more than gloom and desolation, and is able to appreciate its wild beauty and its long and lonely reaches.

Or he may seek to see Scotland in terms of the lives of heroes, and here he will be on rich, fruitful ground, for Scotland has ever been a land of strong individual character, of men who were great *as* men, but who drew much from their national environment. Carlyle, himself something of a crotchety hero, might well have written of them : fighting heroes, like Wallace-wight and Bruce, the warrior king ; zealot-heroes, like Wishart and Knox and the unknown martyrs of the moss-hags, soldier-statesmen, like the noble Marquis of Montrose and, most lovable hero of all, the gallant Bonnie Prince Charlie.

There are heroines, too ; Black Agnes, who

bones the atmosphere of certain places : the peace of the old abbeys, the bravery of Bannockburn, and the infinite sadness that broods for ever over Culloden Moor.

But, being a traveller, he may see Scotland as a land of journeyings, for history itself is, in a sense, a series of journeys, brave, gay, adventurous or sad. He may think of the journeys of the early saints, of Ninian, who, landing on the Isle of Whithorn, first brought Christianity to the rough Picts of Galloway ; or of Columba, who founded the monastery of Iona and sailed up Loch Ness to beard the heathen kings. He may stand upon the battlefields of Bruce or gaze

STEPHENSON

SUNLIT BEAUTY OF A HIGHLAND RIVER

Amid the lovely and little known mountains of Ross, the River Beauly has its several beginnings, and three of Scotland's finest glens pay it tribute. Farthest from the sea are the head waters of the stream which flows down Glen Affric. Another branch runs on the north side of the great bulk of Mam Soul and flows down Glen Cannich. Yet another tributary issues from the Loch Morar and runs through Glen Farrar.

upon the grey walls of the many castles which that dauntless warrior stormed, despite their reputed impregnability. The places of his birth, of his exiled wandering, of his brave victories and of his death are still to be seen.

And what of the sad journeys of Mary Queen of Scots? The places and the roads are still there : Linlithgow Castle, where she was born ; Holyrood Palace, where she was browbeaten by the stern Knox and witnessed Rizzio's murder ; Carberry Hill, where the Lords of the Congregation defeated her ; Lochleven's island castle, scene of one of the most thrilling escapes in

waukin' yet? ") After this smashing victory there were tragic delays, and when the prince finally marched by Carlisle into England, it was too late. He would even have gone on from Derby, if his commanders had supported him, but from that turning-point, his story is a tale of retreat. On Scottish soil again, he won a barren victory at Falkirk, but the relentless pursuit of the English armies forced him farther and farther northward, and in the bitter fight of Culloden Moor, his last hopes of victory were ruthlessly shattered. Even then, his wanderings were not at an end. In Glenmoriston he lived

STEPHENSON

RUGGED PEAKS OF SKYE

The Black Cuillin of Skye, those gaunt, bare hills, weathered and splintered into slender peaks, narrow ridges and soaring crags, have no rivals in Britain for sheer splendour and diversity of form. In this view from the flanks of Sgurr Sgumain, we see Gars-bheinn (pronounced Gars-ven), the southernmost peak of the Cuillin.

history, and Dundrennan, from whence she set out upon the journey that was to lead to her imprisonment, betrayal and death.

But every Scottish road follows or crosses at some point the most romantic road of all, the path of the 'forty-five, down which Prince Charles Edward marched, upon a forlorn hope which came within an ace of success. He landed with seven men at Moidart in the west, and unfurled his standard in Glenfinnan. The chieftains of the clans, reluctant at first, were won by his gallant bearing and flocked to his banner. With a rapidly growing army he swept down on Perth and then took Edinburgh with scarce the firing of a shot. From the capital he sallied out to Prestonpans and cut to ribbons Sir John Cope's army. (" Hi, Johnnie Cope, are ye

amid the rocks and caves, sheltered with selfless loyalty by impoverished men who knew that there was a price of £30,000 upon his head, and in the Isle of Skye he was aided, in one hair-breadth escape after another, by the fidelity of Flora Macdonald. A brave, tragic journey, paved with the dead hopes of loyal men and women.

So we have seen Scotland as a land of glamour and enchantment, an enchantment that touches its hills and its glens, its songs and its stories, its battlefields and its romantic journeys. A journey still remains the most romantic of human enterprises, and it is not for nothing that the ancient Gaelic wisdom gave a special blessing to the traveller : " Blessings go with you ; may a straight path be before you, and a happy end to your journey ! "

W. K. R. NEILSON

THE LANTHORN OF THE NORTH

So Elgin Cathedral was termed. Founded in 1224 by Andrew, Bishop of Moray, the cathedral, in its entirety, was said to be " a building of Gothic architecture inferior to few in Europe." After the Reformation the cathedral was allowed to fall in ruin " as a piece of Romish vanity too expensive to keep in repair."

EDGAR WARD

HISTORIC PALACE OF HOLYROOD HOUSE

Holyrood had its beginnings as a monastery built by David I and later became a royal residence. Of all its regal occupants none has left more tragic memories than Mary Queen of Scots. There she was married to Bothwell within three months of Darnley's death, and there her favourite, Rizzio, was foully assassinated.

DIXON-SCOTT

CATHEDRAL OF AN ANCIENT SEE

Llandaff Cathedral, near Cardiff, claims to serve the oldest see in the kingdom, which was founded, according to tradition, in A.D. 547 by St. Teilo. The present building, of twelfth- to thirteenth-century origin, is unique in that it has no transepts. The triforium, a feature of the thirteenth-century design, is also missing.

WILD WALES

by I. O. EVANS

WESTWARDS of England lies the mountainous, valley-pierced, wave-beaten land of Wales. Though small in size it is unequalled in its beauty and charm. Its mountains are higher than any that England can show, its valleys more beautiful, its coastline more rugged. Round its shores are islands, one a county in itself, others bare rocks just peeping above the tide. It is a land older than its larger neighbour to the east—it is without doubt literally true that the mountains of Wales were immeasurably old when the chalk that forms the Downs and Salisbury Plain was a mere ooze on the bed of the ocean.

If the land itself is older, so equally are its people. The original inhabitants of the British Isles, the swarthy Iberians from the Mediterranean, have left their descendants among them. So, too, have the conquering Celts and the Gaels. Its people traded with the sea-farers of far Phœnicia, exchanging for the products of civilization tin and the spoils of the chase. Its people built the great monuments found all over the land, from great Stonehenge and Avebury to the smaller dolmen and menhir, the Druid's Circle of Keswick and Kit's Coty House of Kent. Its people for a time held at bay even the might of Rome, and were only conquered after a fierce resistance. Its people, later, resisted no less fiercely the Saxon invaders, the Danish pirates, and the raiding Irish bands. When all England was subject to Norman rule, the inhabitants of Wales still for many years remained free.

The " Ancient Britons," as we are accustomed to call them, were by no means the uncouth barbarians whom Cæsar describes, clad only in a coat of blue paint and burning their prisoners alive. We know nowadays just how much faith can be placed in the narrative of a military commander, anxious to " civilize " outlying tribes at the sword's point ! The people who could transport and build Stonehenge, who could cover the countryside with a system of well-surveyed straight tracks, who could hold at bay the Roman legions, were certainly not backward in the arts of life. None the less the Britons learned much from the Romans who conquered them ; when the legions departed they took over something of the tradition of Roman rule, striving to keep at bay the hordes of English who were invading their land.

Fiercely fighting, the Britons were pressed into the highlands of the west and north. At last the *Cymry* (" comrades ") were cut off by the English of Wales, first from those of Cornwall, and then from those of Strathclyde. Yet they were not subdued; Offa's Dyke remains to tell us of the efforts that were made by the rulers of England to keep in bounds the race whose country they had seized. Even the Normans could only hold them at bay by a chain of stern and forbidding strongholds.

Valiant in war, the Cymry were not unskilled in the arts of peace. Their bards had devised elaborate poetic forms, had composed works that would certainly attract attention had they been written not in Welsh but in English. Their Druids formed a mystical priesthood, the secrets of which have not been revealed ; their lore, it

W. F. TAYLOR

AN EDWARDIAN CASTLE
Beaumaris Castle, Anglesey, founded by Edward I in 1293, is now a picturesque ruin with fragments of the gatehouses, the Great Hall and oratory still standing. In 1646 it was surrendered to the Parliament forces.

has been claimed, challenges comparison both in age and in depth with that of ancient Egypt.

Not a county in Wales but is associated with what is romantic—with some gallant episode of history or some imaginative piece of legendary lore. Richest perhaps in such memories is *Môn Mam Cymri*, " Mon the Mother of Wales," which the Romans called Mona and the English Anglesey. It earned its title of the Motherland of Wales, perhaps because of its fertility, feeding with its crops the folk of the barren mountain regions on the mainland, perhaps because it was the Sacred Island, the centre of bardic tradition. Only when the Romans had conquered it did

mighty bounds. . . . Returned from the wars he found that his wife, supposing him dead, had married one of his rivals. Einion first, in the guise of a harper, composed a song reproaching her for her forgetfulness, and then ejected his rival and claimed her for his own.

If Anglesey was the stronghold of Wales, one of its warlike outposts is Lleyn, the peninsula which juts out westwards from North Wales into the Irish Sea. It was easily invaded by the Irish, who conquered it and who have left the remains of their camps to show how they dominated the folk of the land. Here died Vortigern, whom tradition holds responsible for the invasion of

W. F. TAYLOR

AN ANCIENT PRIORY

Penmon Priory, in the north-eastern corner of Anglesey, is said to have been founded in the seventh century. Later it became an Augustinian monastery, and the nave and transept of the cruciform church are Norman. The Prior's Lodging is now a farmhouse, and other remains include the refectory and a dovecot.

they feel their hold on Wales was secure. Many are the cromlechs and menhirs to be found on its surface, monuments whose purpose we can only guess. It was the sacred land of the Druids and when they had departed it was no less sacred to the Holy Men of the Christian church; so numerous are their bones in the soil of their burial place, Puffin Island, that the rabbits turn them up.

Yet there are lighter associations to Mona's Isle. Three stones near Red Wharf Bay mark the Three Leaps by which Einion, Lord of Trefeilir, won his bride. So many were her suitors that they had to *leap* for her—and the victor was Einion, who covered fifty feet in three

Britain by the Angles and Saxons and Jutes. He asked their help to drive away the Picts and Scots —and then discovered too late that they had come to stay. The disgusted Britons turned against him, and he was burned in the Irish fort of Tre'r Ceiri where he had sought refuge.

Of another ruler of Lleyn, King March, it is related that he had horse's ears! To silence his barbers, he used to kill them and bury their bodies in a marsh, but as soon as a pipe was made from its reeds its notes broadcasted his affliction to the world. This monarch was none other than the husband of Iseult, who eloped with Tristram in a manner familiar to all opera-goers. More fortunate was his grandson, who made a

STEPHENSON

SUNSET OVER SNOWDON

From Capel Curig the narrow moorland road to Pen-y-Gwryd runs alongside these lakes in which are often mirrored the splendid peaks of Snowdon. The mountain as seen from this side appears as a group of individual heights arranged around the great " Horse-shoe " of Cwm Dyli. In the centre of the photograph is the double crest of Lliwedd. Y Wyddfa, the highest point (3,560 feet) is hidden in the clouds on the right.

VALENTINE

CAERNARVON'S HISTORIC STRONGHOLD

Most elaborate of Welsh fortresses, this famous castle was begun in 1285 by Edward I. It was not completed until 1322 in the reign of Edward II. This monarch was born at Caernarvon where, it will be remembered, as an infant he was presented to the Welsh, in 1284, as a Prince of Wales who could speak no English.

friend of the birds, feeding them with scraps of meat out of his hand. When a prisoner in the Holy Land, the legend goes, he called to the birds and in gratitude they flew away with him and carried him home to the land of the Cymry.

Not merely the highest and most beautiful part of Wales, but its stronghold and fastness is the mountain-pass of Eryri—or, as the Saxons call it, Snowdonia. Pressed by the invader, the fierce mountain warriors could retreat into its recesses ; the pressure released, they could sweep from the ravines to descend upon some undefended castle or unwary camp. It was here that Llewelyn, the last native Prince of Wales, held out against Edward I, here that he rallied his forces in readiness for the final battle he never lived to lead. No longer stronghold or fortress, no longer, with its threefold peak, the sacred mountain of the Druid, Snowdon still draws through its beauty and grandeur travellers from all over the world. The summit, by tradition, is never completely free from cloud ; and sometimes the wayfarer may see, thrown by the sunlight on the mists below, his own shadow, magnified and enhaloed like the spectres of Germany's Brocken.

The difficulty the English felt in subduing the region is shown by the castles that surround it ; Conway and Harlech may with some reason be claimed as the finest in the world. " Every schoolboy knows" the story of Caernarvon Castle, whether it be historical or not, how Edward I promised to the assembled chieftains of Wales that he would give them a prince born in their own country who could not speak a word of English—and then how he fulfilled his word by triumphantly producing his baby son, cradled inside a shield. According to the early chroniclers, the chiefs received the harmless joke in good spirit, feeling that the young king born among them would wish them well ; and, indeed, until his tragic end he showed sympathy with " his countrymen," strove to remedy their grievances and gave them their own law.

Greatest of Welsh Bards

Conway lives in Welsh story not so much for its castles as for the stream on which it stands. On its waters, 1,500 years ago, was found floating a leather-covered coracle, and in the coracle was a young child. This was no other than Taliesin, the greatest of the Welsh bards. For the bards of old were indeed great ; they were held as of equal rank to a king, of equal holiness to a priest, and among their tunes were traditional

STEPHENSON

CLOUDS ON THE CARNEDDS
Carnedd Dafydd and Carnedd Llewelyn, the bulky round heights rising from the vale of the Llugwy, are second only in height to Snowdon, Llewelyn being 3,484 feet. The photograph was taken above the Devil's Kitchen, near Ogwen, looking across Nant Ffrancon Pass to Pen yr Olwen, a southern spur of the Carnedds.

DIXON-SCOTT

HOME OF LOST CAUSES

Harlech Castle was the last fortress in Britain to hold out for the House of Lancaster in 1468, and the last in Wales to surrender to the Cromwellians over two hundred years later. In the early fifteenth century, Owen Glendower reigned for four years as Prince of Wales before Harry of Monmouth captured Harlech.

" triads," threefold sentences of mystic meaning from the Druid lore. They strung their harps with human hair, and played them with their sharpened finger-nails.

The harp, so the Triads tell us, was the invention of a giant of old, Idris Gawr, himself a bard and skilled in the knowledge of the stars. His chair, or throne, is the mountain of Cader Idris, steeply rising to the south of the Snowdon range. Whoever sleeps in his chair will awake next morning either a madman or else an inspired bard.

Cader Idris overlooks Cardigan Bay, the site of one of those lost lands of which Welsh legend is rich. Off the north coast are other regions said to have been fertile land, with towns and valleys, where the sea now flows, and more than one of the beautiful Welsh lakes is believed to cover with its waters a township now lost. To catch a glimpse of the city plunged beneath Llangorse Lake is a sign of impending death, but no such grim warning attaches to the *Cantref y Gwaelod*, the " lost hundred " hidden by the waves of Cardigan Bay. The bells of Aberdovey, immortalized in a well-known song, give a message not of destruction but of peace.

Idris Gawr, Idris the Great, is not the only legendary figure whose name is associated with the shores of Cardigan Bay. At the Twr (tower) Bronwen, where Harlech Castle stands today, dwelt Bran the Blessed, the hero of a poem by Taliesin the Bard. To him was given, by a giant, a witch, and a dwarf, a bowl or caldron, with strange and wonderful powers. Its touch healed every ill and restored the dead to life— but left them dumb, lest they should reveal the secrets of the other world. Moreover it bestowed poetic genius, with wisdom and knowledge of the arts and sciences. Bardic lore is full of stories of this mysterious vessel, one of the Thirteen Wonders of Britain's isle.

A Turbulent Hero

Bran the Blessed led the Welsh against their foes the Irish, and Harlech Castle figured both in those wars and in those which later ravaged the land. Here was summoned one of the last Welsh parliaments, those of Owen Glendower, the turbulent hero of Cymric freedom. Here was fierce fighting during the Wars of the Roses, and here Margaret of Anjou took refuge. Only after a blockade and after great slaughter did Harlech Castle fall to Edward IV, and to this period is attributed that stirring battle song the *March of the Men of Harlech*.

That Owen Glendower, who summoned his Parliament at Harlech, raised his insurrection not idly but in protest against the injustice of English rule. A common which lay near his home at Glyndyfrdwy was unjustly seized by his Norman neighbour, Reginald de Grey of Ruthin Castle.

CHAIR OF A MIGHTY GIANT

Cader Idris, the impressive height near Dolgelly, is the legendary chair of a giant who was even greater in mind than stature. Composed of volcano rocks, it runs in a long ridge culminating in the precipitous face of Pen-y-Gader (2,927 feet). The view shows the rocky flanks of the north face and the lake, Lln-y-Gader lying at the foot of the crags. The Foxes' Path descends the steep screes on the far side of the lake.

More than that, he was denounced to the king as disobedient and sentenced to be deprived of his lands, and de Grey treacherously tried to capture him during a friendly talk. Ruined, dispossessed, and outlawed, Glendower proclaimed himself Prince of Wales, and his countrymen flocked to his standard, the Golden Dragon. He showed himself a skilled and daring leader and a statesman able to negotiate with barons and kings. The common people spread tales of his supernatural powers, and when the camp of the English king was overthrown by a sudden squall, they held that this was the work of the " spirits " his magic could command. Before he was finally conquered Glendower had made himself the ruler of almost the whole of Wales ; and, suppressed though it was, the revolt showed that the spirit of Welsh freedom was not yet dead.

Although it gave birth to that fiery hero Glendower, the valley of the Dee is one of beauty and peace. It is a region one would wish not merely to visit but to live in, and two of its inhabitants over a century ago attained almost a national reputation. These were the " Ladies of Llangollen," who shunned society and scorned married life ; they made their home in this quiet vale, which they barely quitted for

fifty years. Every traveller of repute who passed through North Wales made a point of visiting them, and they are described in the memoirs of the period as formal and rather mannish in attire, and looking " exactly like the respectable superannuated old clergymen."

To the everyday Englishman Wales means North Wales, the high mountains that centre on Snowdon. Certainly, with its mountains and with Anglesey, it has some claim to be the most romantic as well as the most beautiful region of Wales, but it by no means forms the whole of the principality. The districts to its south have charms of their own.

Bleak Plynlimon

Very different from the craggy heights of Snowdon and Cader Idris, and yet not without appeal in its bleak austere lowliness is Plynlimon. Pumplummon, as it should be called, " the Five Heads," gets its name because it has five summits (beside another supplementary one, Bryn y Llo, " the Hill of the Calf ") ; also from it lead off five rivers, two to travel far afield eastwards and to flow through England before they reach the sea, and the other three to plunge more swiftly westwards to Cardigan Bay. As Borrow in *Wild*

Wales translates for us a Welsh *pennill* (rhyme) :
" Oh pleasantly do glide along the Severn and
    the Wye ;
  But Rheidol's rough, and yet he's held by all
    in honour high."

Certainly Rheidol is worthy of honour, for its
course is spanned by a famous ancient monument
of Wales. Built probably by the residents of
Strata Florida, Pont ar Mynach, " the Monk's
Bridge," has a curious legend attached to it. A
Welsh countrywoman was distressed to find that
a ravine had opened in the ground, separating
her from her cattle and her home. A person in
monkish-looking garb suddenly appeared and
offered to span it with a bridge for her, provided
she would give him the first living thing that
crossed it. Of course she accepted, and the
bridge was built—then in the nick of time she
noticed a cloven hoof peeping out from under
his monkish robe. So instead of crossing it herself she threw a crust of bread over the bridge.
Her little dog dashed over it, and the devil
angrily disappeared, no doubt muttering the
Welsh equivalent of " foiled again ! " That gulf
is the gorge of the Rheidol, a place of impressive
beauty that deservedly draws hosts of visitors to
see it ; that bridge is the arch that spans it, Pont
ar Mynach, still sometimes spoken of as " the
Devil's Bridge."

Farther south, in this Ystwyth Valley, lies
Strata Florida, which Baring Gould calls the
Westminster Abbey of Wales. Here were buried
the most noble of the Welsh princes, the most
eloquent of the Welsh bards; here were preserved
the most precious of the Welsh records. Here
was a church over 200 feet long, greater than any
of Cambria's cathedrals—and now reduced to a
mere shattered ruin.

Two historic battles took place in Radnorshire.
At Caer Caradog the British king Caratacus
made his last stand, heroic though vain, against
the Roman conquerors—even the official military
historian, Tacitus, admits that the deciding factor
was the heavy armour of the legionaries compared
with the uncovered bodies and heads of the
" natives." At Pilleth Owen Glendower inflicted
a crushing defeat on the English forces of Sir
Edmund Mortimer.

A Vanished City

Curious indeed is Llangorse Lake, Llyn
Safaddan, of Breconshire. Not merely is there
beneath its waters one of the vanished cities of
Wales, but its very birds had a magic insight.
On the approach of the rightful Prince of Wales,
so Giraldus Cambrensis informs us, they would
clap their wings and burst into song.

This Giraldus Cambrensis was born, nearly
800 years ago, in Manorbier, Pembrokeshire,
" the fairest spot," he tells us, of the fairest county
of the fairest region of all the lands of Wales.
When Baldwin, Archbishop of Canterbury,

W. F. TAYLOR

" OLD CONWAY'S FOAMING FLOOD "

*So Thomas Gray described the River Conway, here seen in a typical setting near Bettws-y-Coed. Since then
the river and its surroundings have had many admirers. Borrow speaks of " the celebrated Vale of Conway
to which in summer time the fashionable gentry from all parts of Britain resort for shade and relaxation."*

W. F. TAYLOR

STRATA FLORIDA ABBEY

Founded and endowed by the Lord Rhys in 1164, this Cistercian monastery was for two hundred years the Westminster Abbey of Wales. Today its ruins give but faint indication of its former grandeur, but the ornamentation of the western doorway (above) is said to be architecturally unique.

the low-lying lands of Holland to form the Zuyder Zee, a number of the Flemish refugees sought a home in England. Henry I, as a Welsh chronicler nastily puts it, " being very liberal with that which was not his own," gave them southern Pembrokeshire; and in southern Pembrokeshire their descendants remain even to this day.

This change of population in a rich area may be the theme of a strange Welsh legend. A prince saw one day that all the people of his land had vanished, and that a horde of field-mice was raiding his wheat. He caught one of the mice and erected a gallows to hang it. A scholar, a priest, and a bishop strove to ransom the mouse, and the prince realized that they were no other than the enchanter who had laid the country waste. In return for the mouse his country was re-populated, but not, it seems, with its original inhabitants.

St. David's

Right in the extreme west of Pembrokeshire stands St. David's, surrounded by the sea on three of its sides, and the only cathedral town in Britain not served by a railway. By tradition it is here that the patron saint of Wales

travelled through Wales not merely preaching the Crusade but seeking to get the supremacy of Canterbury acknowledged by all four dioceses of Wales, Gerald the Welshman went with him. Part of his job was to be the first to volunteer for crusading if the nobles were slow in coming forward, so as to shame them into " doing their bit " ! This journey he has described in his *Itinerary*, a most interesting book, full not only of strange legends but of descriptions of the scenes and the people among which he passed.

Pembrokeshire, where he was born, is " the Little England beyond Wales. The place-names are English; the speech is English; the accent is English; the appearance of the people is English—throughout almost the whole of south Pembrokeshire (the north and extreme west are Welsh enough). When the sea overwhelmed

was born, and here was one of the earliest centres of British Christianity. For the Gospel was preached and accepted by the British inhabitants of these islands before the coming of the Saxons. Is there not a tradition that it was preached by persons no less than Joseph of Arimathea and St. Paul themselves, the one in the west on the Tor of Glastonbury, the other in the east on the Hill of Ludd? For centuries the Welsh Church was independent of the English, and only very reluctantly did it acknowledge Canterbury's rule.

A curious military episode marks the history of northern Pembrokeshire. During the Napoleonic Wars a thousand odd Frenchmen landed on its coast and advanced on Fishguard, living on the country as they came. The British forces rallied against them, and at the same time a party of Welshwomen gallantly shouldered

VALENTINE

HOMELAND OF A WELSH HERO

The Dee Valley at Glyndyfrdwy, seen above, was the birthplace of the famous Welsh hero, Owen Glyndyr or Glendower as he was known to the English. In the neighbourhood is Glendower's Mount, another memento of the valiant, fifteenth-century rebel who overcame several of the great castles and called Welsh parliaments at Machynlleth and Dolgelly. Of where Glendower died or where he was buried no record remains.

W. F. TAYLOR

HILLS AND THE SEA

The peaks known as The Rivals, here seen across Caernarvon Bay from Nevin, are prominent hills, curiously isolated from the main group of mountains of Snowdonia. On the right-hand summit is Tre'r Ceiri (Giants' Town), the most extensive prehistoric remains in Wales, with fragments of the ancient walls and dwellings. According to legend the British king, Vortigern, fled to these hills after betraying his people to the Saxons.

their broomsticks and marched about on the hill-tops. The French saw them with the red petticoats, their tall hats, and shouldered brooms, mistook them for a hostile army, and surrendered on the spot. In this comic-opera style ended the last invasion of the British Isles.

Parts of South Wales, if not as widely known as the high mountains of the north, are justifiably popular among lovers of fine scenery. Other regions though less frequented are no less attractive. Much of Carmarthenshire is "off the beaten track" and unknown to the holiday-maker, yet its hills and the Towy Valley are beautiful indeed, and the country is full of the oddest legends. At

was Rees Pritchard, a Church of England clergyman of the seventeenth century. In his early life he was an inveterate drunkard; to the scandal of his parishioners he used to be wheeled home from the inn in a barrow. When one day a billy-goat wandered into the inn, it amused the parson to make the creature drunk with a saucer of beer and to watch it staggering about and finally collapsing on the floor. Next evening, when he tried to repeat his little joke, the goat disdainfully turned its back on the drink and walked away. So the vicar realized that the brute beast was wiser than he, and from that time forward he was a reformed man, earnest in

W. F. TAYLOR

RIVER OF BEAUTY

Rising on the slopes of gaunt Plynlimon, the River Wye descends from the lonely moorlands and winds across Wales through scenery of rare beauty, through meadowland, green pastures, and wooded country. The photograph shows the view below Erwood, in Breconshire and the Black Mountains of Brecon beyond.

Llanfihangel Abercowin are the " Graves of the Five Pilgrims " ; so long as their graves are respected the village will be free from poisonous snakes.

At Llandilo is a castle built by Rhodri Mawr, Roderick the Great, one of the few kings who ruled over all Wales—for its different peoples, when not fighting against Roman or Saxon, were too often fighting among themselves, and to this day there is rivalry between the Welsh of the north and those of the south. His grandson, Howel Dda, Howell the Good, drew up a code of laws, based on the customs of the people, to have force over all the land.

Well known among Carmarthenshire characters

the performance of his parochial duties, and leaving the people a book of religious verse known as the *Welshman's Candle.*

Carmarthenshire was the centre, ninety years ago, of some most curious riots. The government had run over the land some excellent highways, liberally embellished with tollgates by which their cost was to be repaid. The tolls aroused much indignation, and a strange new movement appeared, gangs of men disguising themselves as women, tearing down the gates, wrecking the toll-houses, and turning their tenants adrift into the bleak night. In one of these onslaughts a poor old woman was slain, yet the authorities could get no information as to their

W. A. CALL

PICTURESQUE COAST OF PEMBROKE

On either side of the limestone cliffs of Tenby lie the North and South Sands. The South Sands illustrated above extend for a distance of nearly two miles. One of the routes to the Sands, the Merlin Walk, passes over a cave of that name terminating close to its entrance, now almost obscured with sand. Hoyle's Mouth, another cave 100 feet long, is divided in three chambers. From Tenby start the famous Pendine Sands.

ROMAN STEPS

W. F. TAYLOR

In the hills east of Harlech are these so-called Roman steps which, according to tradition, were built for the use of Roman sentries patrolling the pass known as Bwlch Tyddiad. Only in modern times have the steps been termed Roman, and it is more probable that they date from the Middle Ages.

away, Gowerland is a favourite resort for visitors. For the rest Glamorganshire rather scares travellers away. They think of it only as a vast coalfield, where the streams are polluted from the mineral workings and the hills are slag, yet there is romance even in these scarred and ravished hills.

King Arthur

In the mountains of Glamorganshire sleep the minerals that give the county its trade. Yet in them sleep too, so the story runs, King Arthur and his Knights, waiting till the day shall come when they are to rise to rule Britain, to inaugurate a reign of justice and peace. On the Craig-y-Dinas is a cave which leads to the hall where they repose. Whoever enters that cave may bring away from their treasures as much gold as he can carry ; but if he touches the bell that hangs within the cave they will awake and ask: " Is it yet day ? " To this the intruder must reply " Sleep on ; it is still night," whereupon they will return to rest. A villager who was too flustered to think of this watchword was beaten by the knights and thrust treasureless out ; and never again did he discover the entrance to the cave.

instigator. " Rebecca," their male leader, got " her " name merely from the verse of Genesis which says that the seed of Rebekah should possess the gate of their adversaries. The rioters attempted to wreck a workhouse; they succeeded in destroying a salmon weir thought to injure the upper waters of the stream. Then, as suddenly as they had began, the " Rebecca Riots " came to an end.

The Gower Peninsula of Glamorgan has a general resemblance in shape to Pembrokeshire south of Milford Haven ; and it also is " a little England," being largely peopled not by the Welsh but by the Flemings. With its magnificent castle at Oystermouth and its blowhole at Rhosilly, the roaring of which as the waves drive the air through its aperture can be heard seven miles

Monmouthshire, from the strict political point of view, is not a county of Wales but part of the Welsh Marches. Yet it is certainly part of the principality in everything except political convention. Guarding the pass into South Wales, a pass used by invading Roman, Saxon and Norman, is Abergavenny. Its castle has a most unsavoury reputation of being dishonoured by treachery more often than any other in Wales. After Henry II had forced the Norman Marcher Lords and the Welsh princes of the region into apparent amity, its ruler William de Braose invited them to a feast to celebrate. Suddenly he commanded all the Welsh guests to swear to abandon the right of wearing arms ; and when they hesitated he had his men-at-arms cut them down. Afterwards he sent emissaries to murder the wife and infant child of his most influential victim. Acts such as these drove the Welsh into a frenzy of revolt, until at last they stormed the wicked castle and razed it to the ground.

In contrast with this scene of treachery and strife is a neighbouring place of peace, Llanthony Abbey. Its site in the Vale of Ewias, high up in the hills, so forcibly impressed a noble of William II by its solitude that at once he abandoned his military career and turned hermit. In the monastery he founded St. David had a cell; hence its name, which is short for Llanddewi nant Honddu, "David's Church by Honddu stream." Not far from Llanthony is another church in a situation as romantic, Partrishow, with a magnificent rood-screen and a holy well.

From the scenic point of view, Monmouth is famous chiefly because its boundary is formed by the River Wye, with its unequalled scenery, and with many places of note on its banks. Here stand Monmouth, which lent its name to Geoffrey of Monmouth, author of a quite incredible *History of the British Kings*, and which was the birthplace of Henry V—his cradle, and the sword he used at Agincourt, are still preserved; Chepstow, once "the stockaded market" where Saxons and Welsh, when not at war, used warily to barter; Trellech, with its three blocks of red stone supposed to be erected by King Harold. Grandest of all is Tintern Abbey, beautiful even in its decay.

The conquering English spoke of the Cymry as the Welsh, the "strangers," ridiculed their

STEPHENSON

A CHURCH IN THE HILLS

In the Black Mountains of Brecon, at Partrishow, near Crickhowell, is this little church founded in the eleventh century and rebuilt in the days of Henry VIII. It possesses a beautiful rood-loft and a font.

language, lampooned them in a nursery rhyme. Yet they have not destroyed their culture, have not merged the Welsh into themselves. The Cymry of today still keep their ancient language, cherish their ancient tradition, honour the ancient bards and heroes, know themselves as distinct from the Englishmen. But they are not narrowly contemptuous of the "Saxons." Dispossessed from England they yet have their motherland, Wales, where every placename has its meaning, where every hill and valley has its association or its legend. Here the Welsh still live; and thus they fulfil the prophecy of Taliesin the Bard:

"And British men
 Shall be captives then
To strangers from Saxonia's
  strand;
They shall praise their
  God, and hold
Their language, as of old,
But except Wild Wales they
  shall lose their land."

RIVER OF LEGEND

STEPHENSON

One of the most beautiful of Welsh rivers, the Usk, rises in Carmarthen and flows for sixty miles to the sea passing Brecon, an ancient borough and now a cathedral city. In the background of the photograph are the Brecon Beacons (2,907 feet), the highest hills in South Wales.

FELTON

SUPERB TUDOR GOTHIC
Built in 1503-1519 the beautiful chapel of Henry VII in Westminster Abbey is the most exquisite example in England of Tudor Gothic. On each side of the chapel are the stalls and banners of Knights of the Bath.

THE STORY OF LONDON

by MARTIN R. HOLMES

LONDON today is one of the world's greatest ports, and in that fact lies the clue to its origin. In the first place, the Thames estuary, facing the Continent, gave easy access by water into the interior of the island; and in the second place the site of London is the lowest point at which the river can be crossed with comparative ease. Indeed, as late as the twelfth century the Thames was occasionally fordable at London Bridge, and the presence of a hard gravel subsoil on both banks at this point facilitated the construction of the bridge itself. On the other hand, the site of London was largely hemmed in by dense oak forest, of which the forests of Epping and Hainault are time-worn fragments. It was not therefore until the arrival of the Romans in A.D 43, with their overseas interests on the one hand and their engineering skill on the other, that the ford assumed permanent importance as a focus of maritime and overland traffic. The erection of the bridge and of the extensive bridgehead settlements on the sites of the city and of Southwark may be regarded as the outcome of that great event.

The new London or Londinium grew rapidly as a commercial centre, and within a few years of the Roman invasion was already one of the five largest cities north of the Alps. But in A.D. 61 this prosperity received a sudden sharp check. In that year the Iceni, taking advantage of the absence of the bulk of the army in the north, marched on Colchester, and thence proceeded to London where they indulged in massacre and destruction.

The Romans were thus faced with the necessity of rebuilding London. The city was laid out on the usual Roman grid-iron plan, and doubtless on a more monumental scale than had been possible in the first flush of conquest. As in the case of the Great Fire of 1666, the catastrophe of A.D. 61 probably proved, in the long run, beneficial to progress of the city, which now extended from the Fleet river in the west to the site of the present Tower of London in the east.

In the second century, probably in the time of the great empire-builder Hadrian, whose colossal bronze statue once stood in Roman London, the city was girt with three miles of wall and ditch, of which fragments (notably in the courtyard of the General Post Office, St. Martin's-le-Grand) can still be seen.

Our knowledge of the buildings of the new town is limited by the disintegrating effects of post-Roman neglect and medieval or modern reconstruction, which, in succession, have helped in a large measure to obliterate the original Roman street-plan. It is, however, clear that in the lay-out of the main features of the town, consideration was given first to the provision of a forum and the basilica as representing the commercial and administrative aspects of urban

ORIGINAL SIGN 1668

FELTON

A PICTURESQUE SIGN

Outside a rope and sailmaker's shop in Fish Street Hill may be seen this quaint old sign of a "Peterboat and Doublet."

life. This important group of buildings stood on the present site of Leadenhall Market and St. Peter's, Cornhill. The basilica, a long rectangular hall some 500 feet in length, served the combined purpose of Town Hall, Law Court and Exchange. Other public buildings included temples and baths, and a fragment of one of these baths may still be seen under the Coal Exchange in Lower Thames Street.

Roman Housing Problem

Industrial development naturally tended to keep pace with the growth of the city. Building materials were urgently required to house the increasing population; tiles and bricks were manufactured on the spot, and freestone was imported from western England. A vigorous demand for earthenware for domestic purposes led to the use of native wares such as those from Castor and the New Forest, in addition to the imported " Samian " ware of Gaulish origin. This last, with its familiar red glazed surface, has been found in great quantities on London sites, and is well represented in our museums. So also are the large two-handled vessels or " amphorae " in which wine and oil were imported from Gaul and Italy. Equivalent exports were metal, corn, slaves, and probably wool.

With the arrival of the Roman general, Theodosius, in A.D. 368 for the purpose of reorganizing the province after a period of disturbance, the written history of Roman London comes to an end. In A.D. 410, with a hostile army besieging the gates of Rome, the Emperor, Honorius, sent to the " Cities in Britain " a message of despair, advising them to take measures for their own safety. The ensuing period, in respect of civic life, was one of stagnation and decay, due on the one hand to the rupture of economic relations with the Roman world and on the other hand to the chaos resulting from the invasions of the Picts and Scots in the north and the Teutonic incursions in the south and east.

Between the years A.D. 400 and 500 very little is known of the history of London. Excluding a reference in an official Roman list of disputed date, the first mention of London after the fourth century is a reference in A.D. 457 in the

D. MCLEISH

REMAINS OF A ROMAN BATH

Outside the wall of Roman London, on a slight eminence overlooking the Thames, once stood the second-century villa of some wealthy citizen of the ancient empire. On the south side of the Strand, at 5, Strand Lane, may be seen this bath, which is still fed by a spring as it was in the days when the villa was inhabited.

LONDON'S HISTORIC FORTRESS

FELTON

On the north bank of the Thames, at the south-east angle of the Roman fortifications, William the Conqueror founded the Tower of London, and the Keep, or White Tower, dates from his reign. It has served as fortress, palace and gaol and held many illustrious prisoners, most of whom only escaped by way of the executioner's block.

Anglo-Saxon Chronicle according to which, after a fight between the forces of Hengist and the Britons, the latter left Kent and fled to London.

At the end of the sixth century the city was dependent upon Kent, and Augustine's foundation of a bishopric at Canterbury was accordingly followed by the establishment of others at London and Rochester. The site of St. Paul's was consecrated in A.D. 604, the year of Augustine's death, and the continuation of Kentish supremacy is indicated by the fact that Canterbury, and not, as Pope Gregory had intended, London, became the southern headquarters of Christianity in Britain.

The cathedral of St. Paul occupied the summit of the western hill of the city. Close to the cathedral we find the churches of St. Gregory at the west end and St. Augustine at the east end. It is possible that this group of churches stood in alignment from west to east, forming an imposing façade to anyone ascending the hill. It has also been said that not far from the cathedral Ethelred II, in later years, built himself a palace. In Westcheap the folkmote, an assembly of the freemen of London, was held on a site north-east of St. Paul's. This evidence, coupled with discoveries which have taken place in this part of the town tend to show that the " west end " of London had then already established its prestige.

During the eighth and ninth centuries, the London Wall was repaired and strengthened to withstand the Danish attacks which during the latter part of this period became a frequent occurrence in the neighbourhood. But in spite of this ever-present danger, London continued to develop apace, aided no doubt by the paternal rule of Alfred. Under his successors, the town passed largely unscathed through the ravages of the Danes, until, in 1017, together with the rest of England, it finally submitted to them. Of the struggles of this phase, Viking weapons recovered from London sites, and particularly from the foreshore of the river, are eloquent witness.

Tower of London

But throughout these vicissitudes, the city had risen from strength to strength, and the fearless independence which it showed at the time of the Norman Conquest in 1066 it retained throughout its later history. Indeed, the first structure erected by the Normans was designed as a check upon this insubordinate spirit and is today a token of it. The Tower of London, built by King William within the south-eastern angle of the old town wall, and known from its ancient coats of whitewash as the " White Tower," is and has always been outside the civic administration. In the modern system of local government

FELTON

OLDEST CHURCH IN LONDON

St. John's Chapel in the Tower of London, a fine example of Norman architecture, built about 1080, is situated in the White Tower. Edward VI destroyed its many rare and beautiful ornaments.

given to that bridge which was the real nucleus of London. It was during the reign of Henry II that the old timber bridge across the Thames was first rebuilt in stone. The new London Bridge had twenty pointed arches, and the roadway was flanked on either side by shops which in some places were joined above it, completely shutting out the sky. It was considered superior to the Pont Nôtre Dame at Paris and the Rialto at Venice, and an Elizabethan writer named it as "worthily to be numbered among the miracles of the world." On the central and largest pier, a chapel was built and dedicated to a famous Londoner—St. Thomas of Canterbury.

Just outside London, also, lay the important Court suburb of Westminster. Until the disastrous fire of 1834, a considerable part of the medieval Palace of Westminster was still standing, including the famous Painted Chamber, with its elaborate mural decoration. Now, however, almost the only surviving portion is Westminster Hall, built originally by William II and altered under Richard II into its present form. Contemporary with this alteration is the greater part of the nave of the Abbey Church of Westminster, near by. The builders, instead of following the architectural fashion of their own time, designed a nave in the style of a hundred years before, to harmonize with the remainder of the building, as set up by Henry III, and it takes careful observation to tell where the work of the thirteenth century ends and that of the late fourteenth begins.

Abbey of Westminster

The actual Benedictine Abbey of Westminster, which guarded the relics of St. Edward the Confessor, was finally dissolved by Elizabeth, but enough of the buildings remained in the reconstituted Deanery and School to illustrate even in our own day the layout of a great medieval monastery; and the walls of the Chapter House still retain, in some degree, their bright paintings of angels and scenes from the Apocalypse.

It is perhaps only fair to outline very briefly the other side of the picture. The London of those years would appal the sanitary authority of today. Early in the Middle Ages it had easily afforded a home to a semi-pastoral population. The city itself was small, the open country lay

it forms a remarkable and significant enclave of the external Borough of Stepney into the natural territory of the City of London.

Further building in the early years following the Norman Conquest was stimulated by a succession of fires, which destroyed many churches, St. Paul's among them. After this disaster, the citizens set to work to erect the finest church in England—a new St. Paul's, which dominated the city for some 600 years to follow. In 1090 the Church of St. Giles was constructed in the vicinity of Cripplegate, and at about the same date the archiepiscopal palace at Lambeth was begun. Thirty years later there arose just outside the city walls the monastery of St. Bartholomew the Great, founded by Rahere. Today the monastic buildings are gone, and of the church attached to them only the eastern end remains to symbolize the grandeur of the vanished monastic architecture of London.

Amongst secular buildings, priority may be

D. MCLEISH

QUIET PRECINCTS OF THE TEMPLE

Pump Court, seen above, was built shortly after the Great Fire of London. The Temple was originally the seat of the famous Order of Knights Templars. When this order was dissolved the property passed to the Knights Hospitallers of St. John, who leased it in the fourteenth century to professors of the common law.

in easy reach, and it was possible for the Londoner to keep his cattle and pigs within the city and have them driven out every morning to pasture. With the increase in building, however, the pasture land became further and further removed from the heart of the city, and the change had its reactions upon the aspect of the London streets.

The foreign merchant, coming to London on business, would find in it many unexpected savours of the farmyard, and the measures passed again and again to regulate the cleanliness of the streets and the proper housing of cattle, and to check the practice of allowing pigs to feed at random in the gutters, show that the authorities were well awake to the necessity of keeping the pastoral element of the city under due restraint. Regulations exist, moreover, prescribing the digging of cesspools, stone-lined or otherwise, and reprehending the practice of emptying filth indiscriminately into the brooks and streams which still ran uncovered through the city. Notwithstanding these insanitary conditions, it has been roughly estimated that the population of London stood close upon 40,000.

But no description of medieval London would be complete without some mention of that important feature of civic life—the City Company. Gilds, comparable to the modern friendly societies, had existed in Saxon times. It was not, however, until the twelfth century that they became predominantly mercantile. Briefly, the Craft Gilds aimed at establishing a monopoly in each industry by regulating production and distribution for the ultimate benefit of their members. Their position had originally rested on the somewhat unstable footing of an annual rent paid to the Crown, but the granting of a charter of incorporation to the Weavers' Company by Henry II established a precedent of which other companies were quick to take advantage. When this degree of security had been reached, the next step was usually the erection of a permanent meeting place for purposes of business and social intercourse. Of the actual appearance of these city halls, very little is known, since the Great Fire swept away most of them, but they doubtless resembled the old Guildhall.

The chief disadvantage of the gilds in later years lay in the restrictions they imposed upon new industries arising within the city, and their prohibition of any change in wages at a time when economic conditions were altering rapidly. Some of their functions have now become the work of the trades unions, but their social and charitable work is still continued by the Livery Companies of the City of London. These bodies retain their courts, their officers and their customs,

FELTON

RICHARD COEUR DE LION

Within the shadow of the Houses of Parliament stands this statue of Richard I (1189-1199), the crusading monarch whose adventures in the Holy Land and elsewhere have provided themes for many a romantic story.

re-grant of them to his nominees, helped to fill London with unemployed men who had formerly worked on the monastic estates. These were now in part diverted to the use of palatial residences, as when Henry VIII built St. James's Palace on the site of a leper hospital. Elsewhere to meet the needs of the swarming population, more and more houses were erected, and the streets were rapidly darkening on account of the overhanging upper storeys. Sanitation was at its worst, and disease was rife throughout the whole area.

It is impossible to say how long this state of affairs might have continued had not the Great Fire of 1666 provided an effective, if drastic, remedy. After it, little remained of medieval London, and, for the first time for many centuries, there was opportunity for a complete remodelling of the street plan. Wren, full of the ideals of the Renaissance movement, was appointed assistant surveyor by Charles II, and prepared a plan for the town which, owing to the nearsightedness of the authorities, was not adopted. Much of the genius of Wren remains today in his immortal buildings, the cathedral of St. Paul's, and in no fewer than thirty-nine of the city churches, of which St. Stephen Walbrook may be quoted as one of the best examples.

From this time onward London entered into its greater glory. Such buildings as Wren's churches, the additions to the Palace of Hampton Court, and the hospitals of Chelsea and Greenwich,

D. MCLEISH

BURIAL PLACE OF DANES

A site revered by Londoners is that of the Church of St. Clement Danes, Strand, it being the traditional burial place of Harold Harefoot and other Danes.

and some of them, but not all, have their halls. The formal dinners of these companies are survivals of the old social gatherings of craftsmen, and many grammar schools and almshouses, in and about London, have been founded and endowed by the Livery Companies just as the old gilds made provision for educating the children of deceased members, or housing craftsmen overtaken by old age.

A great economic change of early Tudor times was the drift of population from the village to the town, which is reflected in London's town planning, or lack of it. So overcrowded did the city become during the fifteenth and sixteenth centuries, that even the encircling ditch was filled in and built over. The confiscation of monastic lands by Henry VIII, and his

D. MCLEISH

TUDOR BUILDINGS IN HOLBORN

In Holborn may be seen this picturesque façade of Staple Inn, a quaint relic of the streets of old London. This inn is believed to have been a hostel of wool-staplers in the fourteenth century and later became an Inn of Chancery.

EDGAR WARD

THE GREAT DOME OF ST. PAUL'S

The dominant note in this London panorama is St. Paul's Cathedral, Wren's famous masterpiece. In the seventh century there is said to have been a church on this site. This was followed by a Norman structure which, with later additions, was the old St. Paul's. After the Great Fire, Wren planned the present building which was begun in 1675, the last stone being laid in 1710. Many of England's greatest men are buried in St. Paul's.

EDGAR WARD

THE SILVER-DAPPLED POOL

That reach of the Thames on each side of the Tower Bridge has long been famous as the Pool of London. Of old it was the city's shipping centre, but since the building of the Tower Bridge only vessels of moderate dimensions reach the upper portion. Below the bridge begins London dockland, although all except the Surrey Commercial Docks are on the north side, London now handles one-third of Britain's overseas trade.

all grace London today, and afford us an insight into the appearance of the city and its environs in the years of the seventeenth-century Renaissance. The new learning was not solely confined to architecture, but embraced all branches of the arts. Books were published on the town, and from such famous diarists as Pepys and Evelyn we get intriguing sketches and descriptions of the period. From now until the end of the century, London saw a succession of fine new buildings which continued into the early nineteenth century under the skilled hands of such architects as Hawkesmoor, Gibbs, Soane, Dance, Wilkins and Nash.

Fashionable Soho

With the establishment of a more or less permanent court at Westminster, London had become the permanent residential city for fashionable society. The city itself was, and is still, devoted to the merchants—the real aboriginal citizens of London—but residential quarters began to rise towards the west. First Soho was fashionable, as many fine late seventeenth-century houses remain to show us ; then, in the first quarter of the eighteenth century, a new residential district sprang up outside London, about the Oxford Road, and between that road and St. James's the West End came into being. Here was no gradual expansion, but a complete scheme for a new quarter, laid out and planned round its fashionable squares, and in due course, when it was completed, London Society entered and took possession.

By the eighteenth century London had reached a position such as it had never before attained as a centre of the brilliant world of folk and fashion. The clothes of the *ton*, silks and satins, periwigs and lorgnettes, the gay livery of the servants, and above all the interest of the common throng—everything indeed tended to make life colourful. The apparent lightheartedness of the times is shown by the number of amusements which increased each year. It was at this time that the famous pleasure resorts of Vauxhall and Ranelagh were opened and attended by all who were considered, or considered themselves, to be of the élite. Scenes of excess were not infrequent at both these gardens, and, according to both Fielding and Walpole, they were mostly responsible for numerous quarrels and duels.

Even the architecture took on a lighter vein, and the brothers Adam engaged pipers to cheer the Scottish builders of the Adelphi, now unfortunately mainly demolished to make room for

D. MCLEISH

WHERE THE FIRE OF LONDON BEGAN
Fish Street Hill, seen above, is adjacent to Billingsgate. On the left is the base of the Monument, commemorating the Great Fire of 1666. In the background is the Church of St. Magnus the Martyr, rebuilt by Wren.

the growing needs of the metropolis. The Adelphi must have been a pleasant place in the eighteenth century, with the streets leading down to the foreshore through that little architectural gem, the York Water Gate. Furniture too changed in these years, and examples in public and private collections remain to show how the work of Chippendale, Hepplewhite and Sheraton was used to adorn the fashionable London houses.

Many of the famous London clubs owe their

EDGAR WARD

LIONS OF TRAFALGAR SQUARE

On the south side of Trafalgar Square, described as " the finest site in London," stands the lofty Nelson's column surmounted by the huge monument of the famous admiral. Round the base of the column are four bronze lions, designed by Sir Edwin Landseer and erected in 1868 some months after the completion of the column.

inception to the bucks of those days, and their lives are reflected in the delightful caricatures by Rowlandson. The later style of the Adam brothers may be seen to advantage in a number of beautiful door-cases still in existence in the remaining part of the Adelphi, Chelsea and the back streets of Westminster. Their later work, however, tended to over-elaboration and, as is only natural, reaction set in during the early nineteenth century and was reflected in the fashions of the time as well as in the architecture. Such " upstart " places as Kensington, which only fifty years before had been a distinct and separate village, were gradually joined to the West End by a chain of heavy pseudo-Renaissance palaces or by overdone Gothic mansions.

Carlton House Terrace

A redeeming feature of this later period was the work of John Nash which may be seen today in Carlton House Terrace in the Mall. Of the eighteenth century we still have the fine examples of the outer wall of the Bank of England (1733), Somerset House, and many churches including St. Martin's-in-the-Fields and St. Mary-le-Strand by Gibbs. Little need here be said of the nine-teenth-century rebuilding of a great part of London, save perhaps to mention the buildings

by Wilkins—the National Gallery and University College, London. For the rest, the century witnessed what may best be called the gradual " mechanization " of architecture : the use, for example, of machine-made terra-cotta tiles, and of concrete apologetically disguised by façades in the traditional fashion. It has been a common plaint that the fine independent quality of the buildings prior to the introduction of machinery is gone, and the individuality of the streets, except for occasional buildings, is lost.

Many people still remember with amusement the first horse-tram, a very rickety affair on which only the young and foolhardy would risk their lives. The London hansom-cab, growlers, drain-pipe trousers and bustles, would seem strange to us even after so few years. Gone today are the crossing-sweepers and fly-posters of Dickens's day, and with them the picturesque streets which have given way to stately avenues of stone and concrete. Yet change is a symptom of vitality and carries with it its own compensations. The Londoner today, looking at his new London based on steel rather than on stone, is able to find a new beauty in his city both comparable with, and at the same time wholly different from, that of the medieval and Georgian cities which have now so nearly vanished.

MELLOW BEAUTY OF OXFORD AND CAMBRIDGE

by S. E. GUNN

AN American visitor to Oxford is said to have asked a gardener how the lovely college lawns were brought to such a pitch of perfection. "Well," was the reply, "you mows 'em and you rolls 'em, and you mows 'em and you rolls 'em, and you keeps on doing it for about five hundred years, and, well, there you are."

The supreme charm of Oxford and Cambridge is in their mellowness. The historic buildings of seven centuries constitute their glory; their attractiveness is to be found in the atmosphere of rare and dignified maturity which each university has gathered unto itself during the slow passage of unnumbered years. There are more beautiful cities in Britain ; more ancient and more interesting antiquities ; but nowhere so many venerable institutions which for so long have been devoted continuously to the same cause. In the colleges of these two old towns the life of learning has gone on for 700 years. Today, developed, reformed, and brought up to date though it may be, the same life goes on, in essentials exactly as it did in medieval times. Changes and upheavals there have been, periods of dullness and depression, but the lamp of scholarship has never been extinguished, and today, within walls raised to protect it centuries ago it burns more brightly than ever.

In the earlier Middle Ages Paris was the greatest centre of learning in Europe. Its University styled itself the " first school of the

D. MCLEISH

OXFORD'S CURFEW TOWER
Tom Tower, of Christ Church, houses Great Tom, a bell which sounds the curfew every night as a warning that all college gates will shortly be closed.

Church," and from every European country scholars flocked thither to sit at the feet of its famous teachers.

Many came from England. But wars with France and disputes with the Pope arose to hinder English students from crossing to Paris. This, and the development of a national patriotism, led to the assembling, as early as the beginning of the twelfth century, of small groups of scholars at both Oxford and Cambridge.

Oxford, standing on ground protected by the Thames and the Cherwell, commanding an important ford— hence the name—and situated on the borders of the great rival kingdoms of Mercia and Wessex, was a stronghold in Saxon times. Part of the masonry of St. Martin's tower dates from these days, and in the cathedral is the Shrine of St. Frideswide, who founded a priory on the site in the eighth century. Later the town became a point of defence against the Danes, who sailed up the Thames in their long boats.

The royal hunting lodge at Woodstock, only eight miles away, brought the Norman monarchs frequently to Oxford. Under their influence the town flourished and became a centre of court life. A castle arose. Here the Empress Matilda was besieged by Stephen : and from here one wintry night she made her escape, travelling in white across the snowclad ground.

Cambridge too had its Norman castle, though it lacked a priory. It was early an important centre in the fenlands. Like Oxford, it stood

H. FELTON

THE NOBLE TOWER OF MAGDALEN

This imposing structure, 145 feet high, was built between the years 1492 and 1507 at a time when Wolsey was junior bursar at the college. Because of its carefully chosen architectural proportions, it achieves an unusual elegance of form, and in the result this graceful tower has become one of the supreme glories of that beautiful old university city of Oxford. Every May morning a ceremony to the dawn is held on Magdalen Tower.

astride a ford. The main route from East Anglia to the midlands passed through the town. Three great animal fairs were held there, and sea-going ships came up to its wharves, which lined the river along the stretch now bordered by the famous " backs."

Oxford was the first to achieve fame as a university town. Throughout the twelfth century students gathered there, and ere long it was able to boast that it contained the " second school of the Church." It has never been fully

St. Martin's, once the townsmen's church. Its bell summoned the town to fight the scholars, who swarmed out of their lodgings at the sound of the bell of St. Mary's, the University church. At Cambridge the Church of St. Mary the Greater has served both town and gown. Its two organs and moveable pulpit are reminders of its dual purpose.

In 1209 a scholar killed a woman in the streets of Oxford, and the rivalry between town and gown flared up into days of terror and bloodshed.

H. FELTON

KING'S COLLEGE CHAPEL, CAMBRIDGE

Described by Wordsworth as " this immense and glorious work of fine intelligence," Henry VI's Chapel took a century to build, being completed in 1545. Its exquisite roof is undoubtedly the most impressive of its kind. On the right is the Fellows' Building, erected from plans partly prepared by Wren.

understood why scholars were attracted to Cambridge, but by 1209 the schools there were sufficiently developed to receive a large migration from Oxford.

In their earlier days the universities of Oxford and Cambridge were strictly ecclesiastical institutions. The students who thronged the streets wore the clerical gown and hood, and enjoyed the protection of the Church. For the most part they were poor. They indulged in gaming and riotous living, and on occasion played the highwayman to eke out their scanty means. Such conduct led to frequent brawls between " town and gown."

Carfax Tower, at Oxford, is all that remains of

King John, always on the losing side, supported the citizens, the Pope the students. Lectures were suspended, and a papal interdict was placed upon the city. A large band of scholars crossed to Cambridge. There is no reason to believe, as has been suggested, that this migration marks the origin of the latter university.

On St. Scholastica's Day, 1354, Oxford beheld further disastrous riots. The university won, though its halls were ravaged ; and from that date it has possessed powers rendering it independent of the town authorities. For centuries, indeed, the latter were held in almost feudal subjection. Until 1824 the Mayor and Corporation went every year to the University Church—for

D. MCLEISH

OLD COURT OF CORPUS CHRISTI, CAMBRIDGE

The dignified frontage of Corpus Christi College is nineteenth century, but the old court, seen above, with its picturesque eaves overhanging the low-pitched chambers, dates from the fourteenth century when the college was founded. The buttresses were added to strengthen the walls in the late fifteenth or early sixteenth century. A mural tablet on the right is a reminder that Kit Marlowe, the famous dramatist, lived here.

many years clad in sackcloth—to do penance for the riots of 1354.

For long after the rise of the universities there were no colleges. The students lived in lodgings or hostels, or, if they were members of a religious order, in monasteries or friaries. Colleges arose to give lay students a community life like that enjoyed by those resident in religious houses.

Though University College, Oxford, claims to be the oldest foundation, Merton College, Oxford, is generally regarded as the pioneer of the college system which distinguishes Oxford and Cambridge from other universities. Founded in 1264, it was, according to its founder, to be a community of poor scholars living frugally on bread and beer, with flesh or fish once a day. It developed into a residential college, and its organization supplied a pattern generally followed by subsequent foundations. In brief, each college is independent as regards internal administration, yet forms part of the university as a whole.

Merton has retained much of its medieval buildings. The lovely Mob Quad, dominated by the Chapel, takes one right into the heart of early Oxford. From this college John Wyclif was banished to his rectory at Lutterworth, where he organized the movement which gained him a place among the early Reformers.

Peterhouse (properly St. Peter's College), Cambridge, was founded within ten years of Merton; it, too, has still some of its earliest buildings in use.

A Miserable Benefaction

Balliol, another of the earliest Oxford colleges, is named after John de Baliol, who having " unjustly vexed and enormously damnified " the Church was in 1263 ordered by the Bishop of Durham to make provision for poor scholars at Oxford. It is said that all the provision he made was the miserable sum of twopence, and that it was his wife, fearful for the welfare of his soul, who in 1282 decided to endow the college adequately.

Oriel College, Oxford, is said to have been the result of a vow made by Edward II that he would endow a college if he escaped from the field of Bannockburn. All Souls, Oxford, was endowed by Archbishop Chichele. Saddened by the loss of so many lives in the French wars of Henry VI, he established a college which was also a Chantry in which masses were said for the souls of the dead.

New College, Oxford, was founded in the fourteenth century by William of Wykeham to maintain seventy scholarships for boys coming up from his school at Winchester. About a hundred years later King's College, Cambridge, was similarly created by Henry VI to receive boys from Eton. For centuries King's remained exclusively a college of Etonians; it stood aloof from the rest of the university, and claimed the privilege of examining its own candidates for degrees.

Both these colleges stand as magnificent monuments to the vision of their founders. The lovely chapel at King's, begun in 1446, but not completed until 1545, with its gorgeous pinnacles reared high above lawns that slope gently down to the river, is perhaps the most impressive and beautiful sight in Cambridge.

"Tax not the royal Saint with vain expense," cried Wordsworth, and one can well agree, for this "glorious work of fine intelligence" is a gem that could hardly be spared. The glorious great windows of painted glass and the fan tracery of the roof are almost unique in England. Henry projected a college on a like scale of magnificence, but, alas, only the chapel materialized.

New College, like King's, possesses the same superb ecclesiastical atmosphere; its dining-hall has the lines and dignity of a chapel, and the entire college breathes the spirit of the days of Edward III. Its founder was a close friend of the Black Prince.

Corpus Christi College, Cambridge, endowed by the Guild of Corpus Christi, is unique in being the only college founded by the "town." Its Old Court, built in 1377, two centuries later, received Christopher Marlowe, greatest of English dramatic poets before Shakespeare.

A Cardinal's Scheme

One result of the suppression of the monasteries by Henry VIII was a great harvest of college building. In the days of his power Wolsey planned, with the revenues received from a number of suppressed religious houses, to erect a magnificent college at Oxford, to be called Cardinal College. When the downfall and death of the arrogant churchman threatened to interrupt the project, Henry VIII took it up; and Christ Church, grandest of the Oxford colleges, arose as evidence of the monarch's solicitude for learning. "I tell you," he said, "that I grudge no land in England better bestowed than that which is given to our universities. For by their maintenance our realm shall be well governed when we are dead and rotten."

A portrait of Henry VIII hangs in the Great

D. MCLEISH

OXFORD'S RENOWNED HIGH STREET

From Magdalen Tower is obtained this fine panoramic view of Oxford, in which the High Street, thought by many to be the most beautiful in the world, winds its way through the city. In the right-hand corner is Magdalen College, while a little farther up, on the same side, a glimpse can be seen of Queen's College.

Both universities grew strong during the age of the New Learning, and produced many great figures during the unquiet days of the English Reformation. Oxford pioneered the teaching of Greek, not without opposition. Greek, its opponents said, was the language of heresy: and a warden of New College, Oxford, wrote indignantly to Wolsey, " Do you really know that you have given studentships at Christ Church to men who go about teaching Greek? Pray let them be dismissed."

Great Scholars

They were not dismissed. Men like Colet, founder of St. Paul's School, Grocyn, Lily and Linacre, under the patronage of Lady Margaret Beaufort — grandmother of Henry VIII, and founder of Christ's College and St. John's — and Sir Thomas More, expounded the Greek philosophers at Oxford, while Erasmus, the greatest scholar of his day, lived in turn at each university.

At Oxford the famous Dutchman was Professor of Divinity: at Cambridge he lodged for three years at Queens' College, holding the appointment of Professor of Greek. He was not altogether enthralled by the charms of this river-side college which

H. FELTON

PUMP COURT, QUEENS' COLLEGE, CAMBRIDGE

Queens' College, founded in 1446, with its warm red brick buildings, has somehow more the air of a country home than the severe semblance of a seat of learning. Pump Court is often called Erasmus Quad after the writer.

Hall at Trinity College, Cambridge, for he granted a charter to this college in 1546. Trinity, now the largest and richest foundation in either university, began as an amalgamation of several of the older halls. In the Great Court, notable for two lovely gateways, is a seventeenth-century fountain at which the college bedmakers used to fill their pitchers in the days before bathrooms and water-taps.

At Cambridge, Queens' College and St. John's, both built of homely brick, and Jesus with its exquisite chapel, originally that of the nunnery on which the college was founded, are all redolent of the age of the Tudors. Trinity and St. John's at Oxford were founded on suppressed religious houses and endowed by men of the new nobility of commerce.

rears its walls sheer out of the water. Times were bad, and he disliked the college ale. From his rooms in the corner of the first court he wrote to a friend that " he had lived like a cockle shut up in a shell. . . . Cambridge was deserted because of the plague. The expense was intolerable, the profits not a brass farthing."

Among the pupils of Erasmus were John Tyndale and Miles Coverdale, translators of the Bible, and Hugh Latimer. In the ancient church of St. Edward, hard by King's College, Cambridge, Latimer, then attached to Clare, delivered two celebrated sermons in 1529. Twenty-six years later, Latimer and Ridley were burned at Oxford, where the Martyrs' Memorial now stands. Archbishop Cranmer, soon to follow them to the stake, watched from the tower of St. Michael's Church.

The trial of Cranmer took place at the University Church of Oxford, St. Mary's in the High Street, where for centuries the business affairs of the university were conducted. Its fourteenth-century tower, one of the city's landmarks, has looked down on many historic events.

When Archbishop Laud was brought to trial by the Puritans, the figure of the Virgin Mary over the door of St. Mary's was used as evidence of his " Popish " tendencies. John Henry Newman, later to become a Cardinal of the Roman Catholic Church, was Rector of St. Mary's from 1828 to 1843. In 1833 was delivered in this church Keble's " Assize Sermon," generally regarded as the starting point of the Oxford Movement.

The reign of Elizabeth was a happy period for both Oxford and Cambridge. The queen saw plays performed at Cambridge in King's College Chapel, and twice displayed her learning by joking with Oxford students in Latin.

In the year of the Armada was founded Sidney Sussex College, Cambridge. To it came some twenty-five years later one Oliver Cromwell, to find it a nursery of Puritanism. During the Civil War he returned to his university town,

this time to occupy it with troops. He prevented the colleges from presenting their valuable plate to King Charles, and restrained his over-zealous followers from doing too much damage.

Later a certain Mr. Dowsing was sent by the Puritans to examine the Cambridge chapels. In all except those of Emmanuel and Sidney Sussex he found statues to be broken, texts to be removed or " Papist " windows to be destroyed.

Cavalier Oxford

Oxford was strongly loyalist. It was full of Cavaliers : the king lodged at Christ Church, and was made free of the college plate. All Souls surrendered all but one piece.

Magdalen College, Oxford, the famous tower of which is said to have been designed by Wolsey, having fought for Charles I and sheltered Prince Rupert, later turned against James II when he attempted to make Anthony Farmer, a Roman Catholic, president of the college.

To Christ's College, Cambridge, came in 1625 John Milton, a youth of such beauty that he was nicknamed " The Lady of Christ's." While in residence he wrote an epitaph on Hobson the carrier, from whose methods arose the phrase

H. FELTON

ST. JOHN'S COLLEGE, OXFORD

A college for Cistercian monks, founded in 1437 and dedicated to St. Bernard, formerly occupied this site.
It was in the sixteenth century, however, that owing to the generosity of Sir Thomas White, twice Lord Mayor of
London, St. John's College was founded for the Study of Sacred Theology, Philosophy and the Good Arts.

"Hobson's Choice," and who had his stable where now St. Catharine's College stands.

In the books of Magdalene College it is recorded that in 1653 Samuel Pepys was rebuked for "having been scandalously over-served with drink ye night before." The diarist later presented his books to his old college, and the Pepysian Library at Magdalene treasures the manuscript of his famous diary, written in the quaint shorthand invented by its author.

If founding halted during the troubles of the seventeenth century, building went on. Queen's and Wadham at Oxford, Clare and St. Catharine's at Cambridge reflect the orderly dignity of the architecture of these days. Sir Christopher Wren left the mark of his genius on both universities ; some of Nevile's Court at Trinity, Cambridge, probably the bridge next the Bridge of Sighs at St. John's, the Sheldonian Theatre and parts of Queen's, Oxford, were designed by him.

During the eighteenth century the universities fell asleep. The professors, "old sinners who drank and dozed in the College Common Rooms," lived a life of leisured laziness, drawing their incomes from college livings they rarely if ever visited. The Fellow Commoners, for the most part wealthy scions of nobility, bedecked themselves in gold-trimmed gowns and velvet caps, and spent their time in fashionably elegant pursuits. Almost the only mental activity which interested them was politics. Oxford was strongly Tory, Cambridge equally strongly Whig.

In 1750, Gibbon, author of the *Decline and Fall of the Roman Empire*, wrote, "In the University of Oxford, the greater part of the public professors have for these many years given up even the pretence of teaching . . . the Fellows of Magdalen were decent, easy men who supinely enjoyed the gifts of the founder . . . from the toil of reading, or thinking, or writing, they had absolved their consciences."

Yet scholarship did not die. The poor student existed as a Sizar or Servitor, paid his college dues by waiting at table and performing menial duties, and furnished many a name of eminence. In the seventeenth century Sir Isaac Newton

H. FELTON

CORNER OF A FAMOUS QUAD

Christ Church, Oxford, known as the "House," was founded by Cardinal Wolsey and refounded in 1532 under the name of Henry VIII's College. The photograph shows a corner of the Tom Quad, the largest in Oxford, showing the entrance to the dining hall, one of the finest in the country.

was a Sizar of Trinity, Cambridge. Later he was made a fellow of his college—and in his rooms near the Great Gate did much of the work which led to his formulating the theory of gravity.

Forty years later Samuel Johnson, the great lexicographer, became a Servitor at Oxford, but was not able to complete his course owing to poverty. Unlike Gibbon, Johnson in later life defended his university. "That the rules are sometimes ill observed may be true," he said, "but there is nothing against the system."

Religious Movements

During the late eighteenth and early nineteenth centuries the life of the universities was shaken by three great religious movements. Methodism was born when Charles Wesley and a few friends, nicknamed the "Holy Club," began to meet together in Christ Church, Oxford. At Cambridge Charles Simeon of King's, Vicar of Holy Trinity Church from 1783 to 1836, inspired the Evangelical Movement in the Church of England. Oxford, always given to ritualism, was the birthplace of the Tractarian Movement of the 1830's, when Newman, Pusey and Keble attempted to revive the spirit of the medieval church in religious affairs.

Religious revival led to secular reform. During the nineteenth century Royal and Statutory Commissions discussed the affairs of both Oxford and Cambridge. Reforms instituted as a result of

VALENTINE

THE GREAT COURT, TRINITY COLLEGE, CAMBRIDGE

A corner of the spacious quadrangle or Great Court. On the left is King Edward's Gateway. This, the original college entrance, was built in 1427 and then stood near the Fountain. It was removed to its present position in the seventeenth century. On the right is the Great Gateway and between these is the College Chapel.

their reports left the universities as they stand today, in possession of all their historic dignity and rights, fulfilling the same destiny for centuries, but with a far wider range of studies, an efficient examination system, and as at their inception, a large proportion of poor students.

In 1858 Cambridge was thrown open to Nonconformists, and in 1871 all religious tests were abolished. In 1873 and 1875 respectively the famous women's colleges of Girton and Newnham were founded. In 1877 the university made provision for the study of natural science—and within a few years the number of its students had doubled.

Three years previously the Cavendish Laboratory, today the home of advanced physics and the scene of astonishing experiments on the atom and the electron, had been opened. In 1887 came the chemical laboratory, and the progress of Cambridge science has since been marked by such steps as the building of the Psychological Laboratory in 1913, and of the Biochemical and Biophysical Laboratory in 1922, the founding of the Sir William Dunn School of Biochemistry in 1924, and the opening of the Pathological Laboratory in 1928.

The scientific block in Downing Street is surrounded on all sides by centuries-old buildings, yet it does not seem out of place, for the magic of the university dwells not entirely in its age but rather in its serene and imperishable vitality. The spirit of Oxford or of Cambridge is not caught in books and lectures and examinations. It is discovered in a walk down High Street, Oxford, or King's Parade, Cambridge, in a stroll through the gardens of Magdalen, Oxford, or a leisurely drifting in a punt along the " backs " at Cambridge.

Wordsworth's Reverence

Rupert Brooke conveys that spirit in his poem on Grantchester, once a haunt of Byron. It is seen in the affection felt by so many great men for their university. Wordsworth sang almost reverently of Cambridge ; Newman loved Oxford all his life. When on his death-bed Gladstone received a message of sympathy from his old university. Much moved, the aged statesman exclaimed, " There is no expression of sympathy that I value more than that of . . . the God-fearing and God-sustaining University of Oxford."

EDGAR WARD

A WINTER'S TALE

Such scenes as the above may be witnessed on a winter's evening in countless English inns. This picture was taken at " The White Horse," Eaton Socon, the fine old inn on the Great North Road, originally built in the fifteenth century, but refronted about the middle of the eighteenth century. It was possibly the house at which Mr. Nicholas Nickleby and Mr. Squeers partook of a " good coach dinner " on their way north.

THE STORY OF THE INN

by MICHAEL GEELAN •

THE brotherhood of the open road, the lure of light and warmth and food, the precious gift of good companionship, and the magic of welcome—these are things that are inseparable from the story of the inn.

It is a long and captivating story, aglow with legend and tradition, winding its way through hundreds of years of history, through times that were brave and gay, and through times that were brutal, drab and menace-ridden. It is a very human story, very near and dear to the heart of the people and to the soul of these islands.

Seen through romantic eyes, the inn has endured as the sanctuary of the weary, the lonely and the hungry. It has been the rich man's haven and the poor man's solace. Time and time again it has harboured the oppressed and the hounded. Here kings and priests and politicians have found shelter. Here runaway lovers have known the benediction of a host's kindly heart. There lingers still around many of the inns of the countryside the rich and romantic atmosphere of rattling and jingling stage-coaches, of prancing horses and shouting ostlers, of halberd, pike and blunderbuss, of ruff and jerkin and powdered wig, of lace-capped serving maid, of candle-light glinting on fine old brass, of boar's head, sucking pig and cheese-cakes, of jovial, pot-bellied host, waiting, arms akimbo, at the ever-open door.

Through more prosaic eyes another picture is mirrored. A picture of dark and squalid taverns, hot-beds of plotting and corruption, the resorts of rogues and smugglers and highwaymen, where blood flowed with the bad wine, where the price of welcome was gold, and death the penalty of a word out of season. But even these sinister dens had their glamour. Their memories make

romance of a different order. Time has woven around them a halo of colour and story.

One aspect of the inns is that they do not decay into empty shells like the castles and the abbeys. They refuse to be merely relics of the past. The march of time cannot trample down their animation. They still serve. They are alive and vital and intensely human. They are next only to the home in permanency and intimacy, keeping pace with progress while still preserving the character and personality engraven on them by the years. Many have still their flagged courtyards and timbered gables ; Canterbury bells and candy-tuft, columbines and snapdragons, larkspurs and love-in-idleness glorify their walled-in gardens ; amid the cosiness within there is brass and pewter and copper, oaken beams of great age, old prints and horse-pistols hanging on walls as they have done for centuries, and sometimes dark, damp stairways leading to secret passages and mysterious chambers.

From pack-horse to stage-coach, from railway to charabanc, from floors of rushes, sand and sawdust to Turkey carpets, from cakes and ale to cocktails and cherries, the inns have gone, and go their happy, friendly way

"YE OLD FIGHTING COCKS" STEPHENSON
Built on the site of an abbey gateway and close to the Roman city of Verulamium, this octagonal-shaped inn claims to be one of the oldest in the country.

with a background of charm and tradition that helps to make the study of Romantic Britain more than ever fascinating.

Much of the literature of the land is closely linked with the inns. From Chaucer's time until the present day the great writers have found them places for pleasure, work and inspiration. Shakespeare himself was more than once in merry mood at the " Mermaid," and Ben Jonson drank at the " Devil," in Fleet Street. The name of Burns will be for ever associated with the " Tam o' Shanter," at Ayr. The interior of this inn remains much the same as it was in the days of the poet, and is a place of constant pilgrimage among Burns lovers. It was from here, it will be remembered, that Tam set out, "weel mounted on his grey mare, Meg," on his stormy, witch-haunted ride.

Doctor Johnson, who frequented the "Cheshire Cheese," in London, was equally at home in the hostelries of the countryside. At the inn at Burford Bridge, by the silent stream under Box Hill, poor Keats wrote some of his grandest poetry. At the "White Hart," at Whitchurch,

and other of his works there are incomparable pictures of pleasant and fascinating hostelries. Some of them, including the famous "Golden Cross," in Charing Cross, have since been demolished, but many still remain almost as he knew them.

The "Leather Bottle," at Cobham, Kent, displays a hanging sign bearing a portrait of Mr. Pickwick addressing the cronies of his club, with the inscription, "Dickens's Old Pickwick Leather Bottle." The inn's original sign hangs inside, in one of the quaintest little bars in England.

PHOTOCHROM

THE "CAT AND FIDDLE" AT HINTON ADMIRAL

This delightful wayside alehouse is only one of the many interesting inns to be found in Hampshire, and is redolent of an age when the small country inn was content to cater for a purely local need. With low-ceilinged rooms, and quaint windows looking out on the tree-shaded road, it retains its rustic atmosphere.

Newman began his *Lyra Apostolica*. The "Mortal Man," at Troutbeck, has memories of Wordsworth, Coleridge and Southey. Hazlitt nursed his genius and penned many of his greatest essays at the "Winterslow Hut" on the Exeter road. Part of *Robinson Crusoe* was written by Defoe at the "Rose and Crown," at Halifax. Pepys complained bitterly that the "Castle and Ball," at Hungerford, had been "modernized." At the "Royal," at Bideford, Kingsley wrote *Westward Ho!* Addison, Steele and Swift gave vent to their acidity at the "George and Vulture," near Lombard Street, in London. De Quincey writes of the "Lion," at Shrewsbury, in his *Opium Eater*.

Dickens, of course, was a great lover and student of the inns. He knew them in the flourishing coaching days—and in *Pickwick Papers*

The "low-roofed room," of which the great novelist wrote, is still preserved, complete with grandfather clock and antique furniture. Upstairs is the room in which he often slept.

Another inn that is steeped in the Dickensian tradition is the "Great White Horse," at Ipswich. Although the present building dates only from the eighteenth century, the site has been occupied by a hostelry of the same name since 1518. Dickens stayed there when, as a young reporter on the *Morning Chronicle*, he arrived to describe a Parliamentary election. The "Angel," at Bury St. Edmunds, has also been immortalized by Dickens. It was here that Mr. Pickwick heard to his alarm that Mrs. Bardell had issued her writ for breach of promise, here also that Sam Weller had his "halfpenny shower bath" under the pump.

Dickens, like many before and after him, was entranced by the names of the English inns. And they do, indeed, make a strange medley of fact and fancy. Who, with a spark of imagination, can fail to be thrilled and intrigued by such subtle and swinging titles as the " Case is Altered," the " Green Man," the " Quiet Wife," the " Cat and Bagpipes," the " Speech House," the " Rover's Return," the " Bell and Mackerel," or " You Might as Well."

Armorial Signs

Others, less romantic, are more easily explained. The " Lord Nelson," the " Shakespeare," the " Palmerston," the " British Grenadier "— these and their kind were obviously inspired by events and personalities in history, just as the many varieties of " Arms " owe their origin to the armorial bearings of the ground landlords, and the many " Lions," " Bulls " and " Feathers " to heraldic crests. Others, such as the " Wagon and Horses " and the " Pick and Shovel," were undoubtedly based on the trades and callings of the people.

The inn sign itself is often a jolly mixture of the quaint and picturesque. The pity is that so many of the really old and genuine have vanished, ruined by the ravages of the weather, stolen, sold to collectors, forgotten or lost. One of the most remarkable signs ever known in the history of the inn was that of the " White Hart," at Scole. It stretched right across the road and bore twenty-five life-size figures of men and animals fashioned in oak. It is said that its original cost was over £1,000.

The inn sign, of course, has emerged from the days when the people were, in the main, unable to read, when the surgeon-barber, for instance, displayed a striped pole suggestive of a bandaged limb, and traders generally used some manner of symbol to call attention to the nature of their business. The " Bush " was the first of the inn signs, an acceptable explanation being that this

PHOTOCHROM

AN ORNATE ELIZABETHAN INN

The Feathers Inn, a beautiful black and white timbered building with its exquisitely-carved front and fine moulded plaster ceiling is one of the architectural glories of the lovely Welsh border town of Ludlow. Granted a licence in 1521, this inn continues to offer a welcome to the wayfarer.

represented a clump of vine-leaves symbolical of Bacchus.

How old are the oldest existing inns? Many claims are made, but some are so ancient in their origin that documentary evidence is practically non-existent. The " Fountain," at Canterbury, however, must be one of the oldest of all, for inscribed in one of the first visitor's books ever known is the following glowing testimonial from a German visitor—an ambassador—who stayed there in 1129 : " The inns of England are the best in Europe, those in Canterbury are the best in England, and the ' Fountain,' in which I am now lodged as handsomely as I were in a king's palace, the best in Canterbury."

Dating back to the thirteenth century are such

W. F. TAYLOR

THE "SONDES ARMS," ROCKINGHAM

This unpretentious but charming hotel is situated at the foot of a hill about nine miles from Market Harborough, in the middle of what was once the Forest of Rockingham. In front of it is a fragment of the old market cross. Standing on the height above it is an historic castle, parts of which date from the thirteenth century.

EDGAR WARD

A FAMOUS INN OF SOMERSET

This beautiful, half-timbered inn, the " George," at Norton St. Philip, erected early in the fifteenth century, has witnessed many historic scenes. The Duke of Monmouth slept there shortly before the fateful Battle of Sedgemoor. While there he was fired at by a man hoping to gain the £1,000 reward on the Duke's head.

inns as the " George and Dragon," at Speldhurst, the " Angel," at Blyth, and the " Maid's Head," Norwich. The fourteenth century knew the " Green Man," Erdington, the " George," Salisbury, the " Seven Stars," Manchester, and the " Crown," Chiddingfold. From the days of the fifteenth century date hostelries of such age and distinction as the " New Inn," Gloucester, the " Spread Eagle," Midhurst, the " King's Head," Aylesbury, the " Red Lion," Colchester, and the " George," Glastonbury, and from the sixteenth century the " George," Southwark, the " Bull," Long Melford, and the " George," Winchcombe. All of these retain some part, however modest, of their antiquity.

One thing is certain : the inn began with the roads. The Romans knew its hospitality. Next came the Saxon ale-houses, probably crude timber buildings of which no trace remains. That they did exist, however, is a certainty, for there is record of the Saxon rulers making orders for their proper conduct between the years A.D. 600 and 730.

In the early days of travel personages of rank, when moving from place to place, relied upon the hospitality of friendly lords, or arrogantly commandeered the cleanest and most comfortable houses in the towns or villages through which they passed. Those with a less exalted position in life were dependent for food and shelter upon religious establishments which considered it a bounden duty to succour the traveller. To this day such hostels still exist, at least in name. At the " Hospital of St. Cross," outside Winchester, for instance, the traveller may still ask for the " Wayfarer's Dole "—a piece of bread and a drink of beer.

Religious Hostels

As more and more roads were built, as travel increased and there was an unceasing demand for hospitality, a change in the system was inevitable. Many of the religious hostels became inns, and have remained as such ever since. Guest houses which had been erected by lords and gentry underwent a similar transformation. So did the common ale-houses. Thus, in its true and proper sense, was the inn business born.

They were far from elegant, these early inns, and often far from clean. Rough mattress beds

W. F. TAYLOR

THE GALLERIED YARD OF THE "GEORGE" AT HUNTINGDON

When the first inn was erected on this site no one can say. The present edifice modestly displays a mid-Victorian front, but behind this is hidden a courtyard surrounded by buildings which Oliver Cromwell, who lived nearby, must have known as a boy, and the records tell us that the house was even then no longer young.

EDGAR WARD

GALLERY OF THE "BULL" AT LONG MELFORD

For a century prior to 1935, this inn presented a stolid Georgian front to the pretty Suffolk village in which it stands, but in that year a nine-inch brick wall was pulled down revealing a half-timbered façade dating from the fifteenth century. It possesses some noteworthy internal features including exquisitely-carved oak beams, an ancient hearthplace and this picturesque gallery with its uneven roof and long line of windows.

were laid on rush-strewn floors, and it was an ambitious bill of fare that went much beyond bread, beer and soup, and sometimes a little fish. Still, they were cheap. A bed in 1331, for instance, cost only a halfpenny, and good-class travelling expenses would not much exceed a shilling a day for food and accommodation.

Early steps were taken to guard the traveller against imposition; in fact, in 1349, in the reign of Edward III—a very capable administrator as well as a dauntless warrior—a law was passed whereby the inn-keeper who overcharged a guest could be ordered to repay double the amount he had extracted. On the whole, however, the growth of competition had the result, then as now, of keeping prices within much more reasonable limits.

Corruption

In those days, any one could open and conduct an inn, subject only to the casual control of the local justices, whose duty it was to stamp out flagrant abuses. Not until 1550 did the licensing system begin to function, and ever since the inn-keeper has been hedged around by a diversity of laws and restrictions, many of which have not failed to evoke criticism and dislike through the years.

In the days of Elizabeth and James I " mine host " was the victim of a brazen and insidious swindle. Those entrusted with the duty of granting licences and collecting the licensing dues contrived to make a handsome profit for themselves. They fixed their own fees, withheld a considerable percentage of their collections from the State and demanded from the inn-keepers what would be known today as " protection " money. One of these scoundrels, Sir Giles Overreach, did literally overreach himself, with the result that he was brought to the Bar of the House of Commons, deprived of his knighthood and banished.

There was a vast difference in the sixteenth century, between the inn and the tavern. The keeper of the first was prohibited from allowing his house to be used essentially as a drinking place, and the keeper of the second from providing sleeping accommodation. But there were many law breakers who risked severe penalties to gain guilty profits. Many an inn had its " bottle parties " long into the night, and many a tavern sheltered low company, and was the scene of dark plottings for robbery and even murder. Those who may rail at that survival of the war-days, " Dora," will be amused to know, by the way, that the closing hour for intoxicating liquor in those days was eight o'clock in the winter and nine o'clock in the summer.

By the seventeenth century both the inn and the tavern had developed on sound and pleasant lines. Stern supervision was exercised. Offenders were flogged and imprisoned. As a result, most of the unlicensed houses and thieves dens —on the highways, at any rate—were stamped out, and there evolved a splendid code of conduct and hospitality for hosts.

For nearly three hundred years after they were licensed the inns remained without bars or dining-rooms. The " quality " dined and wined in splendid— more or less—privacy, or joined the host and other travellers at a common table. The servants and the common people made the

STEPHENSON

THE "FOX AND HOUNDS," BARLEY

This remarkable sign spans the Old North Road in a Hertfordshire village three miles south-west of Royston. Note also the old-fashioned lantern.

best of things in the kitchen, although, in some ways, this was the most pleasant and friendly place in the house.

The golden age of the inn came with the coaching days. With the beginning of the nineteenth century the inn-keeper assumed a greater dignity and importance. Inns won new reputations for courtesy and service. Both food and accommodation improved. In towns and villages everywhere, as well as on the open road, the inn became a hub of activity by day and by night. The highest in the land stayed there. Lord and squire and clergy were habitués. The bar, the coffee-room and the dining-room were born, and by 1850 the hotel idea was taking shape. Business impetus brought about the Commercial Hotel and the coming of the railroad the " Railway Tavern." These developments were a sorry and crippling blow at the old-time inn, and the wonder is that so many survived it at all. It was generally believed that the railway train would destroy road travel for ever, yet the present century has witnessed a revival of staggering dimensions. The inn is reborn.

What an amazing part the licensed house has played in the public and private lives of the people. Even the modern theatre, with its balconies and boxes, has been modelled on that early courtyard in which strolling players won applause and pennies from the gentry seated at their bedroom windows. The inn has been used as a court for trials and inquests, even as a prison. Politicians have made it their headquarters, and prize-fighters their training camp. To commercial travellers it has been a second home. Even today it is a centre of sporting and social activity, from darts to pigeon racing, from dancing to the slate and loan club. The motorist, the cyclist and the walker alike seek out the best of them for food and shelter.

The stories that can be told of the inns are legion. They come from the forests and the mountains and the lonely sea coasts, from placid villages and thriving cities. There are stories of kings and princes, merchants and paupers, cut-throats and knights-at-arms, scholars and vagabonds. One and all, they mirror the romance that is history.

There is the " Bell," at Barnby Moor, where Dick Turpin is said to have halted to water Black Bess on his notorious ride to York. There is the old Pilchard Inn, on Burgh Island, dating back to 1395, where Tom Crocker, smuggler and pirate, made his headquarters and plotted many a desperate escapade. In the " Pilchard " you can see Crocker's own skull-and-crossbones flag, said to be the only genuine pirate's emblem in existence. A curious feature of this now modern inn is that the timbers of a famous old wooden ship of the line, H.M.S. *Ganges*, have been incorporated into its fabric.

Some Curious Inns

Another hostelry which once echoed with the oaths and hoarse laughter of pirates and smugglers is the old " Lobster Smack," on Canvey Island, now a favourite rendezvous of yachtsmen from Southend and visitors from London. Almost hidden behind a sea wall, with low-beamed ceilings, it is one of the most glorious examples of its kind in the land.

The " Castle," at Taunton is one of the most curious inns in the west. It is actually a real castle, dating back to Norman times, complete

A. DURRANT

THE "MERMAID," RYE

Not least of the architectural treasures of the ancient Cinque Port of Rye is this sixteenth-century inn, situated in a narrow, cobbled street of picturesque red-roofed houses. The " Mermaid," with its gables and timbered walls, is reckoned among the finest specimens of the medieval domestic style in the country.

EDGAR WARD

COURTYARD OF AN OLD COACHING INN

In the old coaching days the courtyard was an essential feature of the inns, and was a scene of bustle and strife when the coach arrived and the horses were changed while the weary passengers sought refreshment, and an opportunity to stretch their cramped limbs. The photograph shows the courtyard of the " Greyhound," at Wincanton, in Somerset, a little town on one of the routes from London to Exeter.

W. F. TAYLOR

AN EXMOOR INN

The " Royal Oak," a rambling old thatched inn, is charmingly situated in the village of Winsford on the River Exe. Winsford, which boasts seven bridges, is a favourite haunt of anglers.

with massive stone walls, battlements, great gate-house and arrow slots. The skill with which this medieval fortress has been converted into an up-to-date hotel must really be seen to be believed.

The names of great men and women and of colourful characters in history are inseparable from the story of the inn. For two hundred and fifty years the " George," at Portsmouth, has been linked with the heroes of naval history. Nelson often stayed there. It was here that he spent his last hours ashore before joining his flagship, the *Victory*, on the eve of Trafalgar. He arrived at six o'clock in the evening, but the public would not let their idol rest until he had shown himself and spoken from an upstair window. Later, when he attempted to escape unnoticed by the back door, he was again mobbed. The shouting throng surged around him, " pressing forward," as Southey tells us, " to obtain sight of his face : many were in tears, and many knelt down before him and blessed

him as he passed." Thus, through the back door of an English inn, through an avenue of English patriots, Nelson went forth to his last encounter.

The " George " is a delightful old house. It has charming two-storey bow windows, and a jumble of out-buildings telling of the coaching days. Inside there is a maze of fascinating stairways, a coffee-room hung with old prints of naval battles and heroes, cellars with cat doors, and a kitchen with an old bake oven.

At the " Talbot," Oundle, there is a staircase which was once a part of Fotheringhay Castle, and is believed to have been trodden by Mary Stuart. Jerome K. Jerome, author of the unforgettable *Three Men in a Boat*, was a lover of the " Bull," at Sonning. It is one of the most picturesque inns in the country, a favourite supper haunt of celebrities.

Death Warrant of a Duke

In 1483, in a room at the " Angel," Grantham, Richard III—who apparently preferred an inn to a palace—signed the death warrant of the Duke of Buckingham. The " Angel " is one of the most spectacular houses on the Great North Road. Its fine stone front dates from the Wars of the Roses, and the gateway is at least a century older. There is a legend that in 1213—two years before the signing of Magna Charta—King John and his nobles rested there. There is also a legend of comedy. In 1706, it is said, the landlord, Michael Soloman, left in his will a legacy of £2 to be paid for the preaching of an annual sermon against drunkenness each Michaelmas Day. And it is still preached !

The " Angel " is one of the three remaining medieval hostels in England, and has been a landmark to millions of travellers along the Great North Road. During the eighteenth century it became a great coaching station. The Royal Mail both to and from London pulled up at the famous fourteenth-century archway, and travellers took their refreshment, as they still do today, in that same room which witnessed the signing of the Duke of Buckingham's death warrant. The rooms below the King's Room, or to give it its modern title, Coffee Room, are distinguished by carved stone ceilings over the windows.

It was from the " Blue Boar," Leicester, that Richard left to die on Bosworth Field, where he fought to the end. At the "Greyhound," Maidenhead, Charles I saw his children for the last time before his execution. In striking contrast was the first meeting, almost a furtive one, of Henry VIII and Anne of Cleves—the "mare of Flanders"—at the "Crown," Rochester. It was then, probably, if he ever did say it, that Henry, taking a long, painful look at this queer woman, exclaimed, "The things I've done for England!"

Rich in sporting associations is the "George," at Crawley, near Copthorne Common and Crawley Downs, the scenes of some of the greatest prize fights in history. When the Prince Regent had popularized Brighton, as many as fifty coaches changed horses within the space of twenty-four hours. Once, when her carriage broke down, the young Queen Victoria, slender and demure, was an unexpected guest, and the royal crest now adorns the hotel staircase. Built from fine old timbers from surrounding forests, the "George" has existed since at least 1615. Even the bathroom and billiard-room are richly panelled. The huge, lofty coffee-room was originally built as an assembly room, complete with stage.

A Famous Fight

Conan Doyle immortalized this famous hotel in his novel *Rodney Stone*. It was at the "George" that Belcher trained Boy Jim for the fight with Crab Wilson on Crawley Down. Crowds came from far and wide to see that contest, and horsemen, vehicles and pedestrians filled the roads. "At Kimberham Bridge the carriage lamps were all lit and it was wonderful, as the road curved downward before us, to see this writhing serpent with the golden scales crawling before us in the darkness. And then at last we saw the formless mass of the huge Crawley elm looming before us in the gloom . . . and the high front of the old George Inn glowing from every door, and pane, and crevice in honour of the noble company who were to sleep within that night."

From the "Red Lion," Colchester, one of the pioneer stage-coaches started as early as in 1756, when one James Unwin advertised that ". . . on Tuesday, 9th March, he sets out from the Red Lion Inn, Colchester, with a stage cart and able horses to be at the Bull Inn, Leadenhall Street, London, on Wednesday, one o'clock," which was exceptionally speedy travel for a wheeled vehicle in those days.

Some idea of the spirit of hospitality—and the human appetite—of the "good old days" is afforded by the following hand-written notice which hangs in the "White Horse," Romsey :

"This day's Bill of Fare will contain
Turbot and Fried Soles, Lobster sauce
Leg of Mutton. 6 Tooth wether
Swanston Lea Lamb and Sparagrass
Grass Fed Beef
And all varieties to satisfy
Inner man."

W. F. TAYLOR

AN OLD GABLED INN

"The Chequers," at Tonbridge, is a reminder of how the Elizabethan craftsmen designed their houses, and is luckily not the only one of its kind in this old Kentish town on the Medway.

The massive timber work in this ancient house is very outstanding, and there is not much doubt that the "White Horse," as an inn, dates back to at least the early sixteenth century, an earlier building having been pulled down in the time of Henry VII.

It is impossible, within the compass of a single article, to explore anything but the fringe of those "realms of gold" that are the "inn-" land. Those hostelries that are mentioned can be picked only at random. Many, many more that are worthy of a place here, must be passed by. It is astounding how many inns there are abounding in romance, beauty and story.

There is the "King's Head," at Chigwell, Essex, which Dickens described as "delicious." It has "more gable-ends than a lazy man would

WALTER SCOTT

ENGLAND'S HIGHEST INN
From the hamlet of Keld at the head of Swaledale, in Yorkshire, a narrow moorland road winds over the bare desolate hills of the Pennines.   At the highest point of the road, 1,732 feet above sea level, there stands a solitary unpretentious whitewashed house.   This is Tan Hill, the highest licensed house in England.

STEPHENSON

AN OLD SURREY HOSTELRY
Opposite the church in the charming Surrey village of Witley, stands the White Hart Inn, an ancient hostelry with tiled roof and tile-hung walls typical of local architecture.   Many famous artists and writers have lived in the neighbourhood, including the painters J. C. Hook and Birkett Foster and the author of " Mill on the Floss " who dwelt at Witley Heights.   In the " White Hart " may still be seen " George Eliot's Corner."

TRUST HOUSES, LTD.

THE "BLACK SWAN" AT HELMSLEY

In the spacious Market Place of the little Yorkshire town of Helmsley stands the Black Swan Hotel, its bold sign of a silhouetted swan being at once noticeable. From its quaint interior and old beams it is evidently an ancient establishment. In the lounge are some fine old pewter plates and dishes and some curious lead weights.

care to count on a sunny day . . . over-hanging storeys, drowsy little panes of glass, and front bulging out and projecting over the pathway." It is old enough for the Court of Attachments to have been held there in 1713. "Very good diet, but very dear," wrote Pepys, after he had spent a night at the "Old George," Salisbury. Here Cromwell stayed on his way to join his army. The records of the "Old George" show that in 1453 a bay window was added at a cost of twenty shillings! The "Angel," at Henley-on-Thames, was originally a monastic rest-house for travellers, and the "Bear and Billet," at Chester, with its half-timbered frontage, richly carved woodwork and leaded windows—it was built in 1664—was once the private mansion of the Earls of Shrewsbury.

A Ponderous Roof

Believe it or not, but there are those who declare that it was at the "Star," Alfriston, on the South Downs, that King Alfred burned the cakes! It is a fine old house, one of its most curious characteristics being that it is roofed with slabs of stone, some of them weighing nearly two hundredweight. In the ballroom of the "White Lion," at Eye, Suffolk, you will find the musician's gallery that is a memory of the old Assembly Hall. Of the "White Lion" it was written a hundred years ago that "dinner was provided at 2s. 6d. a head, including as much wine and punch as each man could swallow." In a loft over the coaching stables at the "Ship," Alveston, there are two ancient machines, an oat-crusher and a bean-kibbler, used to prepare fodder for the coaching horses. The cellars of this inn were undoubtedly used by smugglers.

Standing in solitude in the very centre of the Forest of Dean is one of the most curious inns in England. It is set at the junction of two roads, one of which is of Roman origin and covers a site whereon the ancient Foresters of Dean met to settle their disputes. The name of this inn is "Speech House," and to this day it perpetuates the reason for which it was built some 250 years ago in the reign of Charles II, for the Forest Courts are held there ten times a year.

The meetings are held in the dining-room or courtroom, which contains a raised dais with a railed-off bench for the officers of the court. A notice states when the "Court of Attachment," as it is termed, "will be holden in the Speech House in the said forest at half-past three in the afternoon."

Among the cellars below is to be found a tiny room said to be a cell for offenders against the law, while in an upstairs room a strange octagonal post is claimed to be a whipping post.

There is no end to this story. Windows with sheets of horn in place of glass; bunk-holes for the political refugees of long ago; beer-warmers; an inn where no one can be served more than once each half-hour; a hostelry hollowed out of the solid rock; underground rooms and passages; Roman paving and Dutch tiles—there is surprise and mystery and romance to be experienced by all who choose to explore the inns of other days with which Britain is so richly endowed.

VIOLET BANKS

THE FAMOUS FORTH BRIDGE

By this great feat of engineering, Edinburgh gained a more direct link with north-eastern Scotland. Spanning the Firth of Forth, it was opened in 1890. With the approaches, the total length of the bridge is nearly 1½ miles. The three huge cantilevers provide two main spans of 1,710 feet each and two side spans of 690 feet. The railway runs 157 feet above the river and the top of the bridge is 361 feet above high-water level.

THE CHARM OF EDINBURGH

by ALASDAIR ALPIN MacGREGOR

IF there be in the world any city other than Jerusalem that men might describe as " beautiful for situation," that city surely is Edinburgh, the Scottish capital—a romantic city which has urged the pen of many a poet and ballad-writer; a city through the streets of which innumerable writers have followed the history of an ancient and romantic kingdom; a city along whose flagstoned wynds and closes pass the ghosts of kings and queens, of princes and noblemen, and of the most illustrious of the ordinary common folk, who did so much to make Scotland great.

" By universal judgment," remarked Sir Henry Campbell-Bannerman, " Edinburgh has a place, possibly the highest place, in the small group of the great towns of Europe conspicuous for romance and physical charm." By every Scotsman who knows her, she is regarded as the most picturesque and romantic city in the world — a reputation duly admitted by travellers from every part of the globe. Like Rome, she is a city built on seven hills. Northward, these hills sweep down toward Leith, her ancient seaport, by the shores of the Firth of Forth. Her background is that fine range of green hills known as the Pentlands, a name familiar to all readers and lovers of Robert Louis Stevenson, who spent much of his childhood in the secluded community of Swanston, lying in the shadow of their northern range.

Edinburgh is dominated by that great volcanic mass known as the Castle Rock, which is crowned by the castle itself, and is so precipitous on three sides that, throughout the centuries of warfare between England and Scotland, its summit remained inaccessible to attacking forces except on two occasions.

It is approached by the spacious Esplanade, upon which many of Scotland's great ones were judicially murdered during the Middle Ages. In July, 1538, Lady Jane Douglas, having been convicted of attempting to encompass the king's death, was there consigned to the flames in the presence of her husband and her son.

But not only the well-born and the once-powerful suffered : numerous poor women suspected of being witches were burned there at the stake. So late as the middle of the seventeenth century this custom was still in vogue; and in 1659 five women were brutally done to death for " dancing with the devil."

From the strictly legal point of view the Esplanade is part of Nova Scotia in Canada : it was declared to be so in the reign of Charles I in order that Nova Scotian baronets created in Scotland might be able to " take seisin " of their new territories. It is now adorned with military monuments, including an equestrian statue of Earl Haig.

Within the 15 feet thick walls of the State

D. MCLEISH

JOHN KNOX'S HOUSE

This old building in the Canongate contains many relics of the great reformer. In one room he is said to have worked until shortly before his death. Before Knox's days the house is believed to have been occupied by the last Abbot of Dunfermline.

VALENTINE

THE CANONGATE, TOLBOOTH

In the Canongate, once a fashionable quarter of Edinburgh, stands the Tolbooth. Built in a French style and dating from 1591, it served as a jail and courthouse. There the "Bailies of the Canongate" delivered their verdicts, and it was also a meeting place for the councillors of the burgh.

the short and narrow street known as the Castle Hill, on the left of which stands the quaint cluster of buildings called Ramsay Gardens, built on the site of Allan Ramsay's country house, and on the right of which is situated the south-west house of Castle Hill. Embedded in the masonry of the latter is a cannon ball which was fired from the castle's bastions when, in 1745, Prince Charles Edward's arrival in the city sent a shudder through the Hanoverians and their garrison. Immediately below lies the town house of the Duchess of Gordon, a house which, at a later date, came into the possession of the Bairds of Newbyth. The mother of Sir David Baird, who distinguished himself at Seringapatan, in India, was living here when the news was brought to her that her son was one of the many prisoners chained two-and-two in the gaol at Mysore. "God help the chiel'," she exclaimed, "that's chained tae oor Davie."

St. Giles's Cathedral

After the castle, perhaps the two best-known objects of romantic Edinburgh are St. Giles's Cathedral and Holyrood Palace, the former standing by the Parliament Buildings and the Municipal Offices on the ancient High Street, not very far from the castle itself, the latter situated on level ground at the foot of the Royal Mile, overshadowed by the great igneous masses of Arthur's Seat and the Salisbury Crags. Although to Englishmen, accustomed to cathedrals of great size and extravagance, St. Giles's may appear diminutive, and even unimportant, it must not be forgotten that it is the stage upon which many dramatic scenes in the troublous religious history of a nation, continually at variance on matters spiritual, were enacted. Moreover, few possessing any idea of romantic beauty could fail to be inspired by the graceful lantern tower with its airy crown of stone. Though we have no authentic record of the date at which it was founded, we do know that in the year A.D. 854

Prison, over the Portcullis Gate more than one Scottish nobleman suffered the agonies of imprisonment. It is sometimes known as Argyll's Tower, since the two Covenanting members of that family languished there before going to face the headsman. The legend-shrouded figure of the noble Montrose also darkened its grim portals.

The Citadel, 384 feet above sea level, is on the site of the palace of Malcolm Canmore, the obstinate defier of England's William Rufus. To Canmore's queen the Castle owes St. Margaret's Chapel, a very fine Early Norman edifice.

The view from the castle itself is uncommonly picturesque and romantic. Looking eastward, and downhill, across the Esplanade, one sees

D. MCLEISH

EDINBURGH'S FAMOUS THOROUGHFARE

Often spoken of as the finest thoroughfare in Europe, Princes Street, running from Shandwick Place to the Register House, is about a mile long. One side is lined with municipal buildings, shops and restaurants while the other is flanked by laid-out gardens from which a fine view of the Castle may be obtained.

VIOLET BANKS

WINTER OVER THE CITY

This view from the castle ramparts shows the spire of St. Giles's Cathedral, between Tolbooth and Greyfriars. Beneath its shade are buried the regent Moray, Napier of Merchiston, the Marquess of Montrose and John Knox. Until recently the General Assembly of the Church of Scotland was held in Tolbooth Church.

R.B.—G

DIXON-SCOTT

EDINBURGH CASTLE FROM THE GRASSMARKET

On this rock, Edwin, the seventh-century king of Northumbria, probably had a fortress. Several times the site was held by the English. Bruce dismantled the castle, but Edward III, of England restored it in 1337.

minor alterations were carried out a few years later. Finally, between 1871 and 1883, very great improvements were made, so that the edifice now looks much as it did in pre-Reformation times. The choir (restored in 1873) is a fine example of the fifteenth-century architecture.

A Lively Episode

Of all the episodes associated with this historic and romantic pile, perhaps the one that sticks most tenaciously in the mind of the Scottish schoolboy is that which describes how, on the introduction of Laud's Prayer Book, on July 23, 1637, an old Edinburgh apple-wife named Jenny Geddes interrupted Dean Hannay during the service by seizing her stool and pitching it at his head, exclaiming in so doing : " Out, thou false thief : Dost thou say Mass at my lug ? " History records that the Dean " dooked " just in time, and thus escaped injury. Among the many interesting features of the interior of the cathedral is a brass tablet commemorating Jenny Geddes's act.

In the west wall of the cathedral there is a bronze memorial of Robert Louis Stevenson, to which is added *Requiem*, that haunting poem written by him in warm, Pacific seas, when pining for Edinburgh and the Pentland Hills of Home :

" Under the wide and starry sky,
Dig the grave and let me lie :
Glad did I live and gladly die ;
And I lay me down with a will.
This be the verse you grave for me,
' Here he lies where he longed to be :
Home is the sailor, home from the sea,
And the hunter home from the hill.' "

The author of *Treasure Island* was born at 8, Howard Place, in the old town of Edinburgh. The house itself has now been converted into a museum containing much of literary and romantic interest to those who know Scotland, and perhaps Edinburgh in particular. Among the

there stood upon this very site an ancient place of worship, serving the people of " Edwin's burg," attached to Lindisfarne, and dedicated to the " guid Sanct Geille."

With the Reformation—which, as everyone knows, went to much greater lengths in Scotland than in England—much of the pristine glory of St. Giles's Cathedral departed ; and for well-nigh two hundred years it stood in a forlorn and ruinous condition.

In 1829 the work of " restoration " was begun by an architect who must have lacked all feeling for the beauty of the ancient pile, since he destroyed some of its finest features. Further

VIOLET BANKS

ST. GILES'S CATHEDRAL, EDINBURGH

This, the oldest church in the city, was erected in the twelfth century and partly rebuilt after a fire in 1385. It has experienced many vicissitudes. After the Reformation it lost its forty-four altars and a statue of St. Giles was removed and thrown into the Nor' Loch. During the sixteenth century it was at one and the same time a court of justice, a prison, a school, a workshop, the town clerk's office and a storehouse for the gallows.

exhibits is a fragment of oak that once formed part of the Spanish galleon, *Florida*, lying deep at the bottom of Tobermory Bay. This fragment recalls *The Merry Men*, Stevenson's fascinating story of the storm-kelpies haunting that romantic tideway, the Sound of Mull.

The phrase, romantic Edinburgh, immediately conjures up pictures of her castle, of St. Giles's, of the High Street, which is called the Royal Mile, and, not least, the Palace of Holyrood. From the days of Robert the Bruce, and to all intents and purposes until the Parliamentary

It included the Duchess of Argyll, the Master of the Household, and a few others, not forgetting, of course, Rizzio. As dusk fell, a band of armed men closed in upon Holyrood, since a plot had been arranged between the Earls of Ruthven and Morton and others to murder the queen's favourite. As the guests sat talking and drinking at the supper table, Darnley and his accomplices crept up the narrow staircase leading to the queen's boudoir, where they seized Rizzio. Out of the boudoir they dragged him, and stabbed him to death. The warm body of their

VIOLET BANKS

PANORAMA OF EDINBURGH

From the castle ramparts a fine view is obtained of the city which is declared to be the most beautiful and picturesque in these islands. In the foreground, over the railway line, is the National Gallery, left of which is the Royal Scottish Academy. The isolated Gothic spire is the Scott memorial in Princes Street Gardens.

Union with England in 1707, Holyrood remained the intimate residence of the Stewart kings and their courts. Some were born here: others crowned, married, or buried within its walls. And it was to this palace that, as a symbol of the fact that the Scottish monarch had become King of England, Sir Robert Carey brought a ring for the finger of King James VI.

But of all the romantic associations of this hallowed and storied place, none has the poignancy of those that concern the hapless Mary Queen of Scots.

In one of the several apartments shown to visitors, there occurred on March 9, 1566, a tragedy that had repercussions more serious than were ever anticipated at the time. A little supper party had assembled in the queen's apartments.

victim they are believed to have cast down at the door of the apartment where now may be seen a brass tablet let into the floor. Later Rizzio's corpse was carried downstairs and into Holyrood Abbey. It is said to have been interred there, under the last step. Before long, the burghers and citizens of Edinburgh were clamouring outside the walls of Holyrood, intent on vengeance for their sorrowing queen. Matters were not to be permitted to rest there, however: within a year, Darnley himself was killed in the Provost's House at the fateful Kirk-o'-Field.

Whereas it cannot be proved that Mary herself had anything to do with the planning of this murder, there seems every justification for assuming that she knew her husband's life was in danger. Three months after Darnley's death, and in the very chapel at Holyrood, in which she had married him in 1565, she took Bothwell as her husband.

One of the most romantic apartments visitors to Edinburgh are permitted to see is Queen Mary's bedroom at the Palace of Holyrood, with the door leading to the supper-room just as it was on that evening of ill omen.

In the time of Mary Queen of Scots, Edinburgh and its environs became very French. Evidences of Mary's association with France, and of her employment of French people about her court, are to be found in such names as Picardy Place. Then, on the outskirts of the city, there is a small village called Burdiehouse, which is simply a corruption of Bordeaux House. Here resided many of Mary's French vassals. At this period, sanitation was so little known in Edinburgh that it was customary for its citizens to dispose of their slops and garbage by flinging them out of their windows into the gutters below. This ancient custom was so well established at the time when French influence in Edinburgh was at its zenith, that it gave rise to the familiar street cry, Gardyloo, which is simply a corruption of the French phrase *Gardez l'eau*— mind the water !

Though perhaps one of Edinburgh's least romantic streets, because of its comparative newness, Princes Street is claimed to be one of the finest public thoroughfares in the world. View it from the Castle Rock, or from the slopes of the Mound, backed by the gables and spires of much of the Old Town, with the Firth of Forth

A FAMOUS ALLEY

W. F. TAYLOR

Typical of Edinburgh's many narrow alleys is Advocates' Close, seen above, which gained its name from Sir James Stewart of Goodtrees, who was Lord Advocate of Scotland from 1692-1713.

and the Hills of Fife beyond, bordered by its exquisite gardens and its fine monuments, balanced so beautifully by the columns of the Scottish National Gallery, and you readily will realize how Edinburgh won the name, " the modern Athens." Most conspicuous among the many monuments in Princes Street Gardens is that to Sir Walter Scott—a fitting tribute to that giant among Scotland's writers of romance.

It was during the latter half of the eighteenth century, and the opening years of the nineteenth, that there took place in Edinburgh the intellectual revival that did so much to win for her a place among the most celebrated cities in the world. In those days her roofs gave shelter to such men as Smollett, David Hume, Lord Elibank, Dr. Gregory, James Boswell, Adam Ferguson, Adam Smith, Jeffrey, Brougham, and the immortal Sir Walter. We must not fail to mention also two great women, Lady Anne Lindsay, who wrote that beautiful song, *Auld Robin Gray*; and Jean Elliot who, reflecting on the fate that, on Flodden Field, befell the chivalry of Scotland in 1513, wrote her ballad *Flowers o' the Forest*, of imperishable memory and which, played at times of sadness, is one of the most heart-rending melodies.

Edinburgh's peculiar reputation is in no small measure due to Sir Walter Scott. She has had her vicissitudes—her political ups and downs ; but in the pages of the Wizard of the North her citizens must ever remain the descendants of an imaginative and a virile race, heritors of a brave and romantic past.

DIXON-SCOTT

THE LONG MAN OF WILMINGTON

Carved in the chalk of the Sussex Downs near Wilmington is this huge figure measuring 230 feet from head to toes. Once thought to be the work of the monks of a nearby priory, it is now considered of a much greater antiquity. It has also been suggested it represents a sun god pushing open the doors of darkness.

SOME ANCIENT LANDMARKS

by HAROLD SHELTON

HAVE you ever travelled along the little road which hugs the northern slopes of the Berkshire Downs westward of Wantage? If you have not, you have missed one of England's most romantic journeys. The road drops into a wooded combe, then rises again to a low shelf which overlooks the fertile Vale of the White Horse, for all the world like a chessboard of trim hedge and cultivated field, dotted with tiny copses and a wealth of hedgerow timber. On the other hand the abrupt face of the downs rises imminently to the long line of smooth green hills which stretch east and west as far as eye can reach.

A mile or two farther along the road a fantastic scar appears near the summit of the hill where the ridge is clearly defined against the skyline. As we proceed the scar is transformed into the shape of a galloping horse, elongated and attenuated as though it were the very spirit of motion. This, the famous White Horse of Uffington, is one of the ancient but still undated hill figures of England, about which much has been written of late years, but yet so little is actually known.

Who were the men who fashioned this gigantic figure and for what purpose? Tradition, as ever, is a deceiving wench. It relates that the horse is a monument to King Alfred, who was certainly born at Wantage. It says that the great Battle of Ashdown, in A.D. 871, when the Danes were utterly defeated was fought somewhere in this neighbourhood, whereupon Alfred commanded that a figure of himself upon his charger should be cut in the chalk downs as a permanent memorial of the victory.

If only there were the figure of a man upon the horse we might with greater confidence accept tradition, but there is not the slightest evidence to support it. Rather everything tends to other views. It is more likely that Alfred's horse belongs to the dim period in Britain's prehistory.

There are other facts to support the theory. Along the top of the downs runs the Ridgeway, a prehistoric track which branches off the Icknield Way at the chalk gorge of the Thames and so forms a link in the great chain of ancient roads stretching from the Wash to Salisbury Plain,

W. F. TAYLOR

THE SAXON BOUNDARY OF WALES

Offa's Dyke, which takes its name from the eighth-century Saxon king, once extended from the mouth of the Dee to the estuary of the Severn, a distance of 130 miles. In the twelfth century any Welshman found on the English side of the dyke was liable to lose a foot. The photograph shows a section of the dyke at Montgomery.

the metropolis of the New Stone and Bronze Age civilizations. At the foot of the hill too, lies the Icknield Way itself, also used like the Ridgeway, to communicate with Salisbury Plain. Again, it would seem that this part of Berkshire was a centre of habitation second only to Salisbury Plain. The crest of White Horse Hill is crowned by the double ramparts and ditches of an Iron Age camp. Weyland's Smithy is all that remains of a long barrow of the New Stone Age from which the land has been ploughed or washed away. To the south on the Lambourn Downs only a few miles away, are a group of nearly twenty round burial mounds, whilst stone and bronze implements and ornaments have been found in abundance all over the downland country.

A Prehistoric Monument

Thus with greater confidence we can infer that the White Horse is a monument raised by prehistoric man. If this is so we may conclude that, like almost all the monuments of stone, it was raised in the course of religious devotion. When to that is added the fact that the horse is a sacred sign to many primitive nature worshippers of the east, we see that there is reason to

believe that in this lies the origin of the White Horse.

In historic times the horse has still been associated with traditional observance of a semi-religious kind. The cleaning of the figure took on in medieval days the semblance of a local festival. From the middle of the eighteenth to the middle of the nineteenth century it was cleaned every seven years. There was an old custom by which a cheese called locally the "Manger," was rolled down the precipitous slopes of the hill and chased by the local people. As at the Maypole Festival at Cranham, in Gloucestershire, where also a cheese is rolled down the hill, the winner of the race was regarded as a favourite of the gods.

If we clamber up the steep hillside we shall find ridges immediately below the horse, seven in number with six banks on the south side of a steep ravine, all discernible to the naked eye, which cannot conceivably have been cut for cultivation, for the slope of the hill is much too steep. We can only judge therefore, that these too, had a religious significance.

Evidence of excavation points to the same result, or at least by a process of elimination shows that the figure is unlikely to have been

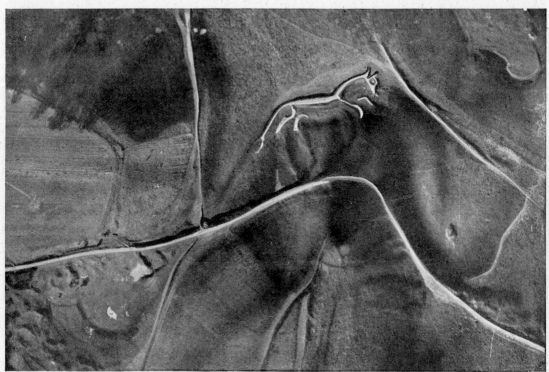

BY PERMISSION H.M. STATIONERY OFFICE AND ORDNANCE SURVEY

BERKSHIRE'S WEIRD WHITE HORSE

Beneath the earthworks of Uffington Castle on the Berkshire Downs is carved this curious figure of unknown antiquity. It is probably the oldest example of such figures in Britain and is considered much more ancient than the days of Alfred the Great, though local legend ascribes it to that monarch's victory over the Danes.

STEPHENSON

WHERE ALFRED DEFEATED THE DANES

Like the Berkshire White Horse, this figure near Westbury, in Wiltshire, is said to celebrate a victory of Alfred over the Danes. Here, in 878, he is believed to have defeated Guthrum. As the horse was modified towards the end of the eighteenth century and again in 1873, it is difficult to ascertain the real age of the work.

cut at any time later than the Bronze Age, which was the age of the round barrows and of the greatest use of the hilltop trackways. There is not the slightest evidence to connect it with the Romans, whilst the horses which appear on some of the pre-Roman Celtic coins are quite unlike the attenuated form of the Berkshire White Horse.

None other of the several horses cut in the chalk downs is ancient. In almost every case the date of their origin is known. In every case too, the horse is picked out in the turf without the symbolical attenuation of the Berkshire figure. So the horse, clearly visible from the main road near Westbury on the northern fringe of the chalk belt, had, records show, been made within living memory, in 1742. The horse at Marlborough was cut about 1804; that at Alton Barnes, in 1812; that at Winterbourne Bassett, in 1835; whilst the one at Wootton Bassett is assigned with certainty to 1864. All these, except the one at Westbury, which for long was thought to be as ancient as the White Horse of White Horse Hill, and attached to itself the same legends about Alfred and the Danes, have been allowed to decay, so that the grass is springing on the bare chalk and may soon cause them to disappear entirely.

The figure of a man mounted on a horse on the side of White Horse Hill overlooking Weymouth Bay just above the village of Sutton

Poyntz, depicts the illustrious George III. In the Cuckmere Valley, a mile or so below Litlington on the Seaford side, we can trace from the other bank the vague figure of a horse, but this, like the crown on the hill above Wye overlooking the Valley of the Stour, in Kent, is very recent. Perhaps the most modern of all are the two crosses cut in the Kentish Downs, one above Lenham, the other beneath the hanging woods of Shoreham Place, over the Valley of the Darent, both of which are War Memorials cut about 1920.

So the tradition of the hill figures seems to go on without pause through the centuries from the period of prehistoric man to the present day. But though the Kent crosses are modern there are two others which may be as ancient as the White Horse of Berkshire.

A Chiltern Landmark

The traveller who crosses the Vale of Aylesbury and approaches the steep escarpment of the Chiltern Hills, near Risborough, cannot fail to see on the hillside the bold, white cross, cut deeply into the green turf and thrown into relief by the dark blur of the beech woods which cover the slopes of the Chilterns southward towards Watlington. The lower part of the cross merges into the huge white scar of a chalk pit, giving a weird effect as though the whole hillside had fallen away under the cross. Four

W. F. TAYLOR

THE MIGHTY GIANT OF CERNE ABBAS

On a Dorset hillside is carved this huge figure with club raised on high. Legend asserts he was an ogre who, after glutting himself with fat sheep from the Vale of Blackmore, lay down in torpor and while he slept the peasants slew him. As an everlasting memorial of their valour, they traced his outline in the hillside turf.

miles away, a bare half-mile from Chinnor Church, is another more regular cross known locally as the Bledlow Cross. Certainly early manuscripts testify that they were not cut within the living memory of any writer. Tradition with curious persistence would have it that they are monuments to more of Alfred's legendary victories.

Pagan Crosses

The measurements of the two crosses have been compared with the result that, allowing for denudation and wear and tear, they seem to have been cut in multiples of a unit of about 58 inches, a unit which applies to the Long Man of Wilmington, to which we shall refer later, and which appears in the measurements of Stonehenge. Can anyone suppose that these are coincidences? Is it not more reasonable to think that the unit is in fact an ancient measure of length which is today unknown.

It might be attractive to suppose that the crosses are of Christian origin, but even that is not plausible, for the cross was reverenced during the Bronze Age of Crete, long before Christianity was known to the world. We must remember that these crosses, like all the ancient monuments, lie near one of the early trackways, in this case the Icknield Way, which seems to point almost conclusively to that same shadowy era known as the Bronze Age.

A well attested legend relates that the White-leaf Cross marks the spot where a medieval road crossed the Chilterns, a theory made more likely by the fact that in the Middle Ages the Chiltern country was a wild countryside with perhaps only this one road crossing it. But we must reject it, along with the legend of the battle between the Danes and the Saxons, if only because the cross is not visible from north or east, but only to a traveller approaching it directly over the vale.

There are two other ancient hill figures in England, the Giant of Cerne Abbas and the Long Man of Wilmington. Their antiquity is as certain as that of the White Horse of White Horse Hill and the Crosses of Whiteleaf and Bledlow.

The Giant of Cerne Abbas is an enormous figure of a man, perhaps with the Long Man of Wilmington one of the largest representations of the human form in the world. He overlooks the pleasant vale in which lies Cerne Abbas, threatening the peaceful countryside with the mighty club which he holds aloft. Of what does he remind you as he frowns down on you? Does he not bring to mind visions of strength beyond human power, and achievements beyond the might of man? If he does, his appearance suggests the same idea that the most learned research can reveal.

A trackway long-lost across the hills belonging to the Bronze or early Iron Age of Britain's civilization leads directly to the Giant. That is the only trace of ancient man that the calcareous uplands of this part of Dorset can show. We cannot be far wrong if we suppose that the Giant's form was cut in the chalk of the down by these peoples. If we look at the manifest signs of his virility we cannot err if we think that he was worshipped as a God of Fertility, before whom young men bowed down and offered prayers to grant them the procreation of many and mighty children to carry on the traditions of their struggling race.

Of the Long Man of Wilmington, in Sussex, there is more legend, but little more fact. As we move up the road which begins by the tree-hung cottages of Wilmington village and climb to a spur of the downs overlooking the Cuckmere Gap he looms above us on the hillside holding two staves, one in either hand. Tradition relates that he was cut by the monks of Wilmington Priory in the Middle Ages, but it seems incredible that in the Middle Ages naked figures should be cut in the downs, still less that the monks of a single priory should offer this strange sign of their devotion. Much more strongly do we incline to the other legend that in ancient days the Long Man was, like the Giant of Cerne Abbas, a God of Fertility, but that the monks of Wilmington were shocked at the manifest marks of his virile nature and set out one night to remove from his form the obscenity which

shocked their consciences, so that today, in the words of the ancient Greek proverb, " He is a man, yet not a man."

This too, is supported by another legend that the form was cut in the downs by the devil who wished to tempt the monks of the priory and remind them of the vigour which they were squandering, but that they in their piety recognized the devil's work and forthwith rendered it a mere mockery.

Many ingenious theories have been evolved to give other accounts of its origin. Sir Flinders Petrie diligently measured the points of the figure and found that the length of the staves was equal to double the distance between them and that the height of the figure was of similar, though not exact, proportion. From this it might be deduced that the staves were set up as a measure of length, but more reasonably we may say that they were cut to a forgotten standard of measurement like the Crosses of Whiteleaf and Bledlow.

Skilful Sculpture

The skill with which the work was done is shown by the fact that from the level of the road the Giant's proportions seem perfectly in accordance with the proportions of man. Yet, in fact, he is almost square. Such is the effect of fore-shortening—an effect which its constructors must have had in mind.

Yet another interpretation suggests that the Long Man's purpose was to mark the longest

STEPHENSON

THE GREAT MOUNT OF SILBURY
A prominent landmark on the Bath Road near Beckhampton is the great mound of Silbury Hill. With a circumference at the base of nearly 1,700 feet and an altitude of 550 feet, it is by far the greatest artificial mound in the country. Several attempts at excavation have produced no clues to its possible origin.

day, for it is only about the middle of June that the sun's rays fall directly on the figure. Before it was defined by white bricks in 1874, it could only then have been visible to an observer in the plain.

The hill figures are by no means the only ancient landmarks undated save by inference. Silbury Hill is another fascinating riddle. It rises abruptly beside the high road from Marlborough to Devizes. At first sight it might well seem a natural hill like one of the tors of Somerset which rise so abruptly and so unexpectedly from the plain. Yet in truth it is wholly artificial—the largest artificial mound in Europe.

An old story similar to one told of the Wrekin, in Shropshire, tells how the devil was walking along the road to Devizes with a sack of earth which he proposed uncharitably to dump on the town, for the devil had a grudge against it on account of its holiness. He chanced, however, to meet a tramp carrying fourteen pairs of old shoes. He inquired of the tramp how far it was to Devizes and the tramp, suspecting his fell design (for he was a holy tramp), told him that he had worn out all the fourteen pairs of shoes since leaving Devizes. In despair the devil (who it would appear was easily deterred from his purpose) emptied his sack there and then, and the mound of earth so formed was thenceforth known as Silbury Hill.

The more critical perhaps will accept this legend no more willingly than the legend of the monks and the Long Man of Wilmington. If so, we must rely once more on inference. Silbury was at first thought to be a gigantic round barrow, a theory supported by the fact that it is near the centre of Bronze-Age civilization and the thousands of round barrows which are found in Wiltshire. Unfortunately there is no sign of interment, nor does it conform to any of the known shapes of burial mounds.

Mound of Mystery

It might be the mound of a Saxon or Norman castle, but alas! there is no record of one in this district. A more recent suggestion is that it is a Roman burial mound, for a Roman road runs nearby and the Roman mounds are certainly larger than any others, as evidenced by the Bartlow Hills, near Ashdon in northern Essex, which excavation has shown definitely to be of Roman origin. In fact, only a complete upheaval of the site could solve the problem, but, to remove such a mass of earth and chalk would require more time and money than any are likely to expend, even in the cause of archæological research.

The various dykes and banks of southern England offer a problem nearly as intriguing. Always they have much the same form, a single bank fronted by a trench, the total height of ditch and dyke combined varying today from a

DIXON-SCOTT

THE WHITE HORSE OF CHERHILL

On Cherhill Down, a few miles west of Silbury and also visible from the Bath Road, is this White Horse which was cut in 1780 by a Dr. Alsop of Calne and which measures 160 feet from head to tail. It stands, however, on ancient ground beneath the ramparts of Oldbury Camp, a prehistoric feature with double banks and ditches.

mere two or three feet to thirty or forty. But before the levelling effect of time and weather when the sides of the ditch and bank were vertical they must have presented a formidable easily-manned defence.

In many places every vestige of the dykes has disappeared. Even so we can trace four main systems of ramparts. Grim's Dyke extends over almost the whole length of the Chiltern Hills. From the Thames it runs in a nearly straight line in the direction of Nettlebed, then taking a zigzag course it passes by Lacey Green and Redland End where a footpath is astride the bank for nearly a mile giving us a splendid view of the now levelled rampart and the ditch facing in the direction of the Thames basin. And so on by Great Hampden and over Berkhamsted Common.

Ancient Boundaries

In the west Offa's Dyke stretches from the Bristol Channel to the Cheshire coast sometimes in Wales, sometimes in England, showing by its very uniformity the hand of a single engineering genius. Where it crosses the high land of Shropshire by Clun it is seen in its finest and most impressive aspect. The Wansdyke extends across southern England for eighty miles from Inkpen Beacon in a more or less straight line into Somerset, through Spye Park and over the Wiltshire Downs. South of the Wansdyke where it passes through Wiltshire we shall find the four mile long stretch of Bokerley Dyke and the less well marked but roughly parallel stretch of Combe Bank.

Finally, in East Anglia athwart the Icknield Way beyond the point where it fords the Cam, we find three parallel lines of dykes, the first traditionally known as the Roman Way, the second the Fleam Dyke and the third the Devil's Dyke which extends from Wood Ditton to Burwell Fen.

Probably there are other similar earthworks, though none which are so clearly marked. It is at least probable that these four systems are of similar date and had a similar purpose. Their traditional names tell us little. The Grim of Grim's Dyke seems to refer to no specific person: he may be the devil; for it has ever been the habit of country people to ascribe to the devil or Cæsar what they could not explain. Or perhaps Grim's Dyke means no more than strong wall, just as the title Graham's Wall is

STEPHENSON

A RELIC OF THE STONE AGE
On a hillside overlooking the Medway between Chatham and Maidstone stands Kit's Coty. Traditionally it is the tomb of Katigern, who was slain in battle, but it is of much greater antiquity.

given to the Roman wall of Antonine, not as some suppose in commemoration of a certain Graham who breached it but rather using the name Graham as typical of a strong man.

In the case of Offa's Dyke tradition is so fixed in attributing the work to Offa, King of Mercia, whilst references to such a work are so numerous that we can perhaps with safety conclude that this was in fact a boundary line dividing the Saxon Kingdoms of England from the Britons of Wales, and raised by King Offa himself. Thus too, we may suppose that Grim's Dyke divided the Saxon villages of the Icknield Way (we know there were many settlements beneath the Chilterns) from the kingdom of the East Saxons whilst the Cambridgeshire dykes may have separated East Anglia from Mercia, and the Wansdyke determined the boundaries of Wessex.

Whether the dykes are Saxon, or as is most improbable Roman, or Celtic, they make a perfect goal for a weekend or a week's walking holiday; for tracing their course and reconstructing it where it has disappeared is as fascinating as any hobby of the countryside.

THE RIVERS OF BRITAIN

by I. O. EVANS

ISLANDS such as ours cannot produce mighty and awe-inspiring rivers, but small as are our streams they have played a tremendous part in the history and romance of our country.

Commerce has been influenced by our river heritage, for London and Liverpool, two of the six main ports of the world, have grown into importance largely through their position upon the banks of comparatively small water courses.

The development of our people has been bound up with our streams. The greatest need of man in his daily life, now and in the earliest days of history, is water both to sustain life and also to facilitate commerce.

Man first settled beside the river shore in order that he might live. He chose a position where the water could be forded so that he might travel from one side to the other with ease, whilst by means of the by-streams, and tributaries, the interlinking rivers developed his trade and solved his question of transport. Time has enlarged the human settlements into great cities, and flung bridges across the river banks, but the urge of commerce and the means of life remain just the same.

Of all the rivers of England that which is most dear, and also of most importance, is the Thames. At Thames Head, in the Cotswold Hills, one of the spots which claim to be the source of London's river, is an old Roman road, the Fosse Way, leading from Cirencester to Bath, and it may well be that many a weary legionary has blessed its waters as he stooped to quench his thirst.

Actually the source of the Thames is not easy

STEPHENSON

A STREAM FROM THE MOORS
The River Ure in Wensleydale receives many tributaries which come rushing headlong down the hillsides. Here is seen Hardraw Force which plunges 80 feet below.

to determine. The spring at Thames Head is frequently dry; this supports the contention that the river actually rises at Seven Springs, near Cheltenham, some ten miles from Cirencester. For the first few miles the Thames follows a tortuous and winding course through peaceful agricultural country until its ever increasing size permits of navigation first by rowing boats and punts and then by larger craft.

The first city of any considerable size is Oxford, but before her grey walls are reached the river flows through Cricklade and Lechlade. Both these towns have a history extending back to Saxon times and speak of fords known in those days. At Kelmscott lived and is buried William Morris, who in *News from Nowhere* immortalized his vision of England as it might be. Farther downstream is Cumnor, the scene of the tragedy described in Scott's *Kenilworth*. Its Hall, now long vanished, was reputed to be haunted by an evil spirit which no exorcism could lay.

The meadows and the old stone bridges glide by, and soon Oxford appears, Oxford, not merely one of Britain's traditional homes of learning but a centre of sporting activity, a cathedral city, a town with over a thousand years of history—and, at the same time, a commercial centre with a flourishing industry. Above all, it is a city of unequalled architectural beauty. The view from Magdalen Bridge will linger long in the memory, and this is but the prelude to its colleges, its castle keep, its cathedral, and its "High."

Abingdon, formerly the site of a mighty abbey —at one time sacked by the townsmen and students

FOX PHOTOS

RIVER OF BEAUTY AND ROMANCE

The Wye is one of the most beautiful and most romantic rivers of Britain. From its source on bare Plynlimon it flows through mid-Wales and through the Marches by Hereford and Ross, by Tintern's lovely ruins and Chepstow's ancient Castle and so to the Bristol Channel. Here the river is seen at Symond's Yat.

of Oxford—impresses the traveller by river or road with its quiet charm, its church, its gabled cottages, its bridge, and its chestnut-trees. Below are villages with old-world names, Nuneham Courtenay the home in 1710 of Simon Harcourt, Lord Chancellor of England; Long Wittenham, with its old " chepeing " or bargaining cross; Wittenham Clumps, the low, rounded hills crowned with beech trees forming a landmark to which the clumps of trees give their name; Clifton Hampden spanning the river with an old toll bridge and a modern red brick structure side by side, and Crowmarsh Gifford boasting a genuine Norman church. From Crowmarsh Gifford the ever widening river pursues its placid course through one of its most interesting geographical features. At this point it forms the dividing line between the counties of Oxfordshire and Berkshire, with Goring on one side and Streatley on the other.

On the Berkshire side the swelling slopes of the downs form an impressive range, while the Chiltern Hills rise on the Oxfordshire bank. The river, slipping along between them, runs through a V-shaped opening which is a landmark from many a hill-top, and so dividing the two ranges forms the beautifully picturesque Goring Gap. From here to Pangbourne is to be found one of the most lovely stretches of the Thames.

The very name strikes a romantic note, for it is here that the Pang bourne or stream, well known for its trout fishing, joins the parent river. The village itself is a little gem of architectural beauty, having preserved many fine examples of old English cottages.

At Reading the river becomes a little more industrialized, but Reading has had a past. The Danes established themselves in this old town, repulsing an attack by no less a warrior than Alfred the Great himself. Here, 600 years ago, an unknown poet, seated perhaps on the banks of the river itself, wrote the earliest English song, the well-known round, *Summer is icumen in.*

Centre of English Tradition

Downstream from Reading the Thames is the paradise of rower and sailing man. Henley with its Regatta, Marlow, Cookham and Maidenhead lead on to Windsor, the seat of royalty, and the town which gave its name to England's ruling family. The mound on which it stands was seized upon by William the Conqueror as the right place at which to establish a castle which should form a western outpost of London. Today it is the centre of English tradition, the birthplace and burial vault of many a royal figure, a home of the reigning monarch, and almost a shrine of pilgrimage for visitors from all over the world.

Not far below Windsor lies the most famous spot in British constitutional history, the island of Magna Charta, where, according to popular belief, King John was forced by his barons to sign the Great Charter which has formed the basis of our political and industrial freedom. This island was supposed to form a neutral

EDGAR WARD

THE THAMES AT PANGBOURNE
" Ne'er saw I, never felt, a calm so deep!
The river glideth at his own sweet will."—WORDSWORTH.

meeting ground for the king and his nobles who were camped on either side of the river, but there is no foundation for this story. In fact the Charter itself gives the signing place as "Runningmede" or Runnymede, a field lying between Egham and the river.

Now the Thames is flowing across the level stretch of fertile soil it has itself brought down from the hills. Here is Hampton Court, the princely residence of the ill-fated Cardinal Wolsey, with its Great Hall, its Haunted Gallery, its Gardens and its Maze. A little farther down the Thames becomes tidal; its course as a river is over, it is merging with the sea.

Here, too, its water becomes polluted, its banks dingy with warehouse and factory and wharf. Gleams of beauty enliven the drabness of the scene, Kew Gardens with its pagoda, the dome of St. Paul's Cathedral, the massive buildings of the New London which is rising before our eyes, the Tower which William the Conqueror built to overawe the city, docks and huge cranes, wharfs, a forest of masts without number, the greatest port in the world. So the river passes through that wide mouth where Viking longships sailed, whence explorers set out to the ends of the earth, where traffic is carried on with every nation in the world. "The Thames" said John Burns, "is liquid history"; and so indeed it is.

Of equal historic interest, and as dear to the heart of every Scot as is the Thames to a

EDGAR WARD

MAPLEDURHAM MILL

Probably few places on the Thames have been photographed and painted so much as this lovely old mill at Mapledurham on the Oxfordshire side of the river, upstream from Reading. Hereabouts is some of the most delightful scenery to be found on the Thames where richly wooded hills rise from the banks of the river.

Londoner, is the River Forth. Contrasting with the gentle smooth-flowing Thames is Scotland's chief river, which rises not among the low hills but on the slopes of the rugged mountains. Ben Lomond, famed in song and story, is its birthplace, and thence it flows eastwards ever through a country rich in historic and literary associations. This is the Walter Scott country, and the scene of *Waverley*; on the shores of Linn Menteith the tragic Mary Queen of Scots spent a part of her childhood. The scenery is as

robbers," by Sir Walter Scott, is now one of the main sources of water supply to Glasgow.

Framed in this lake is Ellen's Island, named after a heroine who defended it and the refugees upon its banks from marauding invaders. Opposite the island is the site of the Silver Strand, now submerged, and on the slope of the mountain is the Goblin's Cave, both famed in Scott's *The Lady of the Lake*.

Both valleys meet at the historic town of Stirling, where many a Scottish monarch held

PHOTOCHROM

SILVER WINDINGS OF THE TAY NEAR PERTH
"' Behold the Tiber!' the vain Roman cried,
Viewing the ample Tay from Baiglie's side;
But where's the Scot that would the vaunt repay,
And hail the puny Tiber for the Tay."—SCOTT.

romantic as its history—lofty mountains, little inferior in grandeur to Ben Lomond itself, rise on either side, and, in the valley between, their crests are reflected in the waters of a chain of lakes.

A few miles to the north is another valley at once more beautiful and more known to fame. Here the hillsides are clothed with the mass of woodland, the silvery birches and darker oaks, that have given the region the name of " the bristly country," the Trossachs.

It is the setting of some of the most romantic and historic episodes of Scottish tradition. At Glengyle at the head of Loch Arklet, Rob Roy the cattle thief and outlaw was born, while Loch Katrine, named Lake Cateran, " the lake of the

his court in the grey castle overlooking the town from its perch of basalt crag. Some little distance from the town one of the most decisive battles in the history of Scotland was fought at Bannockburn.

Soon after leaving Stirling the river widens into an arm of the sea, but still its shores are rich in the memorials of the past. In Dunfermline Abbey lie the remains of Robert the Bruce; and in the palace Charles I was born. As of old, the district still keeps its warlike associations, for on the shores of the Firth is Rosyth naval base. But " Queen of the Forth " is Edinburgh, the "Athens of the north," with its wonderful history, with its castle and its war memorial, Holyroodhouse and Arthur's Seat.

After Thames and Forth perhaps next in importance is the Severn, rising among the peat bogs of black Plynlimon in the range of hills between Cardigan and Montgomery. The district is one of the bleakest and most desolate, yet the Severn is closely associated with the stirring history of the land wherein it is born. Not far from its source is the Cefn Carnedd, an ancient stronghold where the Cymry organized their resistance to the Roman invader, whose station of Caersws is found not very far distant. Near Montgomery is Offa's Dyke, recalling the efforts of the Saxon kings to keep the wild mountaineers from raiding into the fertile plains of Mercia. The Long Mountain nearby is traditionally the site of the last battle for Welsh freedom, during which the insurgent Prince Madog ap Llewelyn was defeated.

Shrewsbury, almost ringed by the Severn and once the seat of the Princes of Powis, fell into Roman and Saxon hands and was many times plundered by the Welsh before Edward I made it the headquarters for his successful war of subjugation ; and here the fiery Hotspur was defeated and slain. The Civil Wars also ravaged the Severn Valley ; and Worcester, from its loyalty to the royal cause, earned its renown as the " ever faithful city."

Still more famous is the Severn's tributary, the Avon. It was near its source that the hopes

STEPHENSON

A RUSHING TORRENT

One of the headstreams of the River Aire emerges from beneath Malham Cove. Here another tributary is seen plunging down into the sublime rift of Gordale.

PHOTOCHROM

THE PEACEFUL EDEN

In the Pennines on the edge of Yorkshire and Westmorland is born the River Eden which flows through the defile of Mallerstang and then across a wide plain by Kirkby Stephen and Appleby and on into Solway Firth. Here is a scene at Armathwaite, where the river flows through beautiful wooded and pastoral country.

of the Royalists were shattered on the battlefield of Naseby in the Civil War. In its valley, at Lutterworth, lived John Wyclif, " morning star of the Reformation " ; while overlooking its waters stands Warwick Castle, a well preserved example of fourteenth-century architecture, and one of the fortress-homes of the feudal nobility.

At Stratford is the birthplace of Shakespeare, one of the most famous of our sons. Here his house, Anne Hathaway's Cottage, and Holy Trinity Church, his place of burial, are preserved.

Below Tewkesbury, the scene of desperate

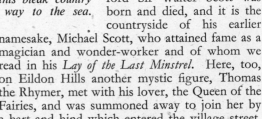
STEPHENSON

RIVER OF THE PENNINES

In the wild uplands dominated by that trinity of Pennine peaks, Whernside, Ingleborough and Penyghent rises the Ribble. From this bleak country it emerges in the softer country of Craven on its way to the sea.

fighting and hideous slaughter in the Wars of the Roses, the Avon unites with the Severn in a mighty river sweeping on past Gloucester with its magnificent cathedral until, so long a Saxon stream, it returns to bathe the shores of the country from which it rose.

Our three " capital " rivers are only the beginning of Britain's waterways. Scotland is deeply pierced with innumerable glens drained by rivers no less beautiful and no less historic than the Forth itself. Greatest of these is the Clyde, best known to us for its clanging dockyards and its factories, and for Glasgow grim and forbidding beneath its pall of smoke. Yet the Clyde with its source among the heather hills and its lovely sea-lochs and its islands is a river of beauty and romance. Long ago its waters reflected the lurid glare of the Beltane beacons which blazed from Tinto, the " hill of fires."

In three magnificent falls the Upper Clyde leaps downwards ; each roaring impressively amidst the rocks and the bracken as at Cora Linn, one of the finest of Scotland's waterfalls.

Down the river from Glasgow is Dumbarton Castle, Dun-Breton, "the hill fort of the Britons." Here, so it is locally held, St. Patrick was born, and there is a legend that the great rock, 650 feet high, is a pebble hurled by the devil at the saint, in a fruitless endeavour to prevent his mission to Ireland.

Near Dumbarton the Clyde is joined by the Leven, which flows from the glorious island-flecked waters of Loch Lomond. These islets are a romance in themselves. Wordsworth was inspired by their beauty to write his ode to the "sweet Highland girl." The MacGregors, notorious cattle raiders, established their stronghold amongst the natural hiding places, and many a pious congregation gathered to hear a sermon preached from the summit of the huge Pulpit Rock.

Rich in memories of " old unhappy far-off things and battles long ago " is the country of the border rivers, the Tweed on the east and the lesser streams flowing into the Solway Firth on the west.

Teviotdale, especially, is rich in interest. At Abbotsford Sir Walter Scott was born and died, and it is the countryside of his earlier namesake, Michael Scott, who attained fame as a magician and wonder-worker and of whom we read in his *Lay of the Last Minstrel*. Here, too, on Eildon Hills another mystic figure, Thomas the Rhymer, met with his lover, the Queen of the Fairies, and was summoned away to join her by a hart and hind which entered the village street.

Border Streams

Teviot flows into Tweed, a stream which though sluggish has witnessed scenes no less interesting than the more spectacular mountain torrents. At Wark Castle, so the discredited legend goes, Edward III founded the Order of the Garter, as he smilingly returned to the Countess of Salisbury the garter she had dropped. Coldstream not merely gave its name to the Guards regiment founded by General Monk, but at one time, like the more notorious Gretna Green, served as an informal registry office for runaway lovers. Berwick, at the mouth of the Tweed,

EDGAR WARD

THE DERBYSHIRE DERWENT

From its source on the bare heights of Bleaklow in the Peak District, the Derwent descends through moorland country, and in the neighbourhood of Matlock flows through a narrow ravine flanked with lofty crags of gleaming limestone.   Characteristic of this part of its course is the above view with the noble mass of High Tor soaring above the stream.   On the side of the glen opposite to the Tor rise the wooded Heights of Abraham.

has the curious distinction of being for certain legal purposes neither in England nor in Scotland.

Among the more northerly of Scotland's streams is the Tay, on whose banks so improbable a person as Pontius Pilate is said to have been born. Though it rises on bare Rannoch Moor, it has several unusual associations with woodland and trees. The woods of Methven sheltered William Wallace; at Dunkeld were planted the first larches to grow in Britain; the "Old Yew of Fortingall" is the oldest of its species in Europe; and Birnam Woods marching on Dunsinane foreshadowed the overthrow of Macbeth.

THE BURE AT COLTISHALL

F. BURFIELD DYER

The Bure, perhaps the best known river of the Norfolk Broads rises near Melton Constable and with many a twist and turn, and often widening into lakes or "broads," it flows through the lowlands to join the Yare.

Perth was formerly the capital of Scotland, and Dundee boasts a church steeple 156 feet high. Yet of all places on the banks of Tay, the most famous is surely Scone, in whose abbey, destroyed in 1559, the ancient kings of Scotland were crowned. The "Stone of Scone" upon which the kings were seated for their crowning was carried off to England by Edward I and now forms part of the Coronation Chair. It is said to be "Jacob's Pillow," upon which he rested his head and dreamed of the celestial ladder, and before it was brought to Scotland was the "Lai Fail" or Stone of Destiny of Ireland.

Natural features take little account of political boundaries, and the rivers of northern England have much in common with those of Scotland. Almost on the border itself rise the Coquet and the Northern Tyne, amidst scenes of bleak desolation, the peat bogs of the high hills. Yet even in these lonelinesses are found the memorials of those who ventured themselves among them, whether for reasons of military conquest or evangelical zeal. Roman milestones mark the paths where the legions trod; and the name of Holystone still commemorates the spot where 3,000 Northumbrians were baptized.

Nor were the terrors of this bleak region purely physical. Two of the names given to the hill where South Tyne rises speak of the awe in which it was held, "Wizard's Fell," "Fiend's Fell"; its other name, "Cross Fell," speaks of the conquest of the powers of evil by the pious monks. The Romans felt these influences, too; for at their station at Chollerford was found the remains of the statue of the God of Tyne.

Fierce Forays

To the harshness of nature and the fears of superstition were added the cruelties of man. We think of the "Border Country" as being the Scottish Lowlands, forgetting that England had its border likewise, and that there were raids from the north as well as from the south. In the river valleys stand the "Peel Towers" where the people might take refuge from the raids and forays of the fierce mosstroopers—strong-walled towers with a space below for the cattle and a room above for the women and children. So the sturdy north countrymen maintained themselves in a region which even the Romans had given up as hopeless, seeking not to conquer it but to keep its wild inhabitants at bay by the device of Hadrian's Wall.

There are other reasons for venturing into wild country than politics and religion. On the valley slopes of the northern hills are found Roman mine workings; and today the name "Tyne" suggests to us a grey industrial area similar to that of Glasgow. At this northern border point the Romans forded the Tyne and built a station known as Pons Aelii, but the foundation of the present city of Newcastle is due to the eldest son of William the Conqueror having built a castle at the same spot after one of his raids into Scotland. Two collections of shacks and shelters on the river's banks,

DIXON-SCOTT

ESS NA LARAGH, GLENARIFF, CO. ANTRIM

Glenariff, one of the far-famed " Nine Glens of Antrim," has two beautiful waterfalls. Ess na Laragh (Fall of the Mares) and Ess na Crub (Fall of the Hoof). Thackeray called this district " Switzerland in miniature," and Washington Irving hoped there to " dream quietly away the remnant of a troubled life."

"shielings," as they were called, have given a name to North and South Shields. At Newcastle, too, Charles I was surrendered to the English Parliamentary forces.

Tees headwaters are noteworthy for the bleak lonely lake, curiously named "The Weel," and for their many beautiful falls, Caldron Snout and High Force. A picturesque medieval bridge and a few shattered ruins mark the spot where "Barnard Castle standeth stately on Tees." Here the name of a deep ravine, Thor's Gill, reminds us of the fierce Vikings who dwelt in this valley, while the remains of Egliston Abbey speak of their conversion by the pious monks.

Down the great valley between the Pennines and Cleveland hills flows the Yorkshire Ouse, gathering one by one many a noble tributary. First comes the Swale from the lonely hills, hurrying down its narrow vale and lapping the base of Richmond's mighty castle. Along the almost parallel valley, the wide green Wensleydale, flows the Ure, fed by lively streams leaping down the hill-sides and itself presenting a series of splendid falls at Aysgarth. Among the Pennine streams perhaps none offers more varied charm than the Wharfe, a bonny lively stream in a rich, romantic vale.

Farther south the streams are more placid from source to sea, yet still they traverse districts at once beautiful and famed in history or legend.

Derwent flows through the limestone regions, passing through caves where the glittering "Blue John" gleams, washes cliffs where the Romans dug for lead, or rises to the surface in a "petrifying spring" that deposits a thick chalky coating on every object immersed in its stream. It carves the rocks into dales no less lovely than those of Yorkshire — Miller's Dale, Tideswell Dale. Dovedale, the finest of all, is the work of the River Dove, in whose waters Izaak Walton fished. Instead of grim castles, palatial mansions stand beside the river banks, mansions like Chatsworth House which housed the unhappy Mary Stuart and her custodian, the Earl of Shrewsbury, no less than five times, and Haddon Hall, the home of Dorothy Vernon and the scene of her romantic elopement.

Where Danes Ruled

On the banks of the Trent stands Gotham, about which is told the unenviable story of the "three wise men" who tried to capture a cuckoo by building a hedge round it. Nottingham, at one time the centre of Danish rule in England, was later divided into two separate boroughs, Norman and English, for the proud conquerors disliked too close an association with the "natives." Owen Glendower of Wales and David II of Scotland were imprisoned in its castle, where later Charles I unfurled his standard

W. F. TAYLOR

HEMINGFORD GREY, HUNTINGDONSHIRE

On the River Ouse, two miles from St. Ives. The church, dedicated to St. James, is an ancient edifice in the Norman and Early English styles, and possesses a register of baptisms dating from 1673. The Manor House, built about 1135, is one of the few Norman buildings of its kind, and the only one continuously inhabited.

in the Civil War. At Gainsborough was moored the fleet of Sweyn, the invading Viking, for here the Trent is a stream of some size famous for its tidal wave, the "eagre."

Hereward

Even more sluggish and more meandering are the waters of the fen country. Yet they win a place in history because of the refuge they afforded to the "last of the English," holding out under brave Hereward against the Norman conqueror behind the muddy streams and the marsh. From a river mouth in these low-lying regions went out another band of lovers of freedom, taking the name of their home town, Boston, half across the world. The streams of Norfolk and Suffolk combine to form those waters so beloved of sportsmen — the Broads; while it was the soft pastoral landscape of the Stour, so he declared, which made Constable a painter.

HUMPHREY AND VERA JOEL

FAIR RIVER OF KENT

Rising in Ashdown Forest, the Medway here seen at Maidstone flows slowly and placidly through the hop fields by Tonbridge and Maidstone, and out by historic Rochester to the Thames estuary. Barges use the river as far as Maidstone.

South of the Thames, and joining it at Chatham, is a veritable gangster amongst rivers, the Medway. Its headwaters have cut their way eastwards into the soft sand and clays, and in doing so they have "captured" many small streams which at one time flowed direct to the Thames. The Medway forms an important adjunct to the Thames and is itself rich in historic and political interest. Chatham, used since the time of Henry VIII as a sea-going centre, is now one of the main naval and military stations of England.

On a hill overlooking the valley is the prehistoric Kit's Coty House, formed of three upright stones capped with a stone 11 feet in length. Legend says that it is the tomb of Katigern and Vortigern, who were killed in the battle with Hengist and Horsa.

The streams which flow from the South Downs, though small, have their historic import. Rye, one of the old Cinque Ports of Sussex, at one time stood at the mouth of its stream, but now, owing to the receding of the sea, finds itself inland. Here too may be seen the turreted Ypres Tower said to have been built in the twelfth century by William of Ypres, Earl of Kent. Arundel Castle beside the Arun was

STEPHENSON

IN THE VALE OF THE USK

Fairest of South Wales rivers and by some people considered a rival of the Wye, the Usk flows by the foot of Brecon Beacons, by Brecon and Crickhowell and down by Abergavenny and ancient Caerleon to the sea at Newport. Between Brecon and Crickhowell it provides many peaceful scenes such as the one above.

originally built to defend the break made by that river through the chalky soil of the South Downs and has withstood more than one siege.

Longer and wilder in their scenery are the West Country rivers which rise on the Devonshire Moors, entering the sea by such tortuous waterways as Plymouth Sound. Of the Dart it is said that each year it claims a life, man one year and maid the next. Exe rises in the north, on heathery Exmoor, but flows southwards almost across the whole of the county.

Severn is not the only fine stream which Wales gives to England. The Wye is renowned for its scenery, for ruined Tintern Abbey and Symond's Yat; beside it Owen Glendower kept his stronghold, made his last stand. At "Wolf's Leap" the last wolf in Britain plunged into its waters. That a dragon should have haunted the vale has its parallel elsewhere, but what are we to think of the hill of Marcle ("miracle") which moved across country with "a loud bellowing noise," doing much damage before it came to rest?

From Wales too we have the Dee, the "holy stream" of the Druids. In its valley, so the story goes, Arthur of Britain spent his early life. It flows through Llyn Tegid, "the lake beautiful," called by the Saxons Bala Lake or Pimblemere, and then eastwards to grey slaty Corwen, past the remains of Valle Crucis Abbey, "the

Valley of the Cross," to Llangollen whose bridge was reputed one of the Seven Wonders of Wales, and by the strange-shaped "Hill of Dinas Bran." So it reaches England and Chester, with its city walls and its ancient "Rows."

The list of Britain's rivers might go on, each with its own beauty, its own legend, its own place on history's page; Usk, with Brecon Castle deliberately destroyed by the townsfolk to avoid the horrors of a siege; Dovey, the bells of its lost city sounding faintly from beneath the wave. The streams of Lakeland, with the Rothay and the Brathay, the crystal Derwent flowing out of Borrowdale, and the lovely Duddon, Wordsworth's "Cradled nursling of the mountains," of these also much might be written.

By historic town and city, through the water-meadows in the wide vales, by many a dreamy village and on towards the narrowing hills, so we may follow these precious streams, dwindling in volume yet assuming a livelier motion as they tumble down the mountain sides.

The rivers of Britain keep the romance and the beauty they have ever held. Placid under the summer sun or whipped to fury by wind and rain, shrinking in drought or spread afar in the winter's flood, rushing bands of silver against the green of the fields or the shadow of the woods, they wind their devious ways to the sea.

CURIOUS CUSTOMS AND CEREMONIES

by I. O. EVANS

IN the soil of modern England we discover fragments of rock or remains of living creatures which speak to us of long-past ages. Among the countryfolk of Britain we equally find customs and ceremonies which recall to us the beliefs and ways of life of our ancestors of long ago. Many and varied are these old-time customs. Some are comparatively recent, derived at least in name from recorded historic events. Some are age-old, older than civilization, older perhaps than the tilling of the soil. Some have come down, almost unchanged, through countless centuries. Some, it is sad to say, have become vulgarized and spoiled. And some have adapted themselves to present conditions and have taken on in this modern age a vigorous new life of their own.

What is more important in the life of beast or man than water? Today, with our Water Boards and our mains, we often overlook its significance—until there comes a drought year to remind us that without water none can live. Our forefathers, with good reason, knew the value of water; the wells from which it came they regarded as sacred. To their waters they attributed a magic power, of healing, of blessing, of cursing. To the wells they resorted, and at the wells they performed solemn ceremonies, "dressing" them with floral decorations; and such ceremonies are still carried out even in our own time.

At Tissington, in Derbyshire, the wells are still dressed each year with impressive ceremony, and with special decorations which have come down from time immemorial. At this village are five wells of the purest

water, bubbling up from far below and keeping the same temperature all the year round: the Town Well, the Holy Well, the Coffin Well, Hand's Well, and Yew Tree Well. Each in turn is visited, every Holy Thursday after church, by clergy, choir and people. At each of the wells a short service is held, with the reading of appropriate passages from the Bible—for are there not Waters of Healing in both the Old and New Testaments?—the chanting of psalms, and the singing of hymns.

TOPICAL

THE TUTTIMEN AT HUNGERFORD

The age-old ceremony of Hock Tide, a survival from the Middle Ages, is still carried out at Hungerford, Berks. This festival is the annual session of the Hock Tide Court. The two tithing men, or Tuttimen, parade the town demanding a coin of the realm from every male over the age of twelve and a kiss from every woman they meet. Tuttimen claiming their kisses.

TOPICAL

A MAY DAY PROCESSION

The annual May Festival is still celebrated in many places throughout the country. Here a procession is seen on the way to the village green at Elstow, in Bedfordshire, where John Bunyan lived. The May Queen, in her flower-bedecked carriage, accompanied by her charming retinue, is preceded in the procession by the May Pole.

Meanwhile the wells have been decorated. Beds of moistened clay are prepared in wooden frames, and in these is worked a picture in a natural mosaic, white grains of rice, reds and blues from flower-petals and berries, greys from lichens and greens from mosses and buds.

Villages of the Plague

This well-dressing is commonly explained as a thanksgiving service from deliverance from the Black Death, which ravaged the villages of Derbyshire, and from which the purity of its wells alone saved Tissington. Students of these matters, however, think it is far older than any medieval plague, though this may of course have revived it ; they consider that it goes back to very early days, that it is similar in idea to the many other customs, all over the world, by which springs and wells are regarded and treated as sacred places. Whatever its origin, the Tissington Well-dressing is a custom that none of us would like to see given up ; it speaks of days and methods of thought other than ours.

Elsewhere in Britain the customs associated with the wells are very different. Among the wishing wells is the Well of St. Keyne, in Cornwall, overshadowed by ash, elm and oak. Whoever, husband or wife, is the first to drink of this well, so the legend runs, will be master of the household for life ! A well-known verse by a former poet-laureate tells of the competition for its waters which used to take place :

" I hastened as soon as the wedding was done,
    And left my wife in the porch-a,
But truly she had been wiser than me,
    For she'd taken a bottle to the church-a ! "

Man shares with the beast the need of water. But one of the earliest things to distinguish man from beast was surely the discovery of fire. To our primitive ancestors this was not, as it is to us, a mere household commodity : it was magic, it was an object of veneration, it was a means of overcoming the powers of darkness and strengthening the brightness of the sun. In our own islands the Bale-fires used to burn at the four seasons of the year, to mark the turning of the sun in the heavens. Today we still like the bright fire at Christmas, even if we have forgotten the Yule Log of tradition, and still we light fires all over the land in the autumn, at almost the time when they used to be lighted long ago. Nowadays we do it, we say, to commemorate Guy Fawkes. But the custom of lighting fires at this time of the year is much older than any Gunpowder Plot.

No period of the year is more impressive even to townsfolk than the spring. Still more is it significant to the countryman, who lives in the midst of burgeoning leaf and new-born lamb, and whose whole life is devoted to them. Spring festivals are known wherever the earth is tilled, and we find them likewise among ourselves. The time-honoured ceremonies of Maypole and Queen of the May seemed in danger of dying out, but now, fortunately, they are being revived. In one place we may see a Maypole erected, as it was in the days of old ; in another a charming little girl is honoured as May Queen. At Minehead, in Somerset, the fishermen parade through the streets a gaily-decorated model of a ship. And at Oxford, ancient home of learning, a service is held to greet the dawn from the summit of Magdalen Tower.

At about the same season, though a few days later, is kept up another picturesque custom. The people of Helston, in Cornwall, one of the most westerly towns in England, deck themselves with flowers and branches and dance processionally through the town. The tune they dance to, like the dance itself, comes down from olden times ; folk dancers know it well. Early in the morning the Furry Dance begins, and in and out through the houses, the doors of which are all left open, the merry dancers go. And as they dance they sing another song whose origin, like that of dance and dance tune, is lost in the mists of antiquity. It tells us of those heroes of olden time, Robin Hood and Little John, of going to the Merry Greenwood, " for to chase O,

to chase the buck and doe." It tells us of an ancient foe of Britain, " those Spaniards that make so great a boast O." It tells us, perhaps, of the real purpose of dance and song and tune, to banish the gloom of the winter and bring the summer home : " For we are up as soon as any day O, And for to fetch the summer home, The summer and the May O, The summer is a come O, The winter is a gone O."

Three paces and hop ; one, two, three, hop. Round the streets and in and out the houses the merry dancers go. " With a hal-an-tow, jolly rumbelow ! " Just as they did long before the Saxons came to the shores of Britain, the Furry Dancers of Helston are bringing the summer home.

Robin Hood and Little John are our hunting heroes, and another custom recalls the days when hunting, and not corn-growing, gave mankind the staff of life. In Abbots Bromley, Staffs, each September may be seen a dance in which Robin Hood, astride on his Hobby Horse, and fair Maid Marian posture and caper with strange-garbed men who bear on their shoulders the antlers of the deer. The crossbow and arrow, those famous weapons of old, are brandished, and the fool, without whom no ancient function was complete, prances about. Moreover the deer represented are not the shy gentle creatures

TOPICAL

HELSTON'S FURRY DANCE

Each year in the ancient Cornish town of Helston homage is paid to the Goddess Flora, when the centuries-old Floral Dance is carried out by couples who dance through the town, in and out of the houses and shops and through the gardens. The photograph shows some of the dancers winding their way through the crowded streets.

hunted and harried by " sportsmen " of today. They are a breed of deer unknown in a wild state in these islands since before the Norman Conquest—they are the great reindeer themselves. Modern savages, explorers tell us, have ceremonial dances in which they dress up as the animals they slay, no doubt to cast a magic spell upon them. So, it seems, did our ancestors of a thousand years and more ago, when they hunted the great antlered deer. The reindeer are gone, and hunting for food has gone—but the Horn collect too. He travelled about the country inquiring about these ancient steps, these quaint costumes and simple haunting tunes. Some he learned just in time to save them from being forgotten ; they had never been written down, the young people would not trouble to learn them, and the old folks who knew them were dying off. He had their steps codified, their music printed ; he formed a special society to carry them on. That student was Cecil Sharp, and the movement he formed was the English Folk

FOX PHOTOS

A WEIRD DANCE AT ABBOTS BROMLEY

The dance of the Deermen is held at Abbots Bromley on " the first Monday after the Sunday nearest to September 4," when twelve Staffordshire yeomen each take a pair of deer's antlers from the parish church and, holding them aloft, dance through the district. The horns were originally used by the poor of the parish.

Dance that our forefathers composed is still danced today. Nor is the dance entirely devoid of religious association, for the traditional garb of the dancers is stored in the tower of the church.

This is by no means the only dance which has come to us through the centuries. It is now nearly forty years since a student chanced to see in an Oxfordshire village one Boxing Day a procession of quaintly-dressed men. One of their number played on the concertina, and the others danced with strange old-world steps. This dance, the observer learned, was danced each year and had been so danced for ages, with the same steps and the same tune. And now it was to be danced as of yore.

The student was interested ; already he had spent much time in collecting old folk-songs, and now, it seemed, there were folk-dances to

Dance Society ; and thanks to him, and his movement, the ancient ceremonial dances have taken on a new lease of life.

These folk dances were no mere means of amusement, no mere social function. They were danced solemnly, with set ritual and to a set tune, as they are still danced in more than one Oxfordshire village. Dressed in white, girt with brightly-coloured ribbons on which tiny bells jingle, their heads covered with broad-brimmed or flower-decked hats, the Morris Dancers stamp and kick and bound, wave their handkerchiefs or clash their staves ; the shrill strains of the fiddle mingle with the tinkling of the bells. So they danced long ago, it is said, to influence the corn and make it grow ; no longer do we think that a dance is magic and can influence the crops, but the dance still goes on.

The Morris is not the only form of dance

FOX PHOTOS

FOLK DANCING AT THAXTED

The ancient timbered Town Hall of Thaxted, in Essex, makes a perfect background for these country dancers. The local members of the Old English Folk Dance Society, which includes some of the hand weavers of Thaxted, are here seen dancing in the main street to the strains of music supplied by a girl fiddler and a drummer.

TOPICAL PRESS

ANCIENT CUSTOM IN COTSWOLD VILLAGE

Every Christmas at Marshfield, a village on the Cotswold Hills in Gloucestershire, this custom, stated to be eight hundred years old, is observed, having been revived after a lapse of some years. On Boxing Day the mummers, here seen setting out on their tour of the village, perform their traditional mumming play.

the country people know. Elsewhere a Sword Dance is more common; the dancers brandish short blunted blades; they dance in a circle, grasp the swords of their neighbours and dance in a chain, leap over the swords, crouch under the swords, link the swords together in a complicated knot and hold it triumphantly on high. Most significant of all, they lay their swords to the neck of one of their number, as though they were about to take his life. Does this ceremony hark back, as certain students of these things tell us, to a time when human sacrifice prevailed, when selected members of the community were ceremonially slain, that their blood should give new life to the harvest, that buried like the corn they should spring again to life in the golden grain?

Gathering Peascods

Morris and Sword Dances are for male teams; for men and women to join in are the Country Dances that we still enjoy. "Longways for as many as will" or in a circle the dancers assemble; they "set and turn single," bow to or "side with" or "arm" their partner; the accompanists go through the old familiar tunes. And so they dance what used to be a celebration of the corn-growing, to a melody that used to be played on the simplest of musical instruments, the tabor and pipe. Some of these dances are

associated with special places, and all, before they were taken up by the townsfolk, used to form an unvarying custom of the harvest home. Religious ideas now forgotten are recalled by some of their motions, for in the round dance of "Gathering Peascods," as the performers rush forward and clap their hands, they are said to be carrying out the old rite of "touching the sacred tree."

At Helston visitors and passers-by are apt to find themselves caught up and carried along in the dance. Still more strange is the experience of those who chance to pass through Hungerford, on the Bath Road, the second Tuesday after Easter. Then, at Hocktide as it is called, a picturesque ceremony takes place. An ancient horn is sounded by the Town Crier, who then parades through the streets in his uniform, summoning the Commoners to attend the Court House. The Hungerford Court of Feoffement is one of the few surviving examples of what used to be a very important feature of medieval life, the Manorial Court, which used to settle disputes arising among the commoners. This Court deals with fishing rights, which are of no small importance to the townsfolk, who find them a useful source of income. The Court itself is of interest to anyone who values the traditional and the picturesque; still more interesting is the outdoor part of the ceremony.

On Hocktide Tuesday two Tuttimen parade the streets of Hungerford. Each carries his ceremonial wand, which he has received from the Constable, a civic office which has come down from of old. The wand consists of a shoulder-high staff, topped with an orange and bedecked with flowers and streaming blue ribbons. By ancient law and custom the Tuttimen are entitled to claim a kiss from every girl they meet, or in default to demand a fine. They make their way through Hungerford, knocking at every door and demanding that all the girls out of the household come out to be kissed; they stop and kiss the girls that they meet. Very seldom, it is said, do the stalwart young Tuttimen have to content themselves with the fine! Meantime the Orange Scrambler, with befeathered hat, distributes gifts to the aged poor in the workhouse and to the children of the town.

Furry Dance and Tuttimen, Bale-fires and Well-dressing are perhaps older than Christianity. Yet the Christian festivals themselves are often celebrated locally with time-honoured rites. At Overton, Gloucestershire, and in other places, are found the Christmas Mummers, the only folk drama that has come down to us from the days of the ancient Mystery Plays. Costumes, words, acting, all are traditional; until recently the " book " of the play was never committed to print, but was passed down through the ages by word of mouth.

The characters of the Mummers vary in different villages and districts. In Wales a " Horse's Head " is sometimes found; an actor is of course concealed beneath it, and creates great merriment as he snaps its lower jaw open and shut. " Twing Twang " perhaps gets his name from the sound of a loosing bow-string, and " Little Johnnie Jack " from the burly henchman of Robin Hood; our Sherwood heroes are honoured everywhere throughout the land. The " Quack Doctor " has his astonishing pills and potions, fit to cure " the itch, the stitch, the palsy and the gout." " Father Christmas " introduces the Mummers and acts as " M.C.," and " King George " is the valiant knight who challenges all the world and overcomes the " Turks " and " Giants " with his wooden sword. In Cornwall there is a very fierce giant indeed:

"Here am I, old Hub-bub-bub
And in my hand I carries a club,
And on my back a frying-pan,
And am I not a valiant man?"

There is much horse-play and fooling about, but the central feature of the little drama is a duel between " King George " and the " Turkish Knight " who of course is left "lifeless " on the ground, only to be restored by the treatment given him by the " Quack Doctor." Here, it is said, is another vestige of the ancient custom of human sacrifice, taking us back to a pre-Christian age.

R. H. RAMSAY

SPECTACULAR FESTIVAL OF VIKING ORIGIN

At the annual festival of Up-Helli-Aa, at Lerwick in Shetland, which celebrates the close of the Yule festival, four hundred Guisers, headed by their chief Guiser Jarl, take part in a huge torchlight procession. A model of a Norse galley is drawn through the streets and burnt by the seashore. The Viking warriors in their galley.

The Danes who ravaged our shores brought their old customs with them, and their ancient methods of honouring their dead leaders are still recalled in the Shetland Islands. In January the Up-Helli-Aa procession makes its way through Lerwick. By the light of the torches a number of armoured Vikings, with their round shields and their winged helmets, drag through the streets a model of an ancient Norse "long ship," with the traditional snake's head and tail at its prow and stern. Other Vikings man the galley, their oars projecting over its sides as though to beat the waves, the shields bearing the crests of the oarsmen being fastened above. High on its deck stands the Guiser Jarl, with his battle-axe and his coat of mail. The bands play the ancient Norse tunes, the rockets blaze overhead, the torches are held aloft; the "long snake" moves forward on its platform, and a double line of flame follows behind.

A Blazing Dragon Ship

The doomed ship moves through the town and reaches the sea front. The torch-bearers circle around, and the islanders, descendants of the ancient Vikings themselves, sing *The Norseman's Home*. The crew leave the ship, the bugles sound and the maroons crash aloft — and the torches are flung into the ship. So the "long-snake" perishes in a blaze of flame, as long

ago a blazing "dragon ship" was laden with the body of some fallen chief, to take him, as though he had been slain in battle, to Valhalla of the Gods.

In the Up-Helli-Aa of the Shetland Islands we find today a survival of the Scandinavian ceremonies of our Norse forefathers; in the Tynwald of the Isle of Man we find, still as active and efficient as ever, one of their "Things," the folk-parliaments by which they governed their communal life. It is thus far older than the Westminster Parliament; it is indeed the oldest legislative assembly our islands possess. Every July the Tynwald assembles to promulgate its laws. A service is held in the church, and then the Lieutenant-Governor of the Island leads a procession to the Tynwald Hill. At the summit of the hill he sits side by side with the bishop; below him are the two dozen members of the Manx Parliament, the House of Keys, and below them the clergy and the officials. If the weather is wet, a tent is set up to cover the assembly; if fine, the ceremony is performed in the open air. An unsheathed sword is held point upwards; the wands of office are given in by the retiring coroners and handed to their successors; the titles of the acts passed during their year are recited in English and Manx, and so they become the law of that tiny land. Thus, much as the Vikings of old settled their disputes and made

TOPICAL

HISTORIC COMMON RIDING CELEBRATIONS

Every June, Selkirk celebrates the granting to the Borough of the Confirmation Charter by James V. Led by the crowds a procession passes through High Street towards the River Ettrick, where the riders gallop away. Here we see the Standard Bearer, holding aloft the Selkirk flag, being welcomed at the Toll after the return.

TOPICAL

SHROVE TUESDAY FOOTBALL IN DERBYSHIRE

The old-established Shrove Tuesday and Ash Wednesday football match is an event which draws crowds to the market town of Ashbourne, in the valley of the Dove. All the town join in the game and here a section of the crowd can be seen playing the ball in the river. Atherstone, Warwickshire, has a similar event.

rules to govern their behaviour, the Manxmen receive their law.

In many villages it is still customary to perform the " Beating of the Bounds," the limits of the parish being solemnly traversed in time-honoured fashion. A similar tradition in the North Country has a grim event behind it. The Border Country is peaceable enough now, and the Scots and the English are fellow-countrymen who find it easy enough to live in common citizenship together. Yet it is not so many years since the Border was the scene of fierce fighting, of merciless outrages and vengeful forays and raids. Soon after their defeat at Flodden, the Scots of Hawick learned that some English raiders were encamped a few miles away. With grim delight they made an attack in the darkness, took the raiders by surprise, killed them or drove them panic-stricken away.

Riding the Marches

So impressive was this victory, following on the crushing defeat of Flodden, that its annual celebration has been continued ever since. A banner, locally held to be that which was carried during the fight, is presented by the town Provost to the Cornet, or leader. Traditional songs are sung invoking the ancient Nordic gods, there is

a procession and a feast. Next morning the members of the ceremonial band rise in the night, as did the raiding party whose triumph they celebrate, and sing a hymn to the rising sun from the bank of the Moat. Another procession is held round the streets and up to the Common which the town received as a reward for the victory ; and this is the " Riding of the Marches " which is observed as a festival and a holiday throughout the town.

Many other ceremonies could be described did space permit. The giving of the Dunmow Flitch to married couples who do not regret their marriage ; the Midsummer Day sunrise-watching from Stonehenge itself ; the Town Crier's contest in Wiltshire ; the bottle-kicking at Hallaton in Leicestershire ; the Forest Courts of Swainmote in the New Forest and at Speech House in the Forest of Dean ; the distribution of oranges and lemons at St. Clements in the Strand—all flourish even in this hustling machine-using age. Such customs are not merely picturesque and quaint. They tell of manners of life and ways of thought other than ours but of manners and ways from which our own have sprung. They may enable us to understand our forefathers, and so they may enable us the better to understand ourselves.

W. F. TAYLOR

THE GIANT'S CAUSEWAY

On the Antrim coast is the Giant's Causeway where a mass of once molten rock has cooled and solidified into innumerable columns of basalt, most of them of hexagonal shape.   Fingal's Cave in the Isle of Staffa, presents a similar formation and legend claims both these outcrops as remnants of a bridge built by an Irish giant.

IRELAND—ISLE OF DESTINY

by MARGARET MAGUIRE

"For, tread as you may on Irish soil
From Antrim's coast to wild Cape Clear,
From east to west no view is found
Without its ruin, rath or mound
To tell of times that were."

TO him who studies it with interest and attention, the face of Ireland reveals a woeful yet wondrous story—the romance of the Irish nation. Century has followed century into the tomb of time, each bearing its burden of "old unhappy far-off things" : but places and place-names, castles and abbeys, round tower and hallowed ruin — these with many other imprints of history remain

"Mute tongues that silent ever speak
Of Ireland's past of grief and glory."

"Isle of Destiny" (Innisfail)—such was the name given it by the Milesians, a Scythian people reputed to have sailed the seas to find their promised land. Tradition, with unusual precision, holds that they first sighted the Irish coast on May 17, in the year 1029 B.C., and hailed it with joy as the island of which Moses had long previously prophesied to their famous ancestor, Gadelius—from whom they were known as the Gaels.

Having defeated, in epic battles, the inhabitants of the island (remnants of many preceding vague waves of colonization), the Milesians settled in Ireland and for more than 2,000 succeeding years their dynasty held sway. One of their monarchs, Ollamh Fodhla, the Solomon of Irish history, instituted (some 1,000 years B.C.) the great national legislative assembly summoned triennially at Tara Hill, in Meath. Tara was, until A.D. 563, the royal place of Ireland and the residence of the Ard-Ri or High King. Today, but a few raths and some grassy mounds and pillars mark the site of the once great heart of a nation.

Christianity dawned on a world almost mastered by Rome. But to Irish soil the Roman Eagle never penetrated. Left to itself, the nation developed its own organization, legislation and institutions. The country was divided, as now, into four main provinces—Ulster, Munster, Leinster and Connacht, each having its provincial king as well as a host of princes of numerous clans.

In Ulster, two splendid palaces are known to ancient history—that at Emania, built in approximately 700 B.C., where now the Navan Fort, two miles west of Armagh, marks the spot ; and that at Aileach by the shores of Lough Swilly where the great ruin, now visited by thousands of tourists, comprises three ramparts of earth mixed with uncemented stones and enclosing a "Cashel" or stone rampart. Cashel, in Tipperary, where stands the "Rock" today, was, in its earliest beginnings, another such royal site.

To this pre-Christian era also belong such stone forts as the mighty Dun Aengus, cresting a sheer 300 feet cliff on Aran Island and Staigue Fort, in Kerry—the most perfect of its kind extant. All over the country there are hundreds of kindred relics—Raths (earthen structures), Cahers (stone structures), Duns (structures on high cliffs), Clochans (stone huts), Crannógs (lake dwellings) and Cairns, Stone Circles and Tumuli (sepulchral monuments).

Worth special mention among such pre-Christian remains are the Lia Fáil (Stone of Destiny) on Tara Hill ; the ancient and interesting group of clochans beside Slea Head, in Kerry ; the Pillar Stones bearing Ogham inscriptions in the old cemetery of Killeen Cormac, in Kildare,

BAINBRIDGE, BELFAST

ST. PATRICK'S STONE

The saint is supposed to have begun his missionary labours in this area, south-west of Carlingford Lough, which includes Downpatrick, where this granite slab is alleged, but on no good evidence, to mark his grave.

W. F. TAYLOR

THE WAVE-BEATEN COAST OF DONEGAL

On the shores of Mulroy Bay stands this little hamlet of Carrigart, far away from the bustle and turmoil of modern civilization. West of the village is the narrow neck of the Rosguill peninsula which thrusts northwards between Mulroy Bay and Sheephaven. In the neighbourhood there are many historical features.

and the Stone Circles at Carrowmore in Sligo, by Lough Gur, in Limerick, and on the Loughcrew Hills, a mausoleum in Meath.

Beds of Diarmuid and Gráinne

In many parts of Ireland one stumbles across " dolmens," more popularly called " cromlechs." These impressive groupings of three or more large unhewn stones supporting a huge flat covering stone were once believed to have been Druid altars, but are now recognized as sepulchral erections dating from the Neolithic or Bronze Age.

Splendid specimens of this feature of Pagan Ireland may be seen at Kilternan, Co. Dublin, the cap stone here measuring 23½ feet by 17 feet, and having six supports ; at Ballymacscanlon, in Louth, where the massive structure is 12 feet high ; at Carrowmore, in Sligo, where there is quite a cluster of cromlechs ; and near Glanworth, Cork, where one of huge proportions has given its name—Labbacully, the old hag's bed—to the surrounding district.

In romantic tradition they are known as " Giant's Graves," and sometimes " Beds of Diarmuid and Gráinne," those legendary lovers who fled from Gráinne's betrothed husband, Fionn MacCool, and were pursued all over Ireland by a revengeful Fionn and his army of Fenians.

The Fianna or Irish Militia headed by Fionn reached the peak point of its glory in the third century A.D. during the reign of Cormac MacArt. Many and marvellous are the stories associated with its fame. The Giant's Causeway at Antrim is said to have been flung across the sea to Scotland by Fionn, to hasten his hostile encounter with a fearsome Scottish rival. Cloughmore (Big Stone) at Rostrevor, was hurled, it is said, by the Scottish Giant at Fionn's head and just missed it ! Fionn retaliated with the Isle of Man which he pulled out of the space now occupied by Lough Neagh. The dolmen at Howth, near Dublin, is pointed out as the burial place of Aideen, wife of Fionn's son Oisin, while Fionn's two moated palaces were situated at the vantage points of Moyvalley, in Offaly, and the Hill of Allen, in Kildare. Scarce a spot in Ireland does not treasure some legend of this renowned Irish Giant.

Yet another great military order, but linked up with the first century A.D. and confined for the most part to Ulster, was the Red Branch Knighthood of which Cuchullain was champion. His name and doughty deeds re-echo in Rathcroghan, where stood the royal palace of Ulster's rival—Connacht, in Cooley, the venue of the Cattle Raid by Maeve, the Amazonian Queen of Connacht, on Slieve Gullion outside Dundalk, where the hero captured the wild fairy steed of

Macha, and at Ardee (the Ford of Ferdia), where for three days Cuchullian was forced to fight his dear friend Ferdia. At Ratheddy, near Dundalk, one may view the "Leaning Stone" to which the champion bound himself that he might die standing. Only when his enemies saw the bird of prey alight on his shoulder did they dare approach. Today, in the General Post Office at Dublin, a beautiful bronze memorial by Oliver Shepherd depicts Cuchullian thus dying tied by his own mantle to the pillar.

The most famous royal burial ground of ancient Ireland was historic Brugh-na-Boinne along the River Boyne. Some of its vast Neolithic tumuli have been excavated, and that at Newgrange, which by its size and the elaborate ornamentation of its interior is one of the most remarkable monuments in Europe, deserves a visit.

In A.D. 432 St. Patrick brought Christianity to Ireland and won a speedy victory for his faith. Thenceforth the face of the nation took on new features readily distinguishable today in the large number of early Christian relics—oratories, churches, round towers, crosses and monastic settlements—which punctuate the countryside. Claims of a pre-Patrician Christian settlement by St. Declan at Ardmore, in Waterford (where there is a perfect round tower that still stands to this day), are supported by the presence there of some very ancient remains of the Oratory, Stone and Well of St. Declan.

All over Ireland there are footprints of Saint Patrick. On Slemish Mountain, when a slave boy, he tended the flocks of a Pagan chieftain. On Slane Hill he kindled the first Paschal fire in Ireland, thus incurring the wrath of the High King and the Druids who summoned him to their presence at Tara. In Cashel he baptized Angus, King of Munster; Armagh he made the site of his cathedral; Croagh Patrick and Lough Derg, to this day centres of unique and vigorous pilgrimages, were his places of penance and in Downpatrick a rough granite slab in the grounds of the cathedral marks his grave.

Irish Missionaries

The seed sown by Patrick bore fruit a hundredfold. From the sixth to the ninth century Ireland was the island of saints and scholars, a beacon light of faith and learning to a Europe engulfed in the aftermath of the great Roman collapse and inundated by the ensuing tidal wave of barbarism. In Ireland monastic establishments flourished everywhere, they were veritable Universities of Piety, Culture and Art. The Irish mission sent preachers and scholars to England and the Continent. Alfred the Great is said to have studied in the Irish schools, and the great Charlemagne summoned their teachers to direct his colleges.

At Glendalough, today a romantic beauty spot in Wicklow, St. Kevin in the sixth century

SLEMISH MOUNTAIN

BAINBRIDGE, BELFAST

Ireland's patron saint, Patrick, is supposed to have tended the herds of his master, Milchu, in the neighbourhood of this mountain near Ballymena, Co. Antrim, and to have beheld visions which inflamed his imagination. A modern biographer states that the scene of his captivity was laid in Connaught, near Croagh Patrick.

DIXON-SCOTT

GLENDALOUGH, CO. WICKLOW: ROUND TOWER AND ST. KEVIN'S KITCHEN

Here in the sixth century, St. Kevin founded the monastic city of Glendalough.   The ruins of seven churches and an almost perfect round tower mark the site.   Legend says that the poor Saint was continually tempted by a wileful maiden and to escape from her he took refuge in the cave now known as St. Kevin's Bed.

I.T.A.

THE "ROYAL AND SAINTLY ROCK" OF CASHEL

The Rock of Cashel in Tipperary is one of Ireland's most ancient landmarks and on its crest are the remains of a number of beautiful medieval buildings.   Here was the royal residence of the Kings of Munster and there are also ruins of a cathedral, the richly decorated twelfth-century Cormac's Chapel and a well-preserved Round Tower, 90 feet high.   According to legend the rock was originally carried to this spot by the devil.

founded his monastic city. Thousands of visitors climb each year the perpendicular rock overhanging the Upper Lake, to see his cave-bed in the cliff face. Seven churches, which may to this day be identified, grew up in this hallowed centre. The sixth century too, and the seventh, saw the setting up of many other famed schools and monasteries. St. Kieran founded Clonmacnois beside the Shannon—today a lovely and venerable ruin. St. Finian was the founder of Clonard in Meath, St. Colman of Kilmacduagh, in Galway, St. Brendan the Navigator of Clonfert, near Clonmacnois and St. Finbarr of lone Gougane Barra at the source of the River Lee. To this Golden Age belong, among many other jewels

above all, their greed and at this time round towers were erected to serve both as watch towers before and as places of refuge during a Norse raid.

These round towers, some of them sadly the worse for history's wear and tear, dot the whole countryside. Careful and studious research has assigned their origin to three distinct periods between A.D. 890 and 1238, and has divided them into four distinct classes, according to their style of masonry and their doorways. The towers range from 50 to 120 feet in height, and are all approximately 16 feet in diameter at the base. They comprise four to five storeys reached by interior ladders and having a doorway several

DIXON-SCOTT

KILLINEY BAY AND THE WICKLOW MOUNTAINS

Many writers have described in glowing words this beautiful bay near Dublin, comparing it favourably with that of Naples. On Killiney Hill, whence the picture was taken, Bernard Shaw wandered as a boy. In the distance is Bray Head, and behind it rise the Sugar Loaf and the hills and glens of the Wicklow Mountains.

of art and architecture, the beautiful Book of Kells (now preserved in Trinity College, Dublin), lovely Gallerus Oratory on the side of Mount Brandon, in Kerry, and the noble High Cross of Monasterboice in County Louth.

The fearsome hordes of invaders known to Irish history as simply "The Danes," threw, towards the close of the eighth century, the first shadows of their fateful comings. In the beginning of their inroads they were mere pirates making intermittent but fierce attacks on various parts of the coast and landing to burn, pillage and plunder. Ecclesiastical settlements, being rich in sacred vessels of precious metals, attracted,

feet from the ground—out of reach of any battering ram, and allowing entrance by a ladder afterwards hauled in by the defenders.

Some seventy of these picturesque structures are now extant but not more than a dozen of them retain their original conical cap. Perhaps the best known to tourists are those at Glendalough (there are two here), Ardmore (in Waterford), Clondalkin (beside Dublin), Monasterboice (in Louth), Antrim (beside Lough Neagh), Devenish Island (on Lough Erne), Clonmacnois (beside the Shannon) and Cashel (upon the Royal Rock). Those at Cloyne (Cork), Killmallock (Limerick), Kildare and Kilkenny

DIXON-SCOTT

CARRICKFERGUS CASTLE, CO. ANTRIM

Probably the most interesting and perfect Norman fortification in Ireland, this castle was completed in the early thirteenth century and has been garrisoned continuously for over seven hundred years. It was for centuries the only castle held by the English in the north. Within recent years it has been completely restored.

DIXON-SCOTT

ST. PATRICK'S CATHEDRAL, DUBLIN

This twelfth-century edifice, which is rich in historical associations, raises its smoke grimed head above the roofs of Dublin's poorest homes. From its pulpit Jonathan Swift, author of " Gulliver's Travels," preached in language as biting as his satires. He died in the deanery and was laid to rest in the cathedral near the woman he loved and may have married. Samuel Lover, the Irish novelist and poet is also buried here.

carry a battlemented parapet erected to replace the conical cap after it had fallen down.

Later the Danish hordes began to come in fuller force and to settle down in sites favourable for maritime cities. So began modern Dublin, Drogheda, Waterford, Limerick and Wexford, whence the new settlers from time to time made marauding sallies into the interior of the country. About the year A.D. 840, a monster fleet under the fierce Thorgils sailed up the Shannon, sacked Clonmacnois and converted the cathedral into a pagan palace. Retribution was wrung from them by Malachy, Prince of Westmeath (he who " wore the collar of gold which he won from the proud invader "), and by Niall, then Ard-Ri of Ireland. But the decisive battle that crushed for ever the power of the Danes as a ruling force in Ireland was that fought at Clontarf outside Dublin on Good Friday, 1014, wherein Brian Boru, High King of Ireland defeated a combined Norse force of some 20,000 strong. Thenceforth the Danes continued to hold some maritime cities in the country, but never after did they aspire to its conquest.

The Vikings

Danish footsteps have left many an imprint in Dublin, particularly in Christ Church Cathedral, a splendid erection founded by the Norse Settlers in 1038, and in St.

W. F. TAYLOR

MUCKROSS ABBEY, KILLARNEY

Within these walls were buried two modern Gaelic writers: Egan O'Rahilly (died 1726), who wrote satires on the Cromwellian invasion; and Owen Roe O'Sullivan (died 1784), whose witty sayings are still current in Munster.

Michan's Church whose vaults have always had curious preservative powers by virtue of which their dead remain undecayed. Reginald's Tower, in Waterford, commemorates these sea raiders too, while such places as Waterford, Wexford, Wicklow, Arklow, Strangford and Carlingford preserve in their names the story of their Scandinavian origin.

To the medieval chapter of Ireland's story date many well-known features of the countryside. Up to the middle of the twelfth century church architecture developed on very interesting lines, a style of elaborate ornamentation and decoration known as the Hiberno-Romanesque having come into use. Well proportioned columns with carved capitals and exquisitely moulded doorways are typical of such churches as Clonmacnois, Killeshin, Aghadoe (Killarney) and Freshford, while that gem of Irish architecture "Cormac's Chapel," on the Rock of Cashel, ascribed to 1127, shows, in its ruin, a richly-carved doorway, a steeply-pitched stone

CASTLE OF THE BLARNEY STONE

This castle at Blarney, Co. Cork, contains the magic " Blarney Stone." By the simple expedient of kissing the stone one is endowed with the ability to " speak with the tongue of men and of angels." The fortress was built by the MacCarthys, Princes of Desmond, and was at one time considered almost impregnable.

roof and intricate external and internal ornament. But the latter half of the twelfth century witnessed a change to the large cruciform edifices in the pointed (transitional) style.

The establishment in Ireland, about this time, of the Cistercian Order resulted in the erection of many monastic structures, which even in their ruins today are very beautiful. Mellifont, sweet as its name, was the first such abbey, and owed its establishment, in 1142, to the bounty of Donagh O'Carroll, the Lord of Oriel. What splendour of scene attended its consecration in 1157! Among the royal guests were Tiernan O'Rourke, Prince of Breffni and his wife Devorgilla, whose abduction by Dermot McMurrough, the ill-famed King of Leinster, was the immediate cause of the Anglo-Norman invasion of Ireland. Almost forty years later, after much prayer and penance, this repentant queen returned to die and be buried within the walls of the monastery.

Bective Abbey, not far from Mellifont and very near to Tara, rose four years after the parent house and became an important centre, its abbot being a Lord of Parliament. Today it slumbers, grey-shrouded in peace by the banks of the historic Boyne. And Jerpoint beside the Nore, in Kilkenny, is another such beautiful group of ruins comprising a church, tower, cloisters and several monuments. Perhaps the most elaborate of these foundations was Holy Cross, near

Thurles—if one may judge from the wealth of detail and exquisite features noticeable in the ruin today. It was once a famed place of pilgrimage, for it enshrined a relic of the True Cross, now treasured in the Ursuline Convent in Cork. Hore Abbey, at the foot of the Rock of Cashel, and the cathedral, on the summit, are of this era, the latter being particularly beautiful and most historic.

Loveliest of Irish Castles

The majority of Irish castles date from the Anglo-Norman span of history and range, in great variety, from the single and simple keep-tower of the invading chieftain to the defensive fortresses—now noticeable in the ruins at Trim, Maynooth, Bunratty, Roscommon and Limerick—and the modernized castles found liberally all over the country. Roscommon, known as " one of the largest and loveliest of Irish castles " was inhabited up to 1691 when it fell in the burnings that followed the Battle of Aughrim. A lovely specimen of the modernized castle is Lismore, overlooking the Blackwater River, in County Waterford. Today the Irish home of the Duke of Devonshire, it stands on a precipitous cliff amid a wealth of foliage that frames its majesty. Another such is storied Malahide Castle, the more than 700-year-old home of the Talbots; and again, Kilkenny, the castle of the Butlers of

Ormonde, on the banks of the " grey-watered " Nore, of which Spenser wrote. Dublin Castle, for more than seven centuries the hub of English rule in Ireland, was erected at the instructions of King John of England, and to this day remains a showplace of the city, although in strict truth, the only portion of the original building extant is the Bermingham Tower, which was used as a State Prison and has its own dread tale of suffering to record. St. Patrick's Cathedral, a very handsome building in the oldest part of the city dates from 1191, but has its chief associations with the eighteenth century.

Drogheda offers a good instance of Anglo-Norman town fortifications. Its walls were strengthened by twenty towers—portions of which still remain, and it was entered by ten gates, of which the only one extant is the impressive St. Lawrence's Gate. This consists of two lofty circular towers of four storeys, between them being a retiring wall pierced, like the towers, with loopholes. Other such fortifications may be identified in their remains at Limerick, Athlone, Drogheda, Clonmel and Waterford.

For place-names of Norman origin, perhaps the most interesting example is Buttevant—in Cork—a corruption of the war cry of the De Barrys—*Boutez-en-avant*—(push forward), in

their attacks and predatory raids around this district.

Tudor days left many a mark inscribed upon the face of Ireland. With the reign of Henry VIII came the dissolution of the monasteries and the confiscation of church lands. Thus were deserted Mellifont, Muckross (in Killarney), Timoleague, Clonmacnois, Durrow, Boyle and a host of other lovely settlements, some of which fell into decay through disuse, some of which were afterwards restored for a brief span and many of which were battered down when they were used as places of refuge and besieged during the numerous battles fought out on Irish soil between the supporters of the Royalist, Roundhead and Williamite sides in the English civil wars of the seventeenth century.

Sir Walter Raleigh

Wars and rumours of wars on the part of " the rebellious Irish " fill the stretch of Elizabeth's reign in Ireland, and many grim landmarks enshrine their memories. Sir Walter Raleigh, who was given large estates in Munster, introduced the first potato and the first tobacco plants to Ireland. His name is echoed in Youghal, where at his house, Myrtle Grove, he entertained the poet Spenser. One can imagine the Lord Mayor of Youghal (Raleigh) and the Clerk to

BAINBRIDGE, BELFAST

THE GAP OF DUNLOE, KILLARNEY

Between Purple Mountain (2,737 feet) and Macgillicuddy's Reeks (3,414 feet), the highest range in Ireland, is this magnificent four-mile long defile. Visitors to Killarney often make the journey through the Gap on ponies. In a valley almost at right angles to it are the Three Lakes, connected by the Long Range Stream.

the Council of Munster (Spenser) reading, in pleasant Elizabethan gardens by the sea, the manuscripts of *The Faerie Queene*, and perhaps of *Colin Clout's Come Home Again*, a work treasuring many references to Munster scenery. For Spenser spent eight years of his life at Kilcolman Castle, an old Desmond stronghold in Cork. It was sacked and burned over his head by the native Irish whom he hated as sincerely as he loved the natural beauty of their country.

In Dublin city, Elizabethan days are recalled by a lovely group of buildings comprising Trinity College, in the heart of the capital. A charter for the foundation of this university was obtained from the queen in 1591, and the lands of the old Augustinian monastery of All Hallows (established by Dermot McMurrough, in 1166, but suppressed in 1538), were granted by the Mayor and Corporation for the new institution. The original Elizabethan erections have alas, disappeared, the oldest surviving block (1722) being the red brick range on the east side of Library Square.

The queen's favourite, Essex, commanded for a time the queen's forces against the Irish chieftains, O'Neill and O'Donnell, but with disastrous results that led to his fateful breach with the queen and consequent death in the Tower of London. From Blarney Castle, just outside Cork City, and renowned for the "Stone of Eloquence" in its battlements, which many come to kiss today, Elizabeth derived a new word to add to the English language. "Blarney," or soft talk, referred to the delays and delusive promises of surrender made by its owner, The McCarthy, to Sir George Carew.

Yet another famed Munster Castle was Dunboy, in the Berehaven Peninsula, on the outskirts of the Atlantic. This ancient seat of the O'Sullivans of Bere was almost shattered to pieces by Carew in one of the most obstinate sieges of history, in 1602. Only a portion of the walls now remain, while of the brave defenders not one survived.

A Pirate Queen

In Western Ireland, in the late sixteenth century, the Corsair Queen, Grace O'Malley (Granuaile), sailed the seas in barques of plunder, a picturesque figure of rude beauty who once called upon Elizabeth's Court (1593) and met her sister queen with calmness and aplomb. Her castles are a feature of the west of Ireland today—strong square keeps of martial aspect. Clare Island was her home and Carrigahooley (Rock of the Fleet) the safe harbour of her pirate galleys.

Cromwell came to Ireland in 1649, to ravage with fire and the sword, the enemies of his dictatorship. For Ireland, with its ever fatal propensity of backing a losing side had, in espousing the Royalist cause, become the final stage of this civil struggle. The Protector's triumphant

BAINBRIDGE, BELFAST

CATHEDRAL OF ST. PATRICK, KILLARNEY
This cathedral was built in the Gothic style after the design of A. W. N. Pugin. In the north transept is a brass to Bishop Moriarty and the three-light east window was a thank-offering from an Earl of Kenmare for the recovery of his only daughter. It is by far the most distinctive building in the town of Killarney.

"tour" of Ireland left a tradition of cruelty which earned him undying hatred. His name became a household word of fear. In Drogheda, which he took by storm, with consequent ferocity, the ruins of the Abbey of St. Mary, as well as the once stout walls of the city, bear testimony to the power of his guns. In the Bull Ring, in Wexford Town, some three hundred civilians, mostly women, were slaughtered by the Ironsides. Several places connected with his cruel campaign carry his name today — Cromwell's Arch, in Youghal, Cromwell's Bridge, in Glengarriff (said to have been built, by his order, in an hour), and Cromwell's Rock, on the River Moy, in Mayo.

Cromwell, having broken the back of his Irish campaign, left it in the hands of his son-in-law, Ireton, and returned to England in 1650. In the subsequent successes of his followers, Limerick, Athlone and Galway were stormed and taken, while Ross Castle, a fourteenth-century stronghold of the O'Donoghue's of Kerry, surrendered in 1652—"the last place in Munster to yield." Today it is a handsome ruin fronting the waters of the Lower Lake. The almost perfect keep consists of a splendid square tower with a spiral staircase to the top.

BAINBRIDGE, BELFAST

THE CURFEW TOWER, CUSHENDALL

From this tower, which stands in the centre of one of the most prettily situated towns in Ulster, the " curfew " is rung every night at seven o'clock. It was originally erected " as a place of confinement for rioters and idlers."

All around there are places and things woven into the legends of storied Lough Leane and the exploits of the great O'Donoghue, "Donal of the Captives," who was the most famed of the Kerry chieftains. One can see the window in the castle, whence he leaped, charger and all, into the lake beneath, to arise every seventh year on the morning of May Day and, mounted on his white horse, ride over the Kingdom of Kerry. The boatmen of Killarney, rowing over Lough Leane, will point out the Island Library of The O'Donoghue, where shelves of rocks hold slabs of rocks, and his Prison Rock, whereto he chained delinquents and left them to starve— but always he saw to it there was plenty of water.

Many scenes of yet another war—that between Kings James and William—were set in Ireland, the decisive battle of this Stuart strife being fought at the Boyne Water on July 1, 1690. The ford where King William's army crossed to the south bank to close with the Jacobites is just outside Drogheda, and nearby is King William's Glen, a leafy place of memories. In this conflict, too, the city of Derry looms important for its historic siege (1689) which lasted one hundred and five days, and was at long last relieved by the Williamite forces who burst the blockade and rescued the exhausted city. The cathedral in Derry is filled with relics and trophies of that amazing and historical siege.

The last siege of this campaign was Limerick (1691) where on the Treaty Stone (in the town today) the famous Treaty of Limerick was signed. King John's Castle, dating from the early thirteenth century, bears some marks of Williamite guns, but the old and lovely cathedral (St. Mary's) remained intact and stands, a silent witness of eight troubled centuries of history.

Under the Georges, Dublin became a splendid city, ranking second in the Empire, next to London in population, extent and magnificence of buildings. The eighteenth century was her "glorious" age, and to those days date the wide streets and beautiful squares and houses so

years to complete. It suffered severely in the civil hostilities following the Anglo-Irish Treaty, but was restored, with little change in its external appearance.

Many visitors to Dublin regard the Customs House, near O'Connell Bridge, as the city's most beautiful building. It was begun in 1781 and took ten years to build. Leinster House, in Kildare Street, formerly the residence of the Dukes of Leinster and now the Dail or meeting place of the Irish Free State Parliament, was built in 1745 from designs by Cassels, while the Bank of Ireland—until the union in 1800 the Irish House of Parliament—dates from 1729, and

DIXON-SCOTT

THE FOUR COURTS, DUBLIN

Erected at a cost of £200,000 during the closing years of the eighteenth century, it is one of Ireland's most impressive public buildings. During the Civil War of 1922 it was seized by the Republican leader, Rory O'Connor, and withstood a siege by the Free State forces under Michael Collins. It has since been restored.

much admired in the Irish capital at the present day. Social gatherings of splendour assembled in the stately Georgian houses—Belvedere House (now a secondary school), Charlemont House (now the Municipal Gallery of Modern Art), and those of Merrion Square, Kildare Street, Stephen's Green, Fitzwilliam Square, Mountjoy Square and Parnell (then Rutland) Square. Many of their walls and ceilings were decorated by Angelica Kauffman.

The City Hall, beside Dublin Castle, was erected in 1769 as the "Royal Exchange." The Four Courts, which is one of Dublin's architectural masterpieces, dates from 1786. This beautiful pile cost £200,000 and took fourteen

is perhaps the proudest proof of eighteenth-century activity in the city. Its east front, with six lofty columns forms one of the most excellent specimens of Corinthian architecture to be seen anywhere.

St. Patrick's Cathedral, though of an earlier age, has eighteenth-century memories of Jonathan Swift its fiery dean "whom fierce indignation lacerated." Goldsmith and Burke are associated with Trinity College, and their statues (by Foley) stand within its railings. Addison lived in Glasnevin, where his house "Addison Lodge" is still to be seen. His favourite walk, along the Tolka Bank, is named "Addison's Walk"; now in the Botanic Gardens. Peg Woffington

DIXON-SCOTT

THE GUILDHALL OF THE WALLED CITY OF LONDONDERRY

Some of the stained-glass windows of this building were presented by the London Companies. It was in 1613 that a charter was granted to certain London trade guilds, grouped as the Irish Society, whereby they became owners of large tracts of Ulster, including Derry, which then added London to its ancient name.

W. F. TAYLOR

THE LOFTY CLIFFS OF MOHER
These rugged cliffs in Co. Clare rise sheer out of the water to a height of 700 feet and extend for five miles. During rough weather the Atlantic waves, higher here than anywhere in the world except Cape Horn, present an enthralling spectacle as they thunder against the rocks. Moher is a veritable bird-lover's paradise.

acted in Smock Alley theatre ; Handel played on the old organ in St. Michan's. The Royal Dublin Society was founded (1731) for the advancement of industry, agriculture, arts and crafts ; the Royal and Grand Canals were constructed and a service of mail packets introduced between Dublin and Holyhead. In effect, the main features of the plan and arrangement of modern Dublin may be said to begin from an Act of the Irish Parliament of 1757 appointing " Commissioners for making a wide and convenient street from the Essex Bridge to the Castle of Dublin." The ample accommodation built at the Docks is yet another testimony to the very far-seeing policy and sound judgment of the eighteenth-century town planners.

Fear of Invasion
To the eighteenth century also, when fear of French naval invasion was rife (and not without cause), belong the many Martello towers which one sees along the Irish coastline, particularly on the east front. Ugly and little-used structures, their purpose was to anticipate attack by fortifying the coast. Those standing at Sandycove, on Dalkey Island, and at Malahide are good examples of the type.

With the Act of Union, in 1800, Dublin ceased to be an independent capital, the seat of Government and the home of a resident aristocracy.

In the nineteenth century, cut off from the mainspring of government, industry and commerce, the city wilted into decay, amid the elegancies of its former independence. This decline was hastened by the opening up of outlying districts by rail and train in the nineteenth century, so that handsome suburbs grew up amid sea and mountains, but at the expense of the city. However, since the establishment of the Irish Free State as a separate political entity (1922) having its independent legislature, the city has thrived, and now bids fair to becoming as handsome and prosperous as, and a great deal more representative of its hinterland than the eighteenth-century capital.

Danes, Normans, English and the original Gaels—these have left most marks upon the face of Ireland today. One can read the story of her rough-hewn destiny in the many monuments of ancient times, and of medieval and modern centuries which are scattered in such rich profusion over her plains and mountains and in the heart of her deep-wooded glens. She has watched the battle smoke of many long centuries drift across the screen of troubled time. She has known trouble and distress and the bitterness of internecine strife. May she have at last emerged, triumphant if somewhat scathed, to reach, in quiet confidence, safe harbour, hard-won but long-enduring !

THE VILLAGE AND ITS STORY

by RUSSELL PAGE

OF all the factors that go towards the making of the English scene the village is not the least important. The red roofs of cottages clustered round a church beyond the water meadows, a ribbon of stone-tiled houses climbing a Cotswold hillside, the bright simplicity of whitewash and slate lightening the bareness of a northern moor—our villages invest our varying landscape with a human element, and now perhaps only in the villages can we clearly trace the slow change in the patterns of our daily life during the last 2,000 years.

To find the first evidences of the English village we must go back a long way. Our earlier ancestors, the Celts, lived as shepherds on the bare downs and hills which rose like islands above the thickly - forested lowlands and the swamps of the un-drained river valleys. Little beyond a few names and well-worn tracks where the daisies still grow thickest remains to tell us of these people except in the west, where in Cornwall and parts of Wales the countryside is peppered with many tiny hamlets showing that these were a people who lived in much smaller groups than the Saxons.

The village was based on an economic necessity. Settlers stopped at a place which offered them a favourable opportunity of gathering their livelihood from the very earth around them. It is hard to imagine trying to make a life with only such things as you could grow. Bread, meat, milk, beer and wool from field and grassland, timber from the forest for furniture, and clay from the river bank for pots and dishes.

As a result the beauty of our villages is a great deal more than skin deep. Implicit in their buildings, their bridges, their mills and fords, their field tracks and their common lands is the accumulated experience of generations of sturdy men working their lands for daily bread and accumulating a deep knowledge of the hard necessities of life.

In the fifth and sixth centuries the Anglo-Saxons came in bands to conquer the Celts or drive them into the far west. They pushed their way up the river valleys in their long boats.

These people were agriculturists rather than shepherds—the bare wolds and hill-tops were less useful to them. They needed well drained land for growing wheat, rye and barley, water meadows for their cattle, good water, and woodlands for fuel and pigs. By the very pattern and placing of most of our villages in the middle of their open fields we can still see how the Saxons and Danes instituted in England the idea of a larger communal agricultural life quite different from the smaller grouping and tiny enclosures of their Celtic predecessors.

By the time the Domesday Book came to be written in 1086, many villagers, owing to successive small waves of invasion, had given up their freedom in return for protection from a local lord, and from this usage grew the "manorial" system on which medieval village life was based. The manor house and the church became the two social centres of the village.

Very soon the village ceased to be a collection of primitive dwelling-places where men and their cattle shared a common roof. The church and the manor linked the village directly to a national life. Under the feudal system the village was a link in the chain that connected the lord of the manor through his overlord to the king and to the idea of central government.

STEPHENSON

A DALE OF ITS OWN

Dent, near the western border of Yorkshire, has a dale to itself and is an example of the stone-built villages that nestle so beautifully in the north country.

The feudal system is reflected to this day in the thousands of villages which cluster round the tower or steeple of the village church, and the manor house. In many places only the manor and church remain close together—the village has grown away towards a road. In other places cottages may have encroached on the manor field and only a dried-up moat or a piece of finely-cut stone incorporated into a barn remain to tell us that here was the great house.

The next great change in village life was due partly to the Black Death, and partly to improved methods of weaving on the Continent. The first was a plague which towards the end of the fourteenth century decimated the population of England. Whole villages were deserted, land fell out of cultivation and by accident of disease the feudal system of land tenure fell into jeopardy. About this time, too, came the increasing demand for fine wool. The English uplands produced the best wool obtainable and landowners were quick to buy up small farms and enclose the common lands to form huge sheep runs. By the reign of Henry VII whole villages had disappeared, rents went up, small tenants unable to pay lost their farms, and the system of large farmers employing landless men as labourers began.

This new system brought into being a new kind of village, the most characteristic of which

still exist almost complete in the Cotswolds. These limestone hills made the best sheep-walks and fine grass and plentiful water made good wool. The same hills were quarried for limestone to build in lasting material such exquisite villages, some large enough to call themselves towns, as Chipping Campden, Broadway and Stanway, Burford and Bourton, Stow and the Swells. Noble architecture in the rigid perpendicular manner reflected the riches of the new kind of landowner and set a new standard.

Birth of England's Hedges

In the eighteenth century the rising price of wheat led to a new revival of arable farming and the great enclosures began.

These Enclosure Acts had enormously important economic reactions on the village, but they are chiefly interesting to us because the present setting of most of our villages dates from this period.

The endlessly shifting shapes of grass and ploughland changing in texture and colour through the seasons, enclosed by quickthorn hedge, punctuated by lines of hedgerow trees—in fact the whole network of field and hedgerow patterned like stained glass in its leading, dates from the late eighteenth century.

One hundred years ago the railway took the traffic off the roads—the factories and towns

HUMPHREY AND VERA JOEL

A PERFECT COTSWOLD VILLAGE

William Morris considered that Bibury, Gloucestershire, was the most beautiful village in England. It is difficult to disagree, for the stone cottages cluster round a meadow and the crystal-clear Coln flows through, a mirror to the beauty on its banks. Paths, walls and cottages seem to grow as if a part of the hills themselves.

STEPHENSON

A VILLAGE OF THE DOWNS

The main street of Alfriston, in the Cuckmere Valley, not far from Eastbourne, is beautified by the timbered Star Inn and the stone pillar that remains from the old market cross. The Star Inn, a sixteenth-century building is, like the nearby Market Cross Inn, noted for its associations with the old-time smugglers.

tempted the people from the villages. Food came across the sea. Our villages became static for nearly a century and changed scarcely in detail.

Now the roads are alive again, but with the new life flowing through the countryside there goes attendant disease. We want to live, perhaps, in a village because we appreciate its beauties, and so we go to the country and with us take electrified railways, petrol stations, main drainage, the " grid," arterial roads and the vast mechanical necessities which we have invented. Until now these elements have seemingly worked only destructively. Can the positive sides of our civilization be used constructively, not only to preserve but to add new life and beauty to our older heritage?

Our villages have been conditioned as well by geography as by history. The hills, the forests, the open river valleys have each produced a special form of living and so a special kind of village. The use of local materials has made the villages seem always part of their immediate setting.

The Wiltshire village built of cob walling and thatched and covered with creepers is directly related to its surroundings, and the stone roofed, whitewashed village in a Yorkshire dale repeats and accentuates the austerity and strength of its background.

In the woodland village of the Sussex Weald the cottages will be framed in oak shaped as it grew in the surrounding woods. The old weather-boarded houses of a south coast fishing village repeat the construction of the boats by which their owners gained a living, and the enchantingly decorative flintwork of many villages on the Norfolk coast is there because flint was easily available for building.

The Stone of the Country

The most remarkable results of geological control over the villages of earlier Englishmen are to be seen in the villages which lie in the great Oolite Belt, that band of limestone which runs half over England from Dorset to Lincolnshire and on into Yorkshire.

Here every village is almost completely stone, yet each a little different, and you can see how slight variations in the quality of the stone have affected the local architecture. On the ridge which runs from Lincoln to Grantham the stone is coarse and hard to work and there are no strata which produce stone roofing slates, so the houses are built of a coarse, uncut stone and roofed in pantiles. In Rutland and Northampton such villages as Ketton, with its superb thirteenth-century church; Geddington, which has an Eleanor Cross; and Colley Weston, famous for its stone roofing slates, reflect in their architecture the fine-textured stone of this district. So again in the Cotswolds, where the roofing stone is of even finer quality, you will see much more play made with gables and a steeper roof pitch.

In districts which were once or still are heavily wooded, villages appear scattered ; since, though the woods may have gone, little clusters of houses tell of ancient clearings in the trees. In open areas villages have tended to cluster together and present a solid face to the winds and rains.

A main road would make the village into a wide street. Broadway, one of the noblest and best-known villages in the Cotswolds, is such a street village.

towards the growth of the village : man's necessities, the slow processes of change and growth, and the physical potentialities of the site.

We can make happy voyages of discovery through the villages of England, our pleasure enriched by understanding something of their growth. There is so much to see on such a voyage that it is difficult to know where to begin.

Since we are exploring an island, perhaps the coast will make a good starting-point. In the south especially, few coast villages have managed to remain as such. Now there is a seemingly endless belt of houses along the shore but just

STEPHENSON

IN HARDY'S WESSEX

Tolpuddle, in the heart of Hardy's Wessex, has other claims to fame than its association with the " Martyrs."
It is typical of the Dorset villages that hug the road running west through Dorchester to Bridport and Exeter.
Trees, thatch, whitewash and local stone are blended into charming cottages that straggle along the roads.

Water supplies have affected the shape and appearance of our villages. In broken, hilly country with many springs one or two cottages would be built round each well. In a wide country where water might be rarer a whole village would grow round one source of supply. It is possibly for the same reason that one sees that most charming of village compositions, a row of cottages parallel to an open stream.

In the Fens every village seems huddled close, a small oasis of large trees and houses in a wide landscape where land and sky melt into each other on the horizon. Here formerly, as on Romney Marsh, only occasional islands of higher ground rising from miles of mere and swamp allowed a safe site for a village.

Such are some of the elements that have gone

inland we can find unspoilt villages still with a salty atmosphere. On Romney Marsh, in Kent, Dymchurch is already bungalow ridden, but fine old churches with clusters of houses set on mounds in the marsh, such as Brenzett with its alabaster figures, are worth a visit.

Winchelsea, although strictly a town (was it not one of the Cinque Ports ?) and now no longer by the sea, we may regard as a village. A place of weather-boarded painted houses nobly situated on a green hill above the marshes, and still entered by a medieval gate, Winchelsea is, indeed, one of the most fascinating of the many treasures of Sussex.

In a fold of the downs lies Alfriston, not a sea village but yet of the sea, for the men of Alfriston were daring smugglers landing their

W. F. TAYLOR

A VILLAGE OF GREY PENWITH

High on the Penwith moors, near St. Ives, Cornwall, Zennor's sombre beauty is rarely seen by the casual tourist. The moor granite has been used for the cottages and it crops up immovably in garden and road. The district is reputed to be so barren that there is a local saying: " Zennor, where the cat ate the bell-rope."

cargoes at Cuckmere Haven and carrying them inland by devious ways to baffle the excisemen.

Alfriston today consists chiefly of a single street of attractive houses including the ancient timbered building of the Star Hill, which was once within the jurisdiction of Battle Abbey and a place of sanctuary for fugitives from justice.

Beaulieu, lost in the New Forest, should be approached by river from the sea. The atmosphere of a great monastery still clings to it, and on the way we pass Buckler's Hard, designed to be a shipbuilding centre in the eighteenth century, but ships ceased to be of timber and Buckler's Hard remains a village of little, formal red brick houses between the slow moving river and the forest.

Now we are nearly into Dorsetshire and, since we may not come this way again, we must go inland a few miles behind Studland to see Corfe Castle, where stone-tiled houses cluster round the ruin-covered mound of the great castle, set dramatically in a sudden gap in the Purbeck Hills.

Once we stray into Dorset we are tempted to wander from one village to the next for here lies many a hamlet of thatched cottages in the neighbourhood of a grey old church, sometimes with a clear little rivulet flowing down the street. Hardy gave fame to some, others may have furbished and bedecked themselves to attract tourists from the holiday resorts, but many remain

plain and unadorned and attractive in their simplicity.

Sydling St. Nicholas, for instance, is as charming as its name, with thatched cottages and a duckpond, and a background of smooth green hills. Also in a hollow in the hills is Cerne Abbas, more famed for the giant, but worthy of note if only for that charming street leading to the church and the abbey gate-house with its beautiful two-storeyed oriel window. Nearer the coast are such places as Upwey, nestling in a soft green valley, and Burton Radstock, a picturesque stone-built hamlet where artists congregate.

Glorious Devon

In Devonshire we come to the land of cream and roses, of colour-washed houses, fuchsia hedges and clusters of blue hydrangeas at almost every cottage door. Dittisham, where the Dart meets the sea, is as good a Devon village as any that slope down to the sea between Exmouth and Plymouth. The upper portion of the village is finely placed on the neck of Gurrow Point above the tidal waters of the River Dart and overlooking its tree-hung banks.

Beyond St. Germains, which seems almost too good to be called a village, the country changes and we are in Cornwall, a county of violent contrast, treeless and wind-swept on the high ground where hundreds of small villages merge with the stone-walled fields, and almost tropical in the sheltered coves on its southern coast. Though there is little of architectural interest these Cornish villages are extremely attractive, and many have odd and often beautiful names.

One of the quaintest of Cornish fishing villages is Polperro, with its little natural harbour round which the houses are irregularly grouped one above the other in picturesque confusion.

I suppose Clovelly is one of the most famous of English villages, though it is always written about as being exactly like Italy. Actually it is like nowhere else. You have to go to realize how intimate it is and how exactly " right " is the cobbled street that tumbles between two rows of cottages stepped one above the other to the smallest harbour possible. The whole place has been exquisitely cared for. It remains a real and a live village, singularly free from unsightly development.

Where Exmoor falls sharply to the sea Lynmouth has grouped its houses most effectively against the steep hillside, and inland from here the hamlets of Brendon and Oare have blended themselves with the valley and the confining hills.

Porlock, attractive as it is in itself, suffers perhaps in comparison with Bossington, a lovely old-time hamlet with soft-tinted cottages, luxuriant gardens and great spreading walnut trees. Bossington in turn must yield homage to Selworthy. Among the trees at the foot of its Beacon, Selworthy's thatched houses, whitewashed church and sixteenth-century cross make a splendid harmony.

The East Anglian Flats

Devon and Cornwall still have a coast dotted with beautiful and unspoilt villages. Their steep geography presents problems beyond the speculative builder's power. Other coasts have been less lucky.

There are, however, in Norfolk a series of coastal villages joined to the sea by tidal creeks winding slowly through the salt marshes to the North Sea. Shifting sands and a new economy have lost them their prosperity, but since they are not actually on the sea they have never grown into seaside resorts.

Farthest east of these, Wells has fine though melancholy deserted wharves; Holkham is famous

EDGAR WARD

A WEST COUNTRY GEM

Dunster is built in a green Somerset valley and the street rises sharply at both ends. On one hill stands the Elizabethan castle, the other being crowned by a tower built two hundred years later. The octagonal Yarn Market comes beautifully into the picture, a quaint and gabled relic of the old town's medieval wealth.

for a great house and the agricultural experiments of Coke of Norfolk which changed all English farming in the eighteenth century. The Burnhams—Burnham Deepdale, Burnham Overy, Burnham Market and the rest—are all exquisitely simple villages of darkest red brick and flint, often roofed with glazed Dutch pantiles, and remarkable for the brilliance of their flower gardens where all sorts of plants grow that one expects only in Devon or Cornwall.

The flat lands of the Fens—South Lincolnshire, Cambridge and parts of Norfolk, Suffolk and Essex—are full of unexplored villages, since the uneventful landscape and the lack of large towns do not encourage tourists.

There is no stone. Houses are almost entirely of plain red brick with pantiled roofs except in Essex where there is a good deal of half timber. The simplicity of these villages is no small part of their charm, and many have beautiful churches.

Castle Acre and Castle Rising, though not in the Fens are specially interesting. The first has its Norman keep and an almshouse for old ladies who still wear a dress styled in the sixteenth century, while Castle Rising is built among the ruins of a castle and great church.

Sole Relic of the Fens

Wicken, in Cambridgeshire, is a typical Fen village, with two greens, a duckpond, an old mill, and hard by it the only remaining patch of original Fen, swamps and meres full of birds and wild flowers. In all this part of the country the valuable agricultural land washes right up to the village. There seems no gentle transition from village to open country where one ends and the other begins.

If you like fine woodwork, whitewash and thatch go to Suffolk and Essex where signposts marked with pleasant medieval names will lead you to quiet, pale villages with wide goose greens set in an uneventful countryside.

STEPHENSON

THE BELL-CROWNED TOWER OF CAVENDISH

Suffolk's pleasant levels are rich in beautiful villages. Cavendish, near the Essex border, is a large one, centred round an extensive green. At one end are the picturesque thatched cottages, shown in the picture, with the church tower rising behind them in a perfect composition. The tower carries a turret, a bell sling and flagstaff.

HUMPHREY AND VERA JOEL

AN OXFORDSHIRE IDYLL

Wroxton, on the Banbury Road, has idyllic corners. It is largely built of tawny stone and thatch, and possesses a beautiful specimen of that ancient village pride, the duckpond. The Abbey, standing in beautiful woods, was founded as an Augustinian priory in the eleventh century by a nephew of the founder of Trinity College, Oxford.

Leaving the levels of East Anglia it will be pleasant to explore the river valleys and the wooded districts.

Albury, Shere and Abinger Hammer, near Guildford, are three typical valley villages. At Abinger Hammer red brick and tile-hung cottages, with their gardens reaching to the road, face the village green through which ripples the Tillingbourne. Overhanging the road is a picturesque clock with the effigy of a village blacksmith to strike the hours.

Shere has an ancient air and the grey shingled spire of its old church stands high above the old timbered cottages. Here too the Tillingbourne adds to the picture, flowing through the village under a little brick-built bridge, its banks lined with graceful drooping trees.

The Weald of Kent, Surrey and Sussex is also full of interest for the village lover and presents many quiet little hamlets with unpretentious but satisfying features.

In Hampshire the valley of the Test is full of thatched and whitewashed villages pleasantly set in water-meadows and backed by the grey-green ridges of chalky hills. Laverstoke and Wherewell are two of the best. Heytesbury is a typical large Wiltshire village on the Avon, and hard by Stonehenge, on Salisbury Plain, is Amesbury, another river village.

Those villages at the gates of a large house often have a special dignity and an air of unity and distinction. Such a one is the pretty village of Penshurst, in Kent, by the historic home of the Sidneys. Not far from here is Chiddingstone, surely one of the loveliest of Tudor villages remaining in England.

Villages of the Road

Ripley, near Harrogate, is a beautiful stone-built village in the Nidd Valley. Castle and village are here closely connected by a common pride in looking their best. Though the houses are mostly without front gardens, window boxes and creepers seem to have a special brilliance against the hard stone of this Yorkshire village.

West Wycombe, in the Chilterns, now safe from decay and spoliation, is in any case a fine example of a roadside village, but it would lose much were it not for the fine park behind it and the romantic eighteenth-century church and mausoleum which loom above the village street.

The villages which owe their importance to road traffic can be found along all the old coaching roads out of London. The weight of eighteenth-century traffic can almost be judged by their frequency and the size of the old inns.

Wansford, near Stamford, now by-passed, has a superb late seventeenth-century inn, a gothic bridge and beyond it the church with an early fourteenth-century spire. Only the few stone houses that are there are needed to complete one of the most satisfying village pictures it is possible to find.

Trumpington and Harston on the Cambridge Road are road villages in a different medium of whitewash and thatch.

Burford is another road village, and since it calls itself the Gateway of the Cotswolds it must be an introduction to those fine stone villages which lie along the limestone belt between Bath and Lincoln. Before we turn north there are places we must not miss in the basin of the Upper Thames, such as Fairford with its famous church, and Lechlade. On the Windrush, like Burford, is North Leach, and nearer Oxford the charming hamlet of Minster Lovel.

The Cotswolds are so full of enchantment that it is difficult to select. Stow-on-the-Wold typifies the hill-top village, Stanway lies under the carp of the hills on the way to Tewkesbury, Broadway has its magnificently wide street of fine architecture. Lower Slaughter and Bourton-on-the-Water both lie by the River Windrush, and in both of them stone cottages and water fall into the happiest compositions. Further south, between Burford and Cirencester, is Bibury. Here is a famous line of cottages called Arlington Row.

Let us follow these stone villages into Oxford-shire. Hidden away in the forest of Wychwood are Shipton-under-Wychwood and Charlbury in the valley of the Evenlode.

Aynho (just into Northamptonshire) on the Banbury-Bicester Road is considered one of the most beautiful villages in the country. It is beautifully kept and one feels its close connection with the great house. Enormous pride is taken in its appearance and plantings of red roses and apricot trees make it unique.

Gems of the Midlands

Off the line into Buckinghamshire is Weston Underwood, a beautiful secluded stone village where Cowper lived. Beyond Kettering and Wellingborough we suddenly come again into an area compact of good stone villages. Rockingham has a wide street uphill from the Welland Valley to Rockingham Castle, once King John's hunting lodge.

Where Rutland, Northamptonshire and Lincoln-shire meet, there are many interesting villages. Duddington and Colley Weston are close together on a ridge above the Welland, near Stamford. From Colley Weston came the stone slates so widely used in past times. A little to the north, in Rutland, is Ketton with the most exquisite of Early English church spires, own brother, surely, to the famous spire of St. Mary's, Stamford, only four miles away.

N. A. CALL

IN THE CATTLE AND CIDER COUNTRY

Weobley, in Herefordshire, is largely composed of black-and-white houses, many using paint where no timber exists. One house is noted as the home of a Mr. Tomkins who achieved fame not only as the father of thirty-two children but also as the originator of the white-faced cattle known the world over as Herefords.

Going north through Grantham towards Lincoln, only Furbeck perhaps deserves to be called a beautiful village, but if we make a wide detour past Heckington towards Boston, we come to Tattershall, a splendid group—brick castle, stone church and low cottages in dead flat country between river and wold.

Perhaps it is such a charming patchwork of different materials as this which has created the average English village, and all over the country where geological limitations are not too severe are villages where half timber, red brick and stone are happily mixed. Elmley Castle, by Bredon Hill, in Worcestershire, is such a village. Worcestershire, Hereford, Warwickshire are full of good composite architecture. In Shropshire black and white work becomes more frequent. Pott Shrigley, although it has an unattractive name, is a charming village between Cheshire and Derbyshire. Sudbury, between Uttoxeter and Derby, is a wonderful village, seeming more remarkable among rather dull neighbours.

The Dales

In the dale country of the West Riding the stone villages reappear, but without the architectural niceties of the Cotswold villages. Here utility rather than grace has been sought. The houses are solidly built to withstand northern blasts. Constructed of local gritstone, walls, floors and roofs of the same material, they present an air of permanence and lasting strength.

Built as they are of local materials, cottage and church, farm buildings, garden walls and the bounding walls of the field, all harmonize with the landscape and often have been woven into a singularly successful pattern.

Many of these northern villages indeed have an appreciable charm. Whether spread round a spacious green as at Reeth in Swaledale, at Bainbridge in Wensleydale, or Arncliffe in the narrow confines of Littondale, or closely huddled like grey sheep in a storm as in the quaint

hamlet of Dent, they appear at one with their surroundings.

One of the loveliest of the dale villages is Burnsall, in Wharfedale, a few miles upstream from Bolton Abbey. Seen from the hillside, with the lively river rippling beneath a substantial bridge, and with the square tower of the old church rising above trim soundly-built

W. F. TAYLOR

A WESTMORLAND MARKET CROSS

The village of Brough is divided into secular and religious departments, one end being called Market Brough and the other Church Brough. Ancient and important fairs are held at the Cross on September 30 and October 1.

cottages, Burnsall, indeed presents an aspect of permanence and imperturbable calm.

Wensleydale contains a number of villages of distinction including Bainbridge, still retaining the stocks on the green, Aysgarth, with its wide street and rose-covered cottages, and Wensley where a venerable elm still shades the green. Best of all perhaps is Castle Bolton on the northern flanks of the dale, a wide street of stone cottages dwarfed by the massive

W. F. TAYLOR

IN A NORTHERN VALLEY

Near the source of the Derwent, on the borders of Northumberland and Durham, is the village of Blanchland, grouped beautifully round the church and framed against wooded hills. The traveller comes upon the village after crossing the moorland, in whose rough heart it gleams like a jewel of grey and green and brown.

walls of the castle, the feudal stronghold of the Scropes.

In Swaledale the little village of Muker lies at the foot of the domed Kisdon Fell with the road running between the houses and the little moorland beck. Here again one sees a happy blending of bridge and church and cottages with the green hillside patterned with stone walls for a background.

The Northern Counties

The east side of Yorkshire also presents some villages of note including Coxwold where a wide street flanked with green between the houses leads up to the church where the author of *Tristram Shandy* once ministered. Bishop Burton, between York and Beverley, is said to be the prettiest of Yorkshire villages, and it is indeed a delightful place. It possesses a large crescent-shaped pond and a chestnut shaded green, and its houses instead of being in a row are dotted about in a most pleasing style.

In the Lake District men seem to have been content with, or even awed by the landscape—the villages offer no competition. Lowther, near Askham, is an exception, since it is an almost unique example of an eighteenth-century planned village. The cottages and the bailiff's house are placed as part of the whole and carried out, all alike in stone with Westmorland slate roofs.

Among the villages of Northumberland I would give Blanchland first place. It is securely hidden in the wooded valley of the Derwent above which rises the bare brown moorlands. The village has grown on the site of the abbey which was founded in 1175, and now occupies what was the outer court of the monastery. The houses and the village inn are arranged round the sides of the quadrangle which is entered on the north through a battlemented gateway. Whether approached by this entrance, or by the bridge which spans the Derwent, one is immediately conscious that here is a village of rare and distinctive beauty.

After giving the palm to Blanchland I remember Bywell on the Tyne. This is a sequestered little hamlet boasting two churches, relics of the days when Bywell consisted of two parishes, for of old it was a busy place, its inhabitants being employed in the ironwork making horse-trappings for the border folk.

Then there is Bamburgh dominated by its mighty castle but there is no end to our quest of beautiful villages.

There are, I am told, 13,000 villages in England. Each has its special qualities, its attractions and charms for someone. All of us have special ties with one or more of them and no two men would agree in their choice of, say, the twelve prettiest villages in the land.

INDEX

S.9/45. 3R.S.   *Printed by Odhams (Watford) Ltd., Watford.*